MUSICAL CREATIVITY: INSIGHTS FROM MUSIC EDUCATION RESEARCH

To Lucy and Marta

Musical Creativity: Insights from Music Education Research

OSCAR ODENA
University of Hertfordshire, UK

ASHGATE

Published by
Ashgate Publishing Limited
Wey Court East
Union Road
Farnham
Surrey, GU9 7PT
England

Ashgate Publishing Company
Suite 420
101 Cherry Street
Burlington
VT 05401-4405
USA

www.ashgate.com

British Library Cataloguing in Publication Data
Musical creativity : insights from music education research. -- (SEMPRE studies in the psychology of music)
   1. Music--Psychological aspects. 2. Music--Performance--Psychological aspects.
   3. Composition (Music)--Psychological aspects. 4. Improvisation (Music)--
   Psychological aspects. 5. Music--Instruction and study--Psychological aspects.
   I. Series II. Odena, Oscar.
   781.1'1-dc22

Library of Congress Cataloging-in-Publication Data
Odena, Oscar.
   Musical creativity : insights from music education research / Oscar Odena.
      p. cm. -- (SEMPRE studies in the psychology of music)
   Includes bibliographical references and index.
   ISBN 978-1-4094-0622-8 (hardcover : alk. paper) -- ISBN 978-1-4094-3768-0
(ebook) 1. Music--Psychological aspects. 2. Creation (Literary, artistic,
etc.) 3. Music--Instruction and study--Psychological aspects. I. Title.

   ML3830.O34 2011
   781'.11--dc23

2011021697

ISBN 978-1-4094-0622-8 (hbk)
ISBN 978-1-4094-3768-0 (ebk)

591058420X

MIX
Paper from
responsible sources
FSC
www.fsc.org   FSC® C018575

Printed and bound in Great Britain by the
MPG Books Group, UK.

Contents

List of figures and illustrations

Figures

Illustrations

List of music examples

List of tables

Notes on contributors

Margaret S. Barrett is Professor and Head of the School of Music at The University of Queensland. Her research investigates the role of music in human cognition and social and cultural development and has addressed issues in creativity, aesthetic decision-making, the meaning and value of the arts for young people, young children's musical thinking and identity work in and through music. A key aspect of Margaret's work has been the development of innovative arts-based inquiry methods in music and music education, leading to the publication of *Narrative inquiry in music education: Troubling certainty* (with Sandra Stauffer; Springer, 2009). Recent and forthcoming publications include *A cultural psychology of music education* (Oxford University Press, 2011) and *Narrative soundings: An anthology of narrative inquiry in music education* (with Sandra Stauffer; Springer, 2012 in press). She is Editor of *Research Studies in Music Education*, and Associate Editor of *Psychology of Music*, and a member of the editorial boards of key journals in music and arts education. A former National President of the Australian Society for Music Education, she has served as a Board member and Research Commissioner of the International Society for Music Education and is its President Elect (becoming President in 2012).

Leslie Bunt trained in music therapy at the Guildhall School of Music and Drama, London, in 1976 after a period of music teaching. Since then he has worked with children and adults of all ages with wide-ranging healthcare needs. He was awarded the UK's first PhD in music therapy (City, 1985) for his outcome-based study evaluating the effects of music therapy with young children with learning difficulties. Leslie has been training music therapists since 1980 and is currently Professor in Music Therapy at the University of the West of England, Bristol where he leads the MA Music Therapy programme and bases his research. He also works as a music therapist in the field of cancer care and is a qualified practitioner and trainer in Guided Imagery and Music. In 1991 he set up the MusicSpace Trust, which created a network of community-based centres for music therapy in the UK and in Bologna, Italy. The UK-based work of MusicSpace continues in the Bristol area. He presents regularly at national and international conferences and is published widely. Leslie is also a conductor. In June 2009 he was awarded an MBE in the Queen's Birthday Honours list for his services to music therapy.

Pamela Burnard (BMus, MMus, MEd, PhD) is a Senior Lecturer at the Faculty of Education, University of Cambridge, where she manages higher degree courses in Arts, Culture and Education and in Educational Research. She is Co-Editor of the *British Journal of Music Education*, Associate Editor of *Psychology of Music* and serves on numerous editorial boards. She is section editor of the 'Creativity Section' in the *International handbook of research in arts education* (Springer, 2007) and the 'Musical Creativity as Practice' section of the forthcoming *Oxford handbook of music education* (Oxford University Press). Her co-edited books include *Reflective practices in arts education* (Springer, 2006), *Creative learning 3-11* (Trentham, 2007) and *Teaching music with digital technologies* (Continuum, 2007). She was on the Board of Directors for the International Society for Music Education from 2004 to 2008 and is currently convenor of the British Education Research Association (BERA) Special Interest Group 'Creativity in Education'.

Sara Carvalho is a Senior Lecturer in the Communication and Arts Department of Aveiro University, Portugal, where she coordinates undergraduate and master's degrees in Music Studies. She is a fellow researcher of INET-MD, and her investigation is balanced between the fields of Music Education and Music Composition. In 1995 she completed her music teacher training degree in Portugal, and she holds an MA (1996) and a DPhil (2000) in Composition from York University, UK. As a composer she is interested in the interaction of Performing Arts as an extension and transformation of musical thinking, and all aspects associated with musical narrative. Her folio has over 30 pieces for solo instrument, small and large ensembles and orchestra, which are played regularly both in Portugal and around the world. Several of her pieces are available on CD, edited by Numérica and Phonedition. Her scores are published by the Portuguese Music Information & Investigation Centre. In the field of Music Education, Sara is researching the influence of creative processes on the development of musical thinking in children. She is a regular presenter at national and international conferences and has numerous publications. She co-convenes the International Conference Performa, held since 2007 at Aveiro University, Portugal.

Su-Ching Hsieh recently completed a PhD at the Institute of Education, University of London, focused on cognition and musical improvisation in individual and group contexts. She has previously worked as a performer specializing in solo piano performance, a freelance composer, a music education workshop leader for children with special needs and an instrumental tutor in primary and secondary schools. She has presented her research in institutions such as the Centre for Multimodal Research (Institute of Education) and the Institute of Cognitive Neuroscience (University College London) and at numerous international conferences including the Guildhall Reflective Conservatoire Conference and the British Psychological Society Annual Conference. Her working papers include 'The Relationship between sight-reading, memorisation and improvisation in those with expertise in different musical genres' and 'Learning to improvise: Experiences of a trained classical musician'. Currently she is working as an independent research consultant for numerous Taiwanese charity organizations that are utilizing musical creativity in the early stage of cancer patients' recovery programmes.

Oscar Odena is Reader in Education at the University of Hertfordshire, UK, where he is the Director of the Doctorate in Education (EdD) programme. He trained as a music teacher in Spain, where he later specialized in psychopedagogy, and holds a PhD from the Institute of Education, University of London, which focused on English secondary schoolteachers' perceptions of creativity in music education. He is a member of the Peer Review College of the Irish Research Council for the Humanities and Social Sciences and a member of the editorial boards of the *International Journal of Music Education, Research Studies in Music Education, British Journal of Music Education* and *Revista Electrónica Complutense de Investigación en Educación Musical*. Oscar has worked in higher education institutions in Spain, Northern Ireland and England. He is the International Society for Music Education Research Commissioner for the UK and Africa (2008-2014) and has co-edited with Gary Spruce the section on 'Music learning and teaching during adolescence' in the forthcoming *Oxford handbook of music education* (Oxford University Press).

Gabriel Rusinek is Associate Professor at the Faculty of Education, Universidad Complutense de Madrid, Spain. He is the coordinator of a doctoral programme in Music Education, and teaches undergraduate and graduate courses. He has presented papers at many Spanish and international conferences and seminars, and has published articles in Spanish journals (*Eufonía, Tavira, Musiker, Doce Notas* and *Aula*) and international journals (*Music Education Research, International Journal of Music Education, Research Studies in Music Education* and *Journal of New Music Research*). He collaborates on the advisory boards of *International Journal of Music Education, International Journal of Education & the Arts* and *Music Education Research*, and is editor of the peer-reviewed open access research journal *Revista Electrónica Complutense de Investigación en Educación Musical* (http://www.ucm.es/info/reciem). Gabriel convenes a yearly research seminar in Music Education (SCIEM) in Madrid, and in 2010 was appointed commissioner for the ISME Music in Schools and Teacher Education Commission.

Frederick A. Seddon currently works as an Enterprise Researcher at the Northampton Business School, University of Northampton, UK, where he conducts research into evaluation procedures for Social Enterprise. He completed his PhD studies in Music Psychology at Keele University in 2001 and worked as a postdoctoral research lecturer in the Psychology Department of the Open University, UK, from 2001 to 2004. Prior to taking up his current research post in January 2010, he worked at the Department of Education, Padua University, Italy, where he conducted research into musical communication, the training of music teachers and the use of technology in music education. He has previously worked as Head of Music in a secondary school, an instrumental tutor in private practice and a university lecturer at undergraduate and postgraduate levels. He was a member of the international advisory board of the journal *Music Education Research* until 2010 and a member of the editorial board of the *British Journal of Music Education* from 2002 to 2007. He has disseminated the results of his research through several articles in international peer-reviewed journals, contributed chapters in edited books on musical collaboration and music education, and presented papers at many international conferences during the last ten years.

José Soares holds a PhD in Music Education from the Institute of Education, University of London. He also holds Master and BA degrees from the Brazilian Conservatory of Music, Rio de Janeiro. He is Lecturer in Music Education at the Federal University of Uberlândia, Minas Gerais State, Brazil. He taught classical guitar to adolescents (13-18) for 12 years at the Specialized Music School, Minas Gerais. His main areas of interests include creativity, research methods and music teacher education. He is currently involved in the research project 'Assuring and enhancing the quality of distance learning music teacher courses in Brazil', funded by the National Council for Scientific and Technological Development (CNPq) and in the project 'Becoming a music teacher in Brazil', funded by the Coordination for the Improvement of Higher Education (CAPES), National Institute for Educational Studies Anísio Teixeira (INEP) and Secretariat for Continuing Education, Literacy and Diversity (SECAD). He has written a number of publications on teacher education and musical development (mainly in Portuguese), and is a member of the editorial board of *Revista ABEM*, the journal of the Brazilian Society for Music Education.

Ana Luísa Veloso completed a Music Education degree at the College of Education, Porto Polytechnic Institute, Portugal, in 2005. She is presently working on her PhD in Music (Education) under the guidance of Dr Sara Carvalho and Dr Graça Mota at Aveiro University, with a PhD scholarship from the Foundation for Science and Technology of the Portuguese Ministry of Science Technology and Higher Education. She currently teaches in the Music Department at the Porto College of Education. She also leads seminars at Aveiro University and at the Porto College of Education for doctoral and master's students in the areas of music and emotions, musical creativity and music composition in the classroom. From September 2004 to December 2007 she taught music education in several public and private primary schools. She has presented at national and international conferences in music education and has published several articles in the domain of music education, and, more specifically, in the areas of creativity, music composition and emotions and the development of children's musical thinking.

Peter R. Webster is the John Beattie Professor of Music Education and Technology at the Bienen School of Music, Northwestern University in Evanston, Illinois. He holds degrees in music education from the University of Southern Maine (BS) and the Eastman School of Music (MM, PhD). He has held various administrative positions in his career, including his current term as Chair of Music Studies at Northwestern. His teaching responsibilities include courses in philosophy of music education, graduate research, music technology and creative thinking in music. He supervises the doctoral programme in music education. His published work includes over 75 articles and book chapters on technology, music cognition and creative thinking in music, which have appeared in journals and handbooks in and outside of music. He is an editorial board member for several prestigious journals and has served as an editor for several projects, including the forthcoming MENC *Handbook of research on music learning* from Oxford University Press. Peter is co-author of *Experiencing music technology*, 3rd edition update (Wadsworth/ Schirmer, 2008), the standard textbook used in introductory college courses in music technology. He is the author of *Measures of creative thinking in music*, an exploratory tool for assessing music thinking using quasi-improvisational tasks.

Graham Welch holds the Institute of Education, University of London Established Chair of Music Education and is Head of the Department of Early Childhood and Primary Education. He is the elected Chair of the internationally based Society for Education, Music and Psychology Research (SEMPRE), President of ISME and past Co-Chair of the ISME Research Commission. He holds visiting professorships at the Universities of Brisbane (Australia), Limerick (Eire), the Royal College of Music and Roehampton (UK) and is a member of the UK Arts and Humanities Research Council (AHRC) Review College for music. His publications number over 270 and embrace musical development and music education, teacher education, the psychology of music, singing and voice science, and music in special education and disability. His publications are primarily in English, but also in Spanish, Portuguese, Italian, Swedish, Greek, Japanese and Chinese. He is on the editorial boards of the world's leading journals in music education, including *International Journal of Music Education*, *Journal of Research in Music Education*, *Research Studies in Music Education*, *British Journal of Music Education* and *Music Education Research*.

Series editors' preface

There has been an enormous growth of research over the last three decades into the psychology of music. SEMPRE (the Society for Education, Music and Psychology Research) is the only international society that embraces an interest in the psychology of music, research and education. SEMPRE was founded in 1972 and has published the journals *Psychology of Music* since 1973 and *Research Studies in Music Education* since 2008, both now in partnership with SAGE (see www.sempre. org.uk). Nevertheless, there is an ongoing need to promote the latest research to the widest possible audience if it is to have a distinctive impact on policy and practice.

The SEMPRE Studies in the Psychology of Music series has been designed to address this need through our very positive collaboration with Ashgate since 2007. The theme for the series is the psychology of music, broadly defined. Topics include (among others) musical development at different ages; musical cognition and context; culture, mind and music; micro to macro perspectives on the impact of music on the individual (such as from neurological studies through to social psychology); the development of advanced performance skills; musical behaviour and development in the context of special educational needs; and affective perspectives on musical learning. The series seeks to present the implications of research findings for a wide readership, including user-groups (music teachers, policy-makers, parents), as well as the international academic teaching and research communities. The distinguishing features of the series is its broad focus that draws on basic and applied research from across the globe under the umbrella of SEMPRE's distinctive mission, which is to promote and ensure coherent and symbiotic links between education, music and psychology research.

We are very pleased to include this text on *Musical creativity: Insights from music education research* in the SEMPRE series. Creativity is a concern to many in the fields of psychology and education, as well as in music, not least because it is a fundamental characteristic of the human condition. It is also central to artistic endeavour and is an aspect of learning and teaching that provokes the most debate. This new edited collection brings together a diverse range of philosophical and empirical studies to shed light on why creativity is so important. Collectively, they provide an important opportunity to reflect on creativity's diverse nature and how it can – and should – be nurtured.

Graham Welch
Institute of Education, London, UK
Adam Ockelford
Roehampton University, UK
Ian Cross
University of Cambridge, UK

Acknowledgements

The first draft of each chapter was independently reviewed by the editor and two additional reviewers, who included a selection of other authors from the book and anonymous external reviewers. Regarding the latter, I am grateful to Michele Biasutti, Tim Cain, Andrea Creech, Norma Daykin, Rui Ferreira, Sergio Figueiredo, Michele Kaschub, Bo Wah Leung, Chris Philpott, Charles Plummeridge, John Richmond, Gary Spruce, Sandra Stauffer and Betty Anne Younker.

I take this opportunity to thank the editors of the book series and the various representatives of Ashgate with whom I have come in contact during the long process from proposal submission to publication. I especially thank Graham Welch for his helpful advice right from the beginning, and the commissioning editors Heidi Bishop and Laura Macy for their support.

Most of all, I am grateful to the authors for their patience and hard work in preparing their chapters and reviews. This was truly a team endeavour and I hope that the authors agree that it was worth the effort.

Oscar Odena

Introduction

Oscar Odena

The dissemination of an increasing number of musical practices through the globalized media does not seem to provide a clearer understanding of musical creativity. This has prompted me to consider a number of questions: what is musical creativity? How might learners of different ages develop it drawing on their innate musicality? What happens when players, amateur and experienced, improvise collaboratively? How is musical creativity used for a variety of purposes, such as in music therapy sessions? These are just a few of the questions examined in this book, which offers insights from research in the fields of music education and related areas including music psychology and music therapy.

In 11 chapters written by an international team of experts, the book celebrates the richness and diversity of the many different ways in which learners of all ages develop and use musical creativity. The contributions have a broad focus on studies of composition and improvisation, but they also consider collaborative performance and practitioner-led research as a way of advancing pedagogical practice. The chapters include examples from four different continents and a variety of settings comprising primary, secondary, studio, conservatoire, university, specialist music classrooms and music therapy sessions.

All the contributions were commissioned specially for this volume. The authors present accounts of new research combined with reviews of previous relevant studies. They consider practical implications in the light of their work, offering ideas for students, teachers, performers, researchers and practitioner-researchers. I believe the authorship of the chapters is well balanced between established writers and early career scholars, whose work I came across when organizing seminars for the Research Commission of the International Society for Music Education and while working at the Institute of Education in London. The limited space available in a single volume means that many relevant authors (some of whom acted as chapter reviewers) could not be invited this time to prepare a contribution.

The 11 chapters in this volume are organized according to three complementary but flexibly constructed sections – *Conceptualizing musical creativity*, *Examples from practice* and *Paths for further inquiry*. As such, some of the contributions could have been included in other sections of the book. Part I contains two chapters with a focus on examining the concept of creativity in music. The opening chapter rethinks the notion of 'musical creativity', advocating for the idea of multiple creativities in music. Chapter 2 presents a study of music teachers' perceptions of creativity in English secondary schools, putting forward a dynamic model for the teachers' development of their perceptions.

Part II, 'Examples from practice', offers seven chapters focused on studies of musical creativity practices and development from early years to adulthood. The first two chapters discuss the preparation of the early years mind for musical creativity, drawing on case studies from Australia and a music composition project with 7-year-olds in Portugal. They are followed by a contribution on the central place of revision as a fruitful teaching strategy in music composition pedagogy, which provides examples from a 12-year-old student in a middle school in the USA. Chapters 6 and 7 discuss the engagement of Brazilian adolescents in composing activities in two specialist schools and the concept of empathetic creativity in music-making, including jazz and classical adult ensemble playing and internet-based collaborations between adolescents in two European countries. Chapter 8 examines cognition processes when learning to improvise in adult individual and group contexts. The section closes with an insightful account of the uses of creativity in music therapy sessions, drawing on illustrative UK-based examples of children with Special Education Needs and adults with cancer.

Part III 'Paths for further inquiry', opens with Chapter 10, a discussion of research questions and designs used in practitioner-led enquiries on collaborative composition, drawing on a number of international studies. Chapter 11 considers some of the common themes emerging from the volume's contributions, including the definition of musical creativity, the provision of musical creativity practices across different countries and the importance of emotional engagement for their effective implementation. The book concludes with some implications for practice and a consideration of issues for further research.

Each of the chapters examines how musical creativity practices are used and developed in particular contexts, offering insights on how creative processes work in music and suggesting ideas on how they might be better facilitated. I sincerely hope that readers will find the examples illuminating and will be inspired to think deeply about the many different ways in which musical creativity can be developed by groups and individuals of all ages, and that this will motivate them to explore further.

PART I
Conceptualizing musical creativity

Chapter 1

Rethinking 'musical creativity' and the notion of multiple creativities in music

Pamela Burnard

1.1 Summary

This chapter explores the question of what constitutes musical creativity. An argument is put forward against the historically linked and limited definitions of high-art orthodoxies that exalt the individual genius and legitimize dominant forms and practices. In presenting some contemporary (i.e. real world and grassroots) practices that support socially constructed views of musical creativeness other than those ascribed by and mythologized by the accepted canon of 'great composers', Bourdieu's theoretical tools and concept of 'practice' and Csikszentmihalyi's 'systems perspective' are used to highlight affinities and shifts in the dominant historical forms of musical creativity, particularly as they arise within differing cultural, social and activity systems. Illustrations drawn from recent studies invite reflection on differing systems and call for a rethink of the concept of musical creativity in music education.

1.2 Introduction

At the beginning of the third millennium, with affordable digital devices like mobile phones, video cameras and MP3 players for recording and sharing, our understanding of what constitutes musical creativity becomes increasingly important in music education. Despite the proliferation of interest in creativity in general – a defining feature of economic life and educational reform and a crucial component of our occupational potential[1] – the problem of what constitutes musical creativity in education remains unresolved. While the dominant romantic values of Western art music favour the individual dimension, popular music favours the social dimension of collaborative and collective practices (Bennett, 2001; Csikszentmihalyi & Wolfe, 2001; Longhurst, 2007; Sawyer, 2003). This is what makes new perspectives on *who* is making the music, *where* it is being made and for *whom* as significant as the generative aspect inherent in practices

---

[1]   This is particularly so in relation to the creative industries, which are knowledge-intensive and require highly skilled human capital.

such as sampling, resampling, mixing, mashing and songwriting as important as composing, arranging, improvising and performing, in the light of contemporary critical theory and cultural history. Competing explanations place a strong emphasis on specific psychological states or processes of individual composers and 'private' characterizations of individual composers working on their own (Sloboda, 1985). But do these ways of explaining musical creativity convey the kinds of collaborative, communal or collective venturing that underpin activity systems at the beginning of the third millennium?[2]

A collective and individualized understanding of musical creativity (one that traces beyond the common forms of composition and improvisation[3]) is an imperative. As Finnegan has argued, although 'the one common form of musical creativity, is musical composition' for which 'this high-art model assumes a canon of accepted composers, notably the "greats" like Bach, Mozart, Beethoven or Chopin' (2007: 160), there are a myriad of differing ways in which musicians, at both ends of the high-art and grassroots spectrum, are creative. What is more, the Western conception of 'musical creativity' becomes increasingly dominant when we seek out what are the values and norms of approval (i.e. what institutions legitimize) for measuring and standardizing its assessment. In making generalizations and claims about what others mean or have meant by musical creativity, I intend this chapter to be understood in terms of the creative work in music as done by individuals. The composer immersed and at one with the act of composing contemporary art music, the arranger of jazz charts, the conductor of scores for Broadway theatre or opera, the songwriter of popular music, the child in the playground composing within children's communities of musical practice or the DJ's performative role in creating distinctive club cultures from the interaction of records, DJ and crowd – each of whom potentially manifest different and distinctive practices of creativity in music or music creativities. Put in another way, to acknowledge that creativity exists in music is insufficient. The singular defined concept of 'music creativity' is outmoded. The argument in this chapter is *not* about the goodness of music creativity or identifying the creativeness of musics, nor is it about the mythologized and manifest forms of creative practice that are generally assumed to be realized by the individual artist as expressions of individual selfhood in specific social, historical and cultural contexts (for these and other related debates, see Burnard, forthcoming). The argument in this chapter

---

[2] **Activity systems** are complex formations involving individuals or subgroups who challenge the assumptions and norms of previous practice by means of reflective appropriation of advanced models and tools for working on an object, raw material or problem space (such as composing, improvising, sampling and so on) at which the activity is directed (Engeström, 1993).

[3] Traditions involving jazz improvisation and insights derived from interviews with professional jazz musicians (Berliner, 1994) and Western art music examples derived from interviews with composers (McCutchan, 1999) provide insights on the plethora of ways in which social groups produce, distribute and consume music in the digital age.

is about broadening the concept of 'music creativity' from its outmoded singular form to its particular manifestations of multiple music creativities.

In music education, judgements are made by teachers about students' written forms of composition at GCSE[4] as well as those compositions that are not notated particularly at AS and A levels, using predetermined criteria (Fautley, 2010). The relationship between institutionalized assessment practices and the sort of creative works that are made in a particular place and time requires analysis. What meanings are attached to the conceptual invention of 'musical creativity' and how is this expressed in articulating the process in educational practice? In the music industry, the collective enterprise of studio practice and the studio producers are predisposed rather than predetermined to act in certain ways (McIntyre, 2008). Practices such as live-coding and sound design in video games produce distinct forms of music creativity which are qualitatively different from the more traditional notions of 'the master work': a high-art orthodoxy that exalts and validates the *individual* and the romantic notion of the Great Composer. With these ideas in mind, the question arises as to what constitutes musical creativity and how we should move forward in the process of rethinking this vexed yet vital concept in music education.

From their earliest childhood experiences, children's global practices exemplify a myriad of forms of musical creativity which are practised and prominent in their spontaneous interactions in playground songs and games (Marsh, 2008), and in their invented song-making, which evolves from their early musico-communicative interaction with others (Barrett, 2006). Young people today are members of a 'computerized generation' whose musical creativity is infused with digital imagery, video games, YouTube, internet sites and a robust commitment to engaging creatively with affordable digital devices for recording and sharing music, particularly out of school (Lamont et al., 2003). Research shows that the lack of congruence between what students are doing outside of school and what we are able to offer them inside of school, along with teachers' narrowly construed views on musical creativity, is the result of an array of factors, the most obvious of which are competing demands and discourses around teaching music, inadequate systemic support and the way creativity is actualized in classroom and studio practice. But, as I will argue, the unique challenge of musical creativity as it relates to music educational systems is to comprehend the multiplicity of forms, fluid roles and meanings defined in contemporary popular musics.[5] There

---

[4]   The General Certificate of Secondary Education (GCSE) is an academic qualification awarded in a specified subject, generally taken in a number of subjects by students aged 14–16 in secondary education in England, Wales and Northern Ireland. See Section 1.6.1 Composing spaces and the dominant discourse of classroom practice for further explanations.

[5]   For example, with **globally spatialized internet forms** of digital and mobile musics we see websites such as 'ccmixter', which declares itself 'a music sharing site featuring songs licensed under Creative Commons where you can listen to, sample, mash-up or interact with music in whatever way you want...[and then] upload your version for

are astonishing illustrations of how technology can connect us to the creativity of world musics and their social meanings in a particular time and place. Young people are engaging in forms of symbolic creativity (Willis, 1977) with the musical modalities of their subcultural and post-subcultural practices, and other music 'scenes'; they attempt to re-invent themselves at both the centres and the margins, real and virtual, of musical globalization and rapid change.

In order to make my argument, I draw on two studies and propose that the lack of alignment between education and what young people bring in response (as they put various forms of musical creativities into practice) can be best understood through a grasp of the most enduring assumptions and canonical challenges that are built into our language and that have shaped policy and practice in music creativity in relation to educational systems (Clarke et al., 2009; Cook, 1998). The sacred concept of 'composition' (the reigning object and activity of the great composers and composition-based approaches to music) is as far removed from most of the world's traditional musics as it is from the globally spatialized internet forms,[6] both of which were *not* originated through formal acts of 'composition'. In order to demythologize the scholarly rhetoric, we need to recognize that it is a human construction, a product of culture, and accordingly varies from time to time and from place to place. We need to ask what 'musical creativity' means to us and think of how we might begin to situate creativity in music and music-making as it is mobilized in practice by social groups.

1.3 Music, education and creativity

One of the enduring beliefs (and hopes) in most societies is that musical creativity has a 'real' and/or 'virtual' existence in children's and young people's everyday lives as a result of societal practices. So, when children enter the music classroom in school for the first time, many of them come with positive attitudes towards creative activity, enjoying it and believing they are creative. There are some who don't seem particularly interested in singing or playing an instrument in a group or the classroom as an activity system, but many parents report that their children create their own music happily and spontaneously at home. Some children may already have started to form views of themselves as music-makers/creators based on support (or lack of support) from pre-school teachers and parents and through comparison with siblings and friends (Butler, 2008). All, however,

---

others to…re-sample' (www.ccmixter.org, accessed March 2010); see also Eric Whitacre's Virtual Choir (www.ted.com/talks/a_choir_as_big_as_the_internet.html), involving 185 voices from 12 countries which join a choir that spans the globe, an astonishing illustration of how technology can connect us.

[6]   **Globally spatialized internet forms** include digital and mobile music, their social networks and the fluid roles in contemporary popular musics between musicians, DJs and audience.

enter as music-makers, cultural creators and culture bearers (Barrett, 2006). All are involved in making unfamiliar combinations of familiar ideas, whether as musical collages or arrangements of known or unfamiliar musics. Creative ideas proliferate.[7]

As children progress through primary school, there will be progressions between those children who exhibit what Bourdieu (2006) terms the 'well-formed *habitus*' and those who do not. There may be some who change from believing that music is something in which everyone can be creative, to believing that specialized talent is needed; children's self-perceptions as composers, songwriters, improvisers or creative performers in music decline to a greater degree than their self-perceptions in other curriculum subjects. They may start to feel less at ease generating original musical ideas; this leads to a loss of motivation for the subject. How teachers act, and how their students participate, how musical creativity is taught as part of school music exerts a strong influence on the way that formative practices are implemented. As they adapt and become accustomed to the school's learning culture and classroom experiences, group compositional and improvisational activity can become bound by routine and conventions, time and resources; the choice and design of tasks is largely determined by the teacher.

As young people progress through the upper secondary school years a 'hierarchy of value' (Cook, 1998) between composing and performing emerges. Music creativity is more often explained as a singular process located within the individual (i.e. that being the composer *as* author is an individualized practice), and in group work within the classroom, contextualized in a social space with a particular time and setting. The community comprises multiple individuals and/or subgroups who share the same object, such as the making of a piece. The division of labour may be shared between the members of the group with the division of power and status distributed evenly or unevenly and norms and conventions that constrain actions and interactions defining the activity system within which the visible actions undertaken within the system are directed towards achieving the goal of composing a piece (for an analysis of the activity system of composing using Engeström's activity system, see Burnard and Younker, 2010).

The social and cultural sites and activity systems in which music creativities arise are increasingly complex and offer up daily reminders, Boden argues, that it involves 'ideas or artefacts that are *new, surprising and valuable*' (2004, p. 2; see Boden's H-creativity[8]). How and where music is being created and consumed will

---

[7]   See Boden (2004) for her two forms of creativity, **P-creativity** and **H-creativity**.

[8]   Boden (2004) asserts that there are two forms of creativity. Being 'P-creative' means coming up with a surprising new idea or artefact that is new to the person who comes up with it (this can happen in three main ways that correspond to the three sorts of surprise: making and appreciating unfamiliar, novel combinations of familiar ideas; exploring conceptual spaces; and transforming the space). Being 'H-creative' means coming up with an idea or artefact that is thoroughly original.

be defined and valued differently in different cultures. In the world (or habitus[9]) of the internet, e-learning and virtual realities, we also have 'virtual fields', the fields of the media and *globally networked or spatialized internet fields*, in which to make digital and mobile music. Social networks and the fluid roles in contemporary popular musics between musicians, DJs and audience feature strongly, as in the use of YouTube. Most recently, an iPhone application called 'Street Orchestra' lets you play classical music with up to 200,000 synched iPhones.[10] While the production and consumption of music and the human experience of music has changed radically, the notion of equally valid creativities through which we can fluidly move is important and yet these features go unrecognized; this is a major threat to, and a potential tragedy for, music education.

1.4 Researching musical creativity

The *particular context* in which the musicians situate the output of creativity (such as Western classical, funk, rock, rap or reggae, and creativity in music is understood and engaged with in the micro-cultures of the family, classroom, studio, street or playground) and the differing systems for creating original music affect how it is studied. Values spill out untidily at every point in the analysis of musical creativity, and it is one of the abiding weaknesses of much mainstream research that it tends to play down their significance in shaping and explaining observable practice.

Depending upon whether scholars are allied to psychology, sociology or humanistic disciplines (such as art history, aesthetics or criticism), they start from different premises. This extends to the ways in which they formulate questions related to musical creativity. Because the subject of research itself is a matter of debate between competing intellectual orientations, researchers differ among themselves in the ways they view society, social actors and processes. Added to

---

[9]   'Habitus' is a Bourdieuan (2006) term denoting both a system of schemata for the production of practices and a system of perception and appreciation of practices which one has acquired, but which has become durably incorporated in the form of permanent dispositions and which implies knowing one's place but also having a sense of the place of others (i.e. the rules of the game).

[10]   The **Street Orchestra** iPhone application is the world's first 'synched' musical experience. This application allows you and your friends to create an orchestra and make music wherever you are. You just choose your instrument, gather your orchestra and join the revolution. While the experience of playing the game does not comfortably constitute a creative act, the creators of the application, at Gothenburg University, have had to create a new method of synchronization using their own note editor in Microsoft .NET. Being the world's first 'synched' musical application in the field has set a new benchmark (see http:// theorchestraapp.com/).

this lack of consensus is the *problem that musical creativity* is conceived differently and constructed differently within different historical practices.

We know creativity in music arises within and depends upon the legitimizing frameworks of public opinion and conventions (i.e. ways of doing something, such as the way musicians use conventional patterns of melody, harmony and rhythm to create emotional tension and release, and thus musical meaning). Yet research evidence is still patchy on what counts as 'musical creativity', the development of the conception of 'musical creativity' itself and what is made of it in educational systems.

As with general creativity, several literature reviews of musical creativity research exist (see, for example, Burnard, 2006a, 2006b, 2007 and Hickey, 2003, 2007 for some of the latest reviews; Webster, 1992 for an earlier review; Deliège & Wiggins, 2006 for a comprehensive discussion interwoven with a distillation of the literature in which musical creativity has been construed, constructed and contested from early childhood through to adulthood). The reviews bring together musicians of various kinds, people in education, in artificial intelligence, in philosophy, sociology, psychology, neurosciences and psychotherapy and provide a variety of perspectives, methods and goals for examining music creativity. Yet the lack of congruence that emerges between research, policy and practice about what renders creativity in music education remains problematic.

The common ground among *social perspectives* is that they are based on the conviction that creativity is vital to all societies, to all fields, domains and cultures. Social perspectives on music education are not, as some have suggested, 'just political'; they represent the lived meanings of musical culture and communities. Interestingly, both Mihaly Csikszentmihalyi and French sociologist and philosopher Pierre Bourdieu investigate the relationship between creativity and cultural evolution. Inspired by the process of species evolution, a 'confluence' of three subsystems has been identified. These subsystems are firstly the *domain*, which includes a set of rules and practices. Any culture is composed of thousands of independent domains, and most human behaviours or activities are affected by rules of some domains. Secondly the *individual*, who is the most important from the psychological perspective, makes novel variations in the contents of the domain and these will be evaluated by the third part of the system, which is the *field*. *Field*s are held by various gatekeepers, such as experts and scholars, who have the rights to choose which variations can be preserved in the domains. Csikszentmihalyi (1999) takes the position that creativity is about adding something new in relation to the culture. The creation by an individual must be legitimized by a member of the group who is qualified to make such a judgement and who is an expert in the domain (see Figure 1.1).

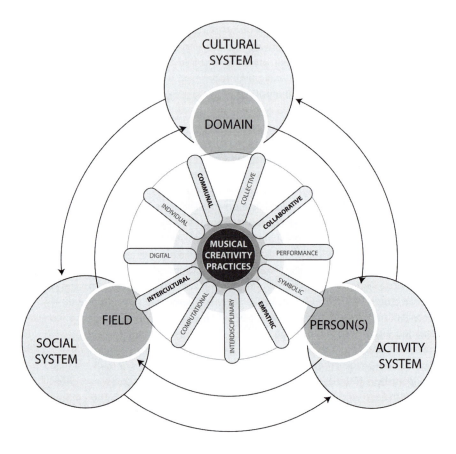

Figure 1.1   A practice perspective for exploring the multiple musical creativities

The *socio-personal* perspective on creativity, as espoused by social psychologist Amabile (1996), suggests creativity arises in all people, including children. Amabile provides us with a *componential model of creativity* in which a number of components converge; these include social environment, task motivation, intrinsic/extrinsic rewards, domain-relevant skills (music aptitude, experience) and creativity-relevant skills (fluency, flexibility, originality). In ground-breaking work, Hickey (2001) has newly adapted Amabile's scheme and applied its tenets to creative musical thinking in the context of musical composition with children in the classroom. From this wellspring of ideas come new ways to view the musical creativity of children and young people.

Studies over many years have shown that creativity assessment is an important aspect of music education and that attention to improving its practice can enhance the learners' achievements and development. Both Webster (2002) and Hickey (2003, 2007; with Lipscom, 2006) introduced ways of addressing this.

1.5 (Re-)conceptualizing musical creativity using the discourse of 'practice'

Given the ontological role of musical creativity to reshape, re-interpret and create anew the human agency in music creativity, it is useful to set the theoretical scene for a socio-cultural view of musical creativity.

Lave and Wenger describe learning as an integral part of 'generative social practice in the lived-in world' (1991, p. 35). Their definition bears analysis: *generative* implies that learning is an act of creation or co-creation; *social* suggests that at least a portion of learning time occurs in partnership with others; and *lived-in world* connotes real world *practices* and settings that make learning more relevant, useful and transferable. Situated musical creativity is generative and it involves acts of creation or co-creation in social contexts. Dynamic communities of practice are seen as critical elements of *situated creativity* (Lave & Wenger, 1991). Thus, musical creativity need not just involve teacher and student but also assorted others, such as other experts from the school, from creative industries, from business and local community artists, and from the digital music world community. Further, *learning communities* are dynamic in that members assume various roles at different times depending on the needs of the learner. For example, a student may be a learner, instructor or coach at any given time during the learning episode. Having previously learned how to scan and place images on a project web page, a student may instruct and coach others (fellow students, parents or friends) through this same process.

Bourdieu (1990) claims musical taste and aesthetic judgement are largely determined by and distributed in a 'field' (e.g. the cultural field) and are related to each other in terms of their synchronistic positioning; they are structured between high and low (that which is deemed to have distinction and confers 'cultural capital' and that which is vulgar). Paradoxically, music educators are sometimes reluctant to reveal their own preferences. Aesthetic value is generated through the relationships between positions rather than through the musical (or art) object in itself. Letting students choose what pieces to compose, what task to undertake or even what creativity looks like provides an opportunity for their teachers to learn what musical creativity looks like from a student perspective and how it engages the student, while, maybe, protecting the teacher from being seen as 'uncool'. Various questions arise: How do teachers value what students have to say about musical creativity? What do teachers value? What criteria are applied by teachers and learners when both are consumers (as listeners, downloaders) and producers (as music-makers and creators)? Both are concerned with the production of judgements: the evaluation of the relative merits of musical objects and discrimination between 'better' and 'worse'.

The production of aesthetic judgements is something that people *do* within a socio-historical context (a field). This field can be described in terms of its structural features and its generative principles (its 'powers'), and it can be understood at the level of the individual in terms of the mediation of habitus. This type of context is conventionally termed a 'canon' and its distinctive feature is that it is extensive in space and time. It is not simply an accumulation of times (musical works) but a dynamic arena for the formulation of endlessly contested and disputed judgements. Music education still promotes a continuing hegemony that favours the 'masterworks' of the past and romantic notions of the lone artist. The full – and different – picture of how the fields of music education and the music industry meet and interrelate remains seriously under-researched. It is in fact impossible to account for the creativities of the music educational world in relation to the music industry unless one looks at the interface between assessment models and the principles underpinning 'musical creativity' as implicitly defined forms and practices that are objectively and subjectively oriented towards certain historical practices.

The notion of 'practice' is particularly relevant here. Bourdieu, a sociologist whose hobby was photography, looked at institutionalized social practices like marriage and education, before he turned his attention to creative practices. His interest in what he calls 'the field of cultural production' led him to analyse the relationship between ways of understanding the world, and the principles behind creative works that are made in a particular place and time and the meanings people attach to what he calls 'practices of distinction'. Bourdieu puts forward a theory of practice which, he argues, is:

> The knowledge we shall call phenomenological…sets out to make explicit the truth of the primary experience of the social world…The knowledge we shall term objectivist…constructs the objective relations…which structure practice and representations of practice…and the theory of practice inscribed (in its practical state) in this mode of knowledge, that we can integrate the gains from it into an adequate science of practices. (1977, p. 3)

This provides an interesting perspective on 'practice' as the locus of musical creativity. What might the practice of musical creativity, inscribed by the popular music composition of an adolescent rock guitarist whose end-products are the result of an originals' band collective effort share with the contemporary classical composer whose creativity is embedded in improvisatory practices? What practice of 'composition' is inscribed when club DJ and crowd interact through records to create unique happenings? What practice of musical creativity is inscribed by DJs who legitimately claim to compose, arrange, improvise and perform combining new and remixed samples, as collectors and players of records in a 'live' club context, where interacting, mediating and orchestrating the crowd establishes an autonomous conceptual discourse of musical creativity?

The problem with definitions as with conceptual discourse (e.g. in articulating 'what is musical creativity?') is that they tend to move from one extreme of the discourse to another. The notion of 'practice', however, engenders musical creativity with overlapping meanings within which the socially and culturally constructed activity systems arise. Yet there is little interaction between educational systems (including academia) and the 'real world' practices of the music and creative industries; each has separate roles and makes separate decisions about what constitutes musical creativity as it is practised. My point here is to argue for the broadening of the concept of 'musical creativity' to include a plurality of equally valid creativities through which musicians may fluidly move or situate within realms of creating and receiving musical artworks and cultural products. What if musical creativities were characterized by their practice, each with its own orienting values and salient features? What if we understood these differing systems for creating original music as autonomous in their own terms? These differing practices would include the following creativities.

Individual creativity allies itself with an ideology of *self-contained individualism* and assumes the high-art model of creativity as the impetus and endeavour of the individual grounded in '*self-responsibility*'. It is commonly believed, especially within the classical music world, that musical creativity is *an embodied practice* involving an individual disposition. Such accounts often feature the self–other binary (see Burnard & Younker, 2004). In contrast, **collaborative (or group) creativity** is grounded in *shared responsibility* which comprehends the actual practices as resulting in joint creative endeavours. Ideas are generated from joint thinking and from sustained, shared struggles to achieve shared musical outcomes and ownership. According to Sawyer (2003), group creativity depends on a shared system of creative conventions; no one can create music without first internalizing the rules and conventions of the domain – a kind of codified practice with emphasis placed on the *significance of relationships*, on synergy in relationships, partnerships and on valuing the other (see Burnard & Younker, 2010). Similarly, **communal creativity** is grounded in a *socially distributed, relationship-oriented* view of musical creativity. The meaning of one's self and self-development occurs '*in relation*' to others rather than being individualized; the process occurs through *mutuality, interaction and exchange* between actors within wider circles of community and creativity and is seen as an ongoing accomplishment of that process (see Lapidaki et al., forthcoming; Odena, 2010).

Empathic creativity allies itself with the idea of empathy in creative musical interaction. Empathy, described by Evan Thompson as 'the involuntary coupling or pairing of my living body with your living body in perception and action' (quoted in Proctor, 2005, p. 5), is important for creativity in musical group interaction in which individuals experience intersubjective communication. What implicates empathy as an emotional capacity is an attribute or quality associated with and occurring in collaborative and communal settings in which creative music-making gains its expressive power from its mimicking facial expressions and body postures of others, facilitating the sharing of musical states (Frith & Frith, 2006). Empathic creativity involves the ability to have emotional and experiential responses to the feelings of others that approximate their responses and experiences. How musical creativity becomes empathically funded and so resonant with empathic meaning is the meaning and value of empathic creativity; a process-oriented activity (see Cross, Laurence & Rabinowitch, forthcoming; Rabinowitch, Cross & Burnard, forthcoming).

Intercultural creativity in music allies itself with cultural construction, and links musical creativity with its cultural surrounds, transforming musical creativity in such a way that the cultural meanings play a vital role in creativity with a commitment to both tradition and change. Forms of musical creativity may be evaluated by society and judged to be creative masterpieces by some or provoke outrage in others with their radical novelty (see Saether et al., forthcoming).

Performance creativity in music, particularly in the more improvisational genres, including jazz, fiddle playing and drumming, is often based on the implicit assumption that all performances are variations. With the prevalence of improvisation in performance, whether using staged or situated techniques, this form of creativity is implicitly socially embedded, interactional and interpretative in nature (see Sawyer, 1997). Similarly, **symbolic creativity in music** (first coined by Willis, 1977) draws on sociological theories for mapping out and reflecting on cultural and subcultural forms of music and the attribution of 'symbolism' to a social activity or humanly produced artefact, which implies a value judgement (see Bennett, 1999, who examines the relationship between youth, style and musical taste and notions of identity that are 'constructed' rather than 'given').

Computational creativity has been defined by Cope as 'initialisation of connections between two or more multifaceted things, ideas or phenomena hitherto not otherwise considered actively connected' (2005, p. 111). This can also apply to networked Web tools for music classroom applications (see the jam2jam social networking site at www.jam2jam.com). Similarly, **collective creativity** allies itself with a particular canon (such as live-coding or electro-acoustic music) and is practised on the intersection of music, interaction and social networking; collective creativity is about building rule-led communities in which performances are contingent, in part, because they are collective; activity is often institutionalized, robust and interdisciplinary (see Tanaka et al., 2005).

Taken together, these differing systems for creating musics form an integral part of generative social practices in the lived-in world: 'generative' in that they describe acts of creation or co-creation; 'social' in that they each occur with social groups or partnerships; 'the lived-in world' connotes real practices and settings that broaden the remit of the term 'musical creativity' and its invariable use in the singular. The notion of a plurality of equally valid creativities through which we can fluidly move and practise multiple music creativities concurrently cuts across the false dichotomies of mind and body, subject and object, feeling and thought, 'high' and 'low' art. These distinct creativities in music, as illustrated in Figure 1.1, are not oppositional but rather seek to broaden the sanitized and singular conception of 'musical creativity' – the preserve of the mythical, isolated Great composer, Great jazzer or Great songwriter (Cook, 1998).

1.6 Examples of musical creativities as practised in and out of classroom settings

Here, I will present two recent studies that report on distinct practices of musical creativity. Each case maps on to and illustrates distinctive realms of the model of multiple musical creativities (see Figure 1.1).

One study is situated in the classroom and illustrates how *collaborative* and *individual creativities in music* are inscribed in primary and secondary practices respectively. The other study is situated within a workshop practice and plays on local historical spaces facilitated by a school–artist partnership, which emphasizes dual conceptions of *individual* and *communal creativities in music*. Each practice concerns practices of musical composition and improvisation with conventional genre demarcations and divisions. Each practice, as insightfully explained by Bourdieu, is 'a *modus operandi* informing all thought and action'; each practice is 'variably constituted by the fields within which their work is disseminated' (1977, p. 18); each has its own status, schemes of action, orientations, rules and codes of behaviour, and can be broken down into individual positions, steps or moves, which integrate into the unity of an activity system. Each practice is an expression of a plurality of equally valid creativities through which students may or may not move fluidly or cut across different forms and ways of locating creativity in their music.

Data from each project are occasionally woven into the narrative; however, the use of evidence is not intended to lead to a conclusion. Rather, I want to present some empirical explorations that serve as illustrations of a more extensive theoretical and conceptual discussion. Each project from which these data are drawn was designed to examine, among other questions, 'what counts as creativity in music'. Each case demonstrates that diverse practices of musical creativity relate not to a fixed external referent in the world that exists prior to the process, but to the construction of a scheme of actions (i.e. a practice) that is socially and culturally situated.

The two studies involve data generation strategies and sites that are described in full elsewhere, but which adopt mixed-methods research: a qualitative interpretative case study and a narrative inquiry approach, respectively. Data sources for one study included e-survey interviews, observations, work samples/ artefacts and reflection on and reconstruction of practice alongside document analysis (see Burnard & Lavicza, 2010). Case study data included transcriptions of primary and secondary students'[11] music-making processes and products, together with the musical notations arising from creative endeavours, and observational and interview data from teachers who evaluated the work (as process) and assessed its outcomes (as products). Interview data, drawn from a post hoc study with artists

---

[11]   Only secondary school data sets are drawn in this chapter. See Burnard and Lavicza (2010) for primary and secondary music and visual arts teachers' conceptions and practices.

who champion contemporary arts practice in educational settings, included pupil perceptions of learning with artists (Burnard & Swann, 2010).

1.6.1 Composing spaces and the dominant discourse of classroom practice

The English education system is based on a National Curriculum (NC) that is divided into four key stages and caters for pupils between the ages of 4 and 16. It is a statutory requirement for all students to study music throughout Key Stages (KSs) 1 to 3. Music becomes an optional subject at KS 4 (ages 14 to 16) with students working towards a General Certificate of Secondary Education (GCSE) examination. There is an Early Years and Foundation Stage (EYFS) framework for pre-school age children, and post-16 courses are offered for those wanting to study music in the post-compulsory sector.

For each key stage, 'programmes of study' specify in detail what pupils should be taught in music, while 'attainment targets' set out the 'the knowledge, skills and understanding' that pupils of different abilities and maturities are expected to have acquired by the end of each key stage. Attainment targets consist of eight level descriptions of increasing difficulty, plus a description for exceptional performance above level 8 (QCA, 2007).

The requirement for schools to promote 'thinking skills' and enable pupils 'to think creatively' and 'become creative' was explicitly presented in the NC and in key policy texts from 1999 onwards. An analysis of the English primary national curriculum (QCDA, 2010) shows the word 'creativity' and its inflections being used more and more frequently in a variety of different contexts.

In music, the concept of collaborative (or group) creativity is often invoked when discussing classroom music-making. Collaborating on group compositional tasks can involve individuals producing their end-products arising from group improvisatory activity. The musical work may be created using ICT or a combination of instruments, voice and music technologies and may emphasize the work of an individual rather than a group or the creation of a piece of music whose formal properties remain largely assessed in terms of quality of performance. Yet the assessment of performance creativity in school music within the primary or secondary school curricula does not have a well-established place in educational practice nor does it form a standard element of pedagogic activity.

Teachers are required to assign each pupil to the most appropriate level of attainment at the end of each key stage (at ages 7, 11 and 14). When music becomes an optional subject, the qualifications are provided by one of three national Awarding Bodies which implement the nationally based subject criteria for music. Standards of attainment at this stage become driven by the quality of students' work in relation to performance descriptors describing minimum standards at key 'grade' points. Hence, the policy context for music education in England can be considered to be nationally prescribed and working within a tightly controlled quality framework.

'Creativity' figures prominently in the EYFS framework, where promoting a child's creativity and critical thinking skills is one commitment to the principles of learning and development (DCMS, 2008). Teachers emphasize the importance of individual and collaborative creativities. Musical creativity is communicated and experienced as the result of creative energies, acts and musical behaviours developed throughout KSs 1 to 3 in the music programmes of study. The focus is mainly on creating and developing 'new' or reworking 'old' and recombining existing elements and musical ideas. The elements of a musical genre are used creatively and incorporated into a shared performance through mainly group composing and improvising. The institutional conditions that frame music creativities' realization, even if the students aren't fully participating, are mainly collaborative practices from KS 1 to 3. At KS 3, the creation of pieces and popular forms becomes increasingly appropriated through individual creativity practices. This focus is a key dimension by means of which pupils' progress is measured in KSs 1 to 3. At KS 3, 'creativity' in music forms a key strand of relevant knowledge and understanding. It is understood to mean using existing musical knowledge and skills for new purposes, in new contexts, and to explore ways in which music can be combined with other art forms. However, there is no direct reference to creativity in the NC attainment levels, which appear more concerned with technical proficiency. The GCSE music subject criteria have 'creative thinking' as a specified learning outcome underpinned loosely by reference to composing skills.

Music teachers are being asked to enhance pupils' creativity through music education while not being required to formally assess the creative aspects of their work or to consider progression in musical skills with reference to 'creativity' itself (Odena & Welch, 2009). In the previous study, music teachers struggle to explain what they understood by being creative in music. They are hesitant in their views about what constitutes a creative response. Generally they relate creativity to musical outcomes more than the process of music-making itself. The secondary teachers choose to relate their understanding of creativity to the assessment objectives from Awarding Body specifications. The word 'creativity' is largely absent from these documents (with the exception of one GCSE music specification) and it is significant that the teachers in this particular study by Odena and Welch (2009) do not identify creativity as a learning outcome or assessment criterion.

In a recent and timely study of Creativity Assessment Practice in the Arts (CAPA), researchers sought to clarify the construct of 'creativity' as perceived and practised by teachers and students (Burnard & Lavicsa, 2010). The CAPA study employed a combination of qualitative data collected by interviews (and contextual observations) and an online survey, distributed via email to key music and visual arts personnel across a range of primary and secondary schools in five local education authorities.

The study focused on the following research questions: (a) What is the construct 'creativity' and how is it expressed in music and visual arts curriculum documents and assessment practices across primary and secondary sectors? (b) How do teachers and students perceive the construct of 'creativity' to be manifested in music and visual arts curriculum documents and assessment practices?

Interview data from four schools (two primary and two secondary) in East Anglia informed the construction and piloting of a questionnaire which was emailed to 300 schools (accessing 120 music/visual arts teachers) recruited to the project from five south-eastern English counties (Cambridgeshire, Essex, Hertfordshire, Norfolk and Suffolk). Instruments included observations (each class was observed, with, where possible, some presentation of pupils' work, primarily for familiarization with the schools, teachers and students and to contextualize the interview questions and analysis); interviews (these included individual face-to-face interviews with the teachers and group interviews with the students from four schools which resulted in approximately 12 hours of interview data for transcription); work samples/artefacts (the collection of documentation of teachers' practices and the inclusion of assessment tasks, work samples, teacher-developed tests, portfolios, critiques, sketchbooks and checklists reflecting the emphasis of assessment of pupil work in music composition, improvisation, performance and listening tasks) and a survey (which included background variables as well as statements (3-5 items per concept for the development of latent variables based on the results of the qualitative study and the literature).

At the end of the survey data collection we received 303 responses that we were able to include in the analysis process. The initial analysis suggests that the majority of teachers (85 per cent) agreed (agreed or strongly agreed on a 5-point Likert scale) that creativity involves taking risks and developing new/unconventional ideas. Nearly two-thirds of participants (65 per cent) implied that creativity can be judged by the value invested in the art process, but at the same time many teachers (40 per cent) believed that creativity is independent of skills. In spite of this creativity can be assessed in the school setting (75 per cent), but this judgement is often subjective (51 per cent). Participants emphasized that assessing creativity is quite difficult and adequate training would be beneficial for their work (74 per cent). However, only 42 per cent reported receiving adequate training and they gained experience through their work, whereas only 55 per cent declared that these experiences qualified them well for assessing creativity.

Conclusions and implications from the analysis include a consideration of the differentiated nature of what 'musical creativity' might mean in relation to classroom-based assessment, where assessment of creativities in music can be practised and how creativity assessment can be operationalized at school levels in and across primary and secondary sectors.

1.6.2 Composing spaces and the dominant discourse of workshop practice

A key element that informed the artists' practice in the Composers' Workshop Project (CWP) was the use of particular spaces as a stimulus and location for creativity. Inhabiting and using a space creatively became an important element of the project. For example, a historic church and heritage sites were locations for the first stages of the project, which later expanded in scale to become a performance in a cathedral.

The project took place on whole days (e.g. inset days), in twilight sessions or on weekend residential courses. One of the key principles that underpinned the artists' approach was the selection of spaces for workshops. The selection of spaces included sites of local significance such as museums, historic buildings, galleries, outdoor landscapes, cathedrals, churches and heritage sites. These sites were selected from within the local area, inspired by the local mythology and community, and were seen as a source and stimulus for ideas. Discussion about the selection of the site provided the starting point for workshop activity. For pupils to engage meaningfully in music composition, like artists, they need to explore how sounds play out, and ideas arise differently, in different spaces. The opportunity to engage, draw inspiration from and be liberated by the sound and space of a particular site, building or environment was a central component within these artists' practice. The artists provided opportunities for pupils to experience at first hand the spatial and temporal properties of a church, a cathedral or hillside, with the intention of exploring how such environments shape the creative process. Furthermore, the different spaces enabled pupils to engage in creative dialogues and develop their own unique creative responses. This was a central and necessary element of the workshops. Learnt assumptions about sound, its organization and the spatial qualities of spaces were challenged. The idea was to stimulate pupils to see and hear things differently. Each workshop culminated in a performance of group and individual compositions inspired by and performed within each site.

The CWP was rooted in assumptions about the context of composing and, by extension, how artist-led facilitation of learning might occur in out-of-school and after-school workshop settings. The workshops were organized as a meeting place where the artists and pupils could participate in brainstorming, experimenting, exploring, improvising, composing and performing original pieces together. The pupils characterized their experience of working with artists as a sense of community-building. They were able to situate themselves within local places and spaces and 'bond' as a community of musicians. They talked of performing, improvising and composing music that was 'local'. The activities were essentially collaborative in nature. A repertoire of means for making and creating new music was developed between them. The practice of music-making seemed more culturally significant to these pupils because they were required to respond to a brief about a local landscape or create works inspired by a local space. The idea of creating pieces in, and for, particular local contexts, as a contemporary practice, seemed to have a profound effect on the pupils. There were many references to the term 'community' and its relationship to understanding, performing and creating music together. The aims were to compose and perform pieces inspired by and created in diverse settings within the local community. The project culminated with a public performance of newly completed pupil compositions created specifically for a cathedral concert presented by some 200 pupils to an audience of parents, family, friends and local school communities (for full account of the project, see Burnard and Swann, 2010).

1.7 The case for rethinking practices in music education

Discussions about what counts as creativity in music and musical creativity are likely to be accompanied by emotion, tradition, mainstream interests and ideology. Bourdieu (1984, p. 16) claimed that musical taste and aesthetic judgement are largely determined by social status. Paradoxically, music educators are sometimes reluctant to reveal their own preferences. There is much to learn from letting students choose or negotiate the kinds of creativities in music education they would like implemented in music programmes; listening to the students helps to decide which approaches are likely to succeed and which are best avoided.

There is an inherent contradiction between calls for more creativity in education and curricula that are becoming increasingly narrow and focused on testing and bureaucratic 'accountability'. Both teachers and their students need to learn about musical creativity as a situated cultural and social activity. We need to reshape and redefine musical creativity in ways that both children and adults can relate to.

We need clearer conceptions of creativity and greater coherence and rigour in curriculum policy documents if creativity is to be a meaningful part of the curriculum. We need radical change to the music curriculum, particularly to reduce prescription, improve coherence and invest more power in teachers and pupils to develop practices engendered by greater self-awareness of the multiple individuals and/or subgroups who share the same social and cultural constructions of musical creativity, to consider new ways of engaging learners in contemporary arts practices and to co-construct conceptions of what constitutes situated forms of musical creativity. One part of these changes should be to develop a rationale for the primary and secondary music curriculum from an explicit position informed by research and scholarship. A persistent problem with the curriculum has been the failure to identify an authoritative definition of musical creativity and use this as a means to ensure greater coherence in articulating how creativity is to be taught and learned. A stable definition and coherent representation of its meaning in the music curriculum is a necessary first step in addressing the challenges for assessing creativity. Although we have shown that, in the academic literature, there are contested views about definitions, there are also clear lines of agreement that could form the basis for a more rigorous and coherent representation in the curriculum.

In recognizing the existence of and need for more than one common form in which musical creativity can be practised in music education, educators need to clarify, work with and promote different ways in which to create original music and music-making practices in the classroom and studio. We need not explain what one mode of musical creativity *is* but rather ask what constitutes the practices on which multiple creativities of music and music-making are based. We need to hold more than one mode of musical creativity, such as written composition, in mind. We need to ask *which music*, from *what* social, cultural and activity system it arises, and *who* are the groups, musicians or artists that support and inform it. In recognizing the multiple creativities in the music and music-making practices of children and young people, judgements should be consciously and deliberately interrelated.

Creative practices need to be considered in the light of the domain, field and activity systems within which they arise. The relative importance of differing systems for creating music, the sensational experience of creating music, the diversity of practices (and performative acts) of creating music and the necessity of translating these understandings into language that can be communicated to others in the weighting of criteria across the field will require rethinking the conceptions of music and creativity in musics, along with the kinds of creativities manifest in music-making in music education; a positioning in the field of music education in relation to the music industry from which music-specific creativities – in practice and theory – need to be reciprocal and interrelated. Music educators, practitioners and researchers need to broaden their conceptualizations of creativities in music in such diverse fields as psychology, sociology, musicology, ethnomusicology and education. We need to accept the inappropriateness of a singular definition of what constitutes creativity in musics. We need to legitimate goals to push and be pushed forward in developing pedagogic practices and contexts of artistic inquiry, positioning them within the discourse of research. The common denominator, for carrying out inquiry into the social construction of music creativities and for identifying what renders distinctive creativities in music, is that a sense of creative self and creative identity is constructed out of the discourse of music creativities as cultural production.

This in turn will lead us to think of the music classroom as an activity system in which local, regional, sub- and cross-cultural conceptions of music creativities are the rule and the engine of changing ideas about the sensational experience of diverse forms of creative processes and how they are rendered differently in different musics.

References

Amabile, T. (1996). *Creativity in context*. Boulder, CO: Westview Press.

Barrett, M. (2006). Inventing songs, inventing worlds: The 'genesis' of creative thought and activity in young children's lives. *International Journal of Early Years Education*, 14(3), 201-220.

Bennett, A. (1999). Subcultures or neo-tribes? Rethinking the relationship between youth, style and musical taste. *Sociology*, 33(3), 599–617.

Bennett, A. (2001). *Cultures of popular music*. Buckingham: Open University Press.

Berliner, P. (1994). *Thinking in jazz: The infinite art of improvisation*. Chicago: University of Chicago Press.

Boden, M. (2004). *The creative mind: Myths and mechanisms*. London: Routledge.

Bourdieu, P. (1977). *Outline of a theory of practice* (trans. R. Nice). Cambridge: Cambridge University Press.

Bourdieu, P. (1984). *Distinction*. London: Routledge & Kegan Paul.

Bourdieu, P. (1990). *The logic of practice*. Cambridge: Polity Press.

Bourdieu, P. (2006). The forms of capital. In H. Lauder, P., Brown, J.-A. Dillabough & A. H. Halsey (Eds.), *Education, globalization and social change* (pp. 105-118). Oxford: Oxford University Press.

Burnard, P. (2006a). The individual and social worlds of children's creativity. In G. McPherson (Ed.), *The child musician* (pp. 353-375). Oxford: Oxford University Press.

Burnard, P. (2006b). Understanding children's meaning-making as composers. In I. Deliège & G. Wiggins (Eds.), *Musical creativity: Multidisciplinary research in theory and practice* (pp. 111-133). New York: Psychology Press.

Burnard, P. (2007). Perspectives on and routes to understanding musical creativity. In L. Bresler (Ed.), *International handbook of research in arts education*. Dordrecht: Kluwer.

Burnard, P. (forthcoming). *Music creativities in real world contexts*. Oxford: Oxford University Press.

Burnard, P. & Lavicza, Z. (2010). Primary and secondary music and visual arts teachers' conceptions and practices of Assessing Creativity in the Arts (ACA): Developing the ACA questionnaire. In G. Mota & A. Yin (Eds.), *Proceedings of the ISME 23rd Research Commission Seminar 25-30 July, North East Normal University, Changchun* (pp. 107-111). Changchun, China: ISME Research Commission.

Burnard, P. & Swann, M. (2010). Pupil perceptions of learning with artists: A new order of experience? *Thinking Skills and Creativity*, 5(2), 70-83.

Burnard, P. & Younker, B. A. (2004). Creativity and individual composing pathways: Perspectives within a cross-cultural framework. *International Journal of Music Education*, 22(1), 59–76.

Burnard, P. & Younker, B. A. (2010). Towards a broader conception of creativity in the music classroom: A case for using Engeström's activity theory as a basis for researching and characterizing group music-making practices. In R. Wright (Ed.), *Sociology and music education* (pp. 165-192). Farnham: Ashgate.

Butler, R. (2008). Evaluating competence and maintaining self-worth between early and middle childhood: Blissful ignorance or the construction of knowledge and strategies in context? In H. W. Marsh, R. G. Craven & D. M. McInerney (Eds.), *Self-processes, learning and enabling human potential* (pp. 193-222). Charlotte, NC: Information Age Publishing.

Clarke, E., Dibben, N. & Pitts, S. (2009). *Music and mind in everyday life*. Oxford: Oxford University Press.

Cook, N. (1998). *Music: A very short introduction*. Oxford: Oxford University Press.

Cope, D. (2005). *Computer models of musical creativity*. Cambridge, MA: MIT Press.

Cross, I, Laurence, F. & Rabinowitch, T. (forthcoming). Empathy and creativity in group musical practices: Towards a concept of empathic creativity. In G. McPherson & G. Welch (Eds.), *The Oxford handbook of music education*. Oxford: Oxford University Press.

Csikszentmihalyi, M. (1999). Implications of a systems perspective for the study of creativity. In R. J. Sternberg (Ed.), *Handbook of creativity* (pp. 313-335). New York: Cambridge University Press.

Csikszentmihalyi, M. & Wolfe, R. (2001). New conceptions and research approaches to creativity: Implications of a systems perspective for creativity in education. In K. Heller (Ed.), *International handbook of giftedness and talent* (pp. 81-93). New York: Pergamon.

Deliège, I. & Wiggins, G. (Eds.) (2006). *Musical creativity: Multidisciplinary research in theory and practice* (pp. 146-167). New York: Psychology Press.

Department for Culture Media and Sport (2008). *Statutory framework for the early years and foundation stage* – see www.standards.dcsf.gov.uk/eyfs (accessed 10 November 2010).

Engeström, Y. (1993). Developmental studies of work as a testbench of activity theory. In S. Chaiklin & J. Lave (Eds.), *Understanding practice: Perspectives on activity and context* (pp. 64-103). Cambridge: Cambridge University Press.

Fautley, M. (2010). *Assessment in music education*. Oxford: Oxford University Press.

Finnegan, R. (2007). *The hidden musicians: Music-making in an English town*. Cambridge: Cambridge University Press.

Frith, C. D. & Frith, U. (2006). How we predict what other people are going to do. *Brain Research*, 1079, 36-46.

Hickey, M. (2001). An application of Amabile's Consensual Assessment Technique for rating the creativity of children's musical compositions. *Journal of Research in Music Education*, 49(3), 234-244.

Hickey, M. (Ed.) (2003). *Why and how to teach music composition: A new horizon for music education* (pp. 113-38). Reston, VA: MENC.

Hickey, M. (2007). Assessing creativity: An oxymoron. In T. S. Brophy (Ed.), *Assessment in music education: Integrating curriculum, theory and practice. Proceedings of the 2007 Florida symposium on assessment in music education* (pp. 191-200). Chicago: GIA Publications.

Hickey, M. & Lipscom, S. (2006). How different is good? How good is different? The assessment of children's creative musical thinking. In I. Deliège & G. Wiggins (Eds.), *Musical creativity: Multidisciplinary research in theory and practice* (pp. 97-110). New York: Psychology Press.

Lamont, A., Hargreaves, D. J., Marshall, N. & Tarrant, M. (2003). Young people's music in and out of school. *British Journal of Music Education*, 20(3), 229-242.

Lapidaki, E., de Groot, R. & Stagkos, P. (forthcoming). Communal creativity as socio-musical practice. In G. McPherson & G. Welch (Eds.), *The Oxford handbook of music education*. Oxford: Oxford University Press.

Lave, J. & Wenger, E. (1991). *Situated learning: Legitimate peripheral participation*. Cambridge: Cambridge University Press.

Longhurst, B. (2007). *Popular music and society*. Cambridge: Polity Press.

McCutchan, A. (1999). *The muse that sings: Composers speak about the creative process*. Oxford: Oxford University Press.

McIntyre, P. (2008). Creativity and cultural production: A study of contemporary Western popular music songwriting. *Creativity Research Journal*, 20(1), 40-52.

Marsh, K. (2008). *The musical playground*. Oxford: Oxford University Press.

Odena, O. (2010). Practitioners' views on cross-community music education projects in Northern Ireland: Alienation, socioeconomic factors and educational potential. *British Educational Research Journal*, 36(1), 83-105.

Odena, O. & Welch, G. (2009). A generative model of teachers' thinking on musical creativity. *Psychology of Music*, 37(4), 416-442.

Proctor, J. D. (2005). Introduction: Rethinking science and religion. In J. D. Proctor (Ed.), *Science, religion, and the human experience* (pp. 3–23). New York: Oxford University Press.

Qualifications and Curriculum Authority (2007). *Music: Programme of study for Key Stage 3 and attainment target*. London: Department for Children, Schools and Families & Qualifications and Curriculum Authority.

Qualifications and Curriculum Development Agency (2010). *National Curriculum* – see http://curriculum.qcda.gov.uk/ (accessed 29 December 2010).

Rabinowitch, T., Cross, I. & Burnard, P. (forthcoming). Between consciousnesses: Embodied musical intersubjectivity. In D. Reynolds & M. Reason (Eds.), *Kinesthetic empathy in creative and cultural practices*. Portland, OR: Intellect.

Saether, E., with Mbye, A. & Shayesteh, R. (forthcoming). Intercultural creativity: Using cultural meetings as a prompting force for creative learning and change. In G. McPherson & G. Welch (Eds.), *The Oxford handbook of music education*. Oxford: Oxford University Press.

Sawyer, K. (Ed.) (1997). *Creativity in performance*. Greenwich, CT: Ablex.

Sawyer, K. (2003). *Group creativity*. Mahwah, NJ: Erlbaum.

Sloboda, J. (1985). *The musical mind: The cognitive psychology of music*. Oxford: Oxford University Press.

Tanaka, A., Tokui, N. & Momeni, A. (2005). *Facilitating collective musical creativity*. Sony Computer Science Laboratory Paris – see www.csl.sony.fr/downloads/papers/2005/tanaka-05a.pdf (accessed 29 December 2010).

Webster, P. (1992). Research on creative thinking music: The assessment literature. In R. Colwell (Ed.), *Handbook of research on music teaching and learning* (pp. 266-278). Reston, VA: MENC.

Webster, P. (2002). Creative thinking in music: Advancing a model. In T. Sullivan & L. Willingham (Eds.), *Creativity and music education* (pp. 16-34). Canada: Britannia Printers and Canadian Music Educators' Association.

Willis, P. (1977). *Learning to labour*. Farnborough: Saxon House.

Chapter 2
Teachers' perceptions of creativity

Oscar Odena and Graham Welch

2.1 Introduction

This chapter draws on a four-year qualitative investigation of creativity in music education with particular reference to the case study perceptions of six secondary school teachers in England. In addition to discussing the findings, the main contribution of the chapter is the consideration of a new generative model of how the teachers' thinking about creativity may develop over time.

The following section reviews the recent surge of 'creativity' in education research and policy. In sections three and four the research questions, theoretical framework and research methodology are outlined. The case study teachers' perceptions of creativity and the influence of their backgrounds on their perceptions are discussed in sections five and six. The final two sections present the generative model of the teachers' thinking and consider some educational implications.

2.2 'Creativity' in education research and policy

'Creativity' is a recurrent topic in education, as exemplified by the work of special interest groups (for instance the British Educational Research Association Special Interest Group Creativity in Education), government departments and advisory committees (Department for Culture Media and Sport, 2006; National Advisory Committee on Cultural and Creative Education, 1999; Scottish Executive, 2006). Researchers' interest in creativity produced a considerable number of investigations in the 1960s and 1970s. While there was a subsequent decrease following this initial surge, interest in creativity has remained consistent and has in fact peaked again in the last decade in many Western countries (Burnard, 2007; Craft & Jeffrey, 2008; Díaz & Riaño, 2007; Hickey, 2002; Kaufman & Sternberg, 2010; Webster, 2009).

As observed elsewhere (Odena, 2001b), there are at least two generic concepts of creativity co-existing: the 'traditional' and the 'new'. The traditional is ascribed to people who contribute significantly to a field and whose contributions are recognized by the community, such as successful adult composers, painters or sculptors. The significance of this traditional perspective in a school context tends to focus more on the output (such as interpretation within the 'canon') rather than the creative process. This implies that although the work of 'the masters' is a source of inspiration and is often studied in educational institutions, such exceptional standards of quality are difficult to reproduce. Other authors have called it *historical creativity* (Boden, 1990) or *big C* creativity (Craft, 2001). In contrast, the 'new' concept (in the sense of being contrasted to the 'traditional') is related to a psychological notion of imaginative thinking and has broad applications in the school context (Savage & Fautley, 2007). Within this latter concept, creativity is defined as imagination successfully manifested in any valued pursuit. Confusion arises when accounts of the new concept are presented as if they were characterizations of the traditional one, as for example when we try to assess young people's musical products using historical creativity criteria.

Taking this situation into account, there are issues that need further consideration. For instance, the term 'creativity' and how creativity might be identified in music classrooms are rarely examined in the literature. A few studies indicate that teachers of arts subjects usually interpret creativity and its teaching in personal terms (Fryer, 1996), while the English National Curriculum devotes a fourth of its requirements for music to developing *creative skills* in the guise of composition and improvisation (Qualifications and Curriculum Authority, 2006). In England, music is a compulsory classroom subject until age 14 and an optional subject subsequently between the ages of 14 and 18. Even though musical creativity practices have a long tradition, which go back to the 1970s experimental work of Paynter and his contemporaries (Mills & Paynter, 2008), having a statutory curriculum does not appear to guarantee a harmonized perception of these practices. For example, concerns have been raised about the standards of composition in generalist schools (Odam, 2000) and on the need for teachers to have more composition and improvisation knowledge if they are to engage fully with the students' composing processes (Berkley, 2001). Other research has suggested that the musical value of improvisation is context and genre sensitive in the lives of music teachers and musicians. For example, an Economic and Social Research Council study of postgraduate musicians undertaking a one-year specialist full-time course to become secondary music teachers in England found that they rated the ability to improvise much more highly than final year undergraduate music students (Hargreaves & Welch, 2003; Welch, 2006). In another example, a recent investigation into the nature of teaching and learning in higher education music studies (the Economic and Social Research Council *Investigating Musical Performance* Project) reported differences between classical and non-classical musicians in their attitudes to improvisation, with the latter (folk, jazz, rock musicians) rating the ability to improvise on their instrument significantly higher, not least because of differences in expected performance traditions (Creech et al., 2008; Welch et al., 2008).

In addition, the term 'creativity' is often used in music education statutory guidelines in two different ways: (a) describing composition/improvisation activities and (b) highlighting the value of creativity as a desirable thinking style. Examples of this duality are evident in the Curriculum for Northern Ireland (Department of Education Northern Ireland, 2006), the National Curriculum for

England (Department for Children Schools and Families & Qualifications and Curriculum Authority, 2007) and the curriculum in Catalonia, Spain (Generalitat de Catalunya, 1992). In England, it is proposed in the secondary school curriculum that the teaching of music increases 'self-discipline' and 'creativity'; consequently pupils need to learn 'to create, develop and extend musical ideas' to make progress in composing skills (Department for Children Schools and Families & Qualifications and Curriculum Authority, 2007: 178-187). Furthermore, the Qualifications and Curriculum Authority (2009: 1) provides specific ways in which the teaching of music is believed to contribute to the development of 'Personal, Learning and Thinking Skills', observing that 'learners can develop as creative thinkers' through analysis and evaluation, selecting 'imaginative ways of working'. Hence, the term creativity is sometimes conveyed to mean a thinking style and at other times to imply activities in composition and/or improvisation.

2.3 Research questions and theoretical framework

This chapter draws on a four-year, case study-based investigation, which focused on creativity in music education with particular reference to the perceptions of six teachers in English secondary schools (Odena, 2004, 2005, 2007a). Two of the original research questions are considered:

1. What are these schoolteachers' perceptions of creativity?
2. In what ways do these teachers' musical and professional experiences influence their perceptions of creativity?

Initial analyses of the first question as well as a description of the influence of the teachers' backgrounds on their viewpoints at the time of data collection are reported elsewhere (Odena, Plummeridge & Welch, 2005; Odena & Welch, 2007). This chapter specifically explores, in the light of recent literature, how the answers to these questions interact in the formulation of a new generative model of the teachers' thinking on creativity in music education.

The initial investigation was divided into four stages and has been subsequently expanded to include other very recent research findings. The four stages were (a) examination of the meanings attached to the word 'creativity' and review of previous studies; (b) discussion of the methodological assumptions underpinning the research; (c) data collection and exploration using thematic analysis; and (d) the drawing of implications. The first stage literature review took a historical consideration of the variety of foci of previous research. Depending on the field of knowledge (aesthetics, musicology, psychology or education), several approaches to the study of creativity have been used, focusing on (i) the characteristics of the creative person, (ii) the description of an appropriate environment for developing creativity, (iii) the study of the creative process and (iv) the definition of the creative product (Odena, forthcoming). In a few studies and meta-analyses of previous enquiries, up to three of these four approaches are evident (Fryer, 1996). In music education research a similar pattern of approaches appeared, with authors discussing the characteristics of creative students (Goncy & Waehler, 2006), the students' composing/improvising processes (Burnard & Younker, 2004; Fautley, 2005; Kennedy, 2002; Seddon & O'Neill, 2003), the environment most conducive to skills development (Berkley, 2004; Byrne & Sheridan, 2001; Glover, 2000) and the assessment of musical products (Green, 2000; Priest, 2006). Therefore, the subsequent fieldwork embraced an emergent fourfold framework that was used for researching case study teachers' perceptions of creativity in music education, focusing on Pupil-Environment-Process-Product.

2.4 Methodology

The participating teachers were deliberately selected following a maximum variation approach (Lincoln & Guba, 1985) on the basis of the combined characteristics of their personal backgrounds and their schools' socio-geographical situation. Their classrooms were videotaped for between three and five hours during lessons involving composition and improvisation activities with students aged 11-14 years. Teachers were interviewed at the beginning (prior to the videotaping) and at the end of the study. In the final interviews, they watched extracts of their lessons and discussed these with the researcher. This video elicitation interview technique had been developed in an earlier pilot study involving three teachers from different schools, which were not included in the final group (Odena, 2001a). All final interviews were understood as in-depth conversations with a purpose that were loosely structured around the videotaped extracts. Up to 30 minutes of short video extracts were selected for each teacher, summarizing their three to five hours of lessons. The aim of these extracts was to allow the teachers to reflect on what happened during the unit of work in terms of the different students in the class, the classroom environment and the students' processes, products and assessment. For reasons of confidentiality, the selection of extracts was not validated by external observers. Instead teachers were asked to comment on the selection at the end of the interviews and all participants agreed that the extracts contained a good summary of what happened during the unit of work. During the interview the interviewer stopped the video after each extract and gathered the teacher's views of what went on during the lesson, using open-ended questions such as 'Would you explain what happened there?' When appropriate, they were also asked to expand or clarify any comments they made relating to the four Pupil-Environment-Process-Product areas.

Interviews were fully transcribed and were analysed using thematic analysis with the assistance of the specialist software NVivo (Odena, 2007b, 2010). This involved a thorough process of reading, categorizing, testing and refining, which was repeated by the first author until all categories were compared against all the teachers' responses, and the overall analysis was discussed with a colleague researcher. Over 87 per cent of the full transcripts – which included the interviewer's questions – were categorized, and two independent researchers read randomly selected parts of the interviews to confirm the reliability of the categorization. Participants were also invited to answer a Musical Career Path questionnaire, derived from Burnard (2000). Employing an undulating line drawn on a single sheet, teachers were asked to write down, in each bend of the line, specific instances that they considered crucial in the direction of their musical and educational lives (see example in Figure 2.1).

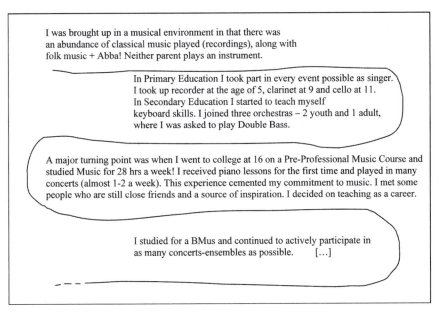

I was brought up in a musical environment in that there was an abundance of classical music played (recordings), along with folk music + Abba! Neither parent plays an instrument.

In Primary Education I took part in every event possible as singer. I took up recorder at the age of 5, clarinet at 9 and cello at 11. In Secondary Education I started to teach myself keyboard skills. I joined three orchestras – 2 youth and 1 adult, where I was asked to play Double Bass.

A major turning point was when I went to college at 16 on a Pre-Professional Music Course and studied Music for 28 hrs a week! I received piano lessons for the first time and played in many concerts (almost 1-2 a week). This experience cemented my commitment to music. I met some people who are still close friends and a source of inspiration. I decided on teaching as a career.

I studied for a BMus and continued to actively participate in as many concerts-ensembles as possible.   [...]

Figure 2.1   Extract from Sarah's Musical Career Path response sheet

Participants were asked to complete the Musical Career Path response sheet answering the following question:

> Thinking back over your life experience, please reflect on specific instances, or critical incidents, which you consider have influenced the direction of your musical live. Brief annotations may be included about any experience that precipitated a change of direction or any influential incident. Please reflect upon your experiences of music studying, making and teaching, at school, with friends and family as well as within the community, and elicit particular incidents and experiences which influenced your career path.

By completing this exercise instead of asking a predetermined list of questions, we intended to gather illustrative examples, maintaining a qualitative-naturalistic research approach (Eisner, 1991). We guaranteed anonymity to participants by assuring them that the videotapes would not be disclosed in the future and that their names would be changed when reporting the study's results. Moreover, in the following sections, confidential information such as years, school and university names are omitted and the gender of one participant has been changed. The teachers' own words are incorporated in the main text in inverted commas.

Overall, the six teachers had fairly contrasting backgrounds. Patrick, the Head of Music in a well-resourced comprehensive school, studied classical performance (piano and viola) as well as a 'conventional' music degree, in which the only composition that he 'ever did' was 'a pastiche of nineteenth-century harmony and counterpoint' (his Musical Career Path is included in Figure 2.2 later in the chapter). Emma learned the piano and sang 'with parents from the age of 6', but stopped her formal music training at 13. At college, she wrote songs, joined a rock band and toured Europe. She had worked as a singer and studio engineer and was currently teaching part-time in a comprehensive inner-city school, and conducting vocal workshops as a freelancer. The third teacher, Laura, remembered arranging songs as a teenager at the piano. She went to a Performing Arts College at 16, studied for a Music and Drama degree at university, majoring in composition, and had experience playing and teaching abroad. She was the head of a small department in an inner-city multicultural comprehensive in an economically deprived area. James, the fourth participant, learned to play the recorder and the cornet at school. At university he specialized in flute as part of his Music and Drama degree and undertook a teacher education course in which he became acquainted with 'world music', but was not taught 'how to go about composing'. He was teaching at a comprehensive school in a rural area. The fifth participant, Elaine, had classical piano training from an early age and studied for a Music degree at university, which did not include 'original composition'. Elaine was the head of a well-resourced department at a comprehensive school in a rural area. The sixth teacher, Sarah, played the recorder, clarinet and cello as a teenager and then went on to study for a Music degree while being a clarinet instrumental teacher. Sarah was the Head of Music at a comprehensive school on the UK's south coast and was also playing regularly in an orchestra and with local jazz groups.

2.5 The teachers' perceptions of creativity

In the long conversations that followed the viewing of the videotaped lessons, teachers talked not only about the students' work, but also about the government's statutory music guidelines and the mixed feelings experienced when watching themselves on TV. For the purpose of this chapter, we focus here on the participants' talk on the creativity of their students. Twenty-two categories and subcategories that referred to the fourfold framework (see Table 2.1) emerged from the analysis of the interviews. The participants' perceptions exemplified, although in different ways, the idea of creativity as a capacity of all students. They viewed creativity in terms of what Craft (2001) described as 'little c' creativity and earlier Elliott (1971) characterized as the 'new concept', where creativity is imagination as successfully displayed in any valued pursuit. Although participants did not agree on how creativity was to be defined, they expressed illuminating views about creative pupils, the environment for creativity, the creative process and creative musical products.

Table 2.1   List of categories (with subcategories in italics) of the teachers' perceptions of creativity emerging from the interviews

Pupil	Environment	Process	Product
1 Personal characteristics	6 Emotional environment *7 Motivation*	15 Different activities	20 Assessment 21 Originality
2 Individual learning *3 Adaptor students* *4 Innovator students*	*8 School culture* *9 Teachers' role* *10 Teaching methods* *11 Time requirements*	16 Group processes 17 Improvisation-Composition	22 Music style and conventions
5 Home background	12 Physical environment *13 Complaints and proposals for improvement* *14 Classroom settings*	18 Structured process 19 Unstructured process	

The similarities and differences between the literature on creativity and these teachers' perceptions (in relation to the second research question) have been explored elsewhere (Odena et al., 2005). Major issues that emerged included the pupils' learning styles, the music school culture and the positive group dynamics. Four of the six teachers observed that pupils experienced music activities with different ways of learning. Borrowing Entwistle's terms (1991), some pupils preferred to work following small steps in a 'serialist' style of learning, while others learned in a 'holist' way, taking the activity as a whole. The former can be compared with 'adaptor' pupils and the latter with 'innovator' pupils (Brinkman, 1999). For the adaptor type of student, closed activities with a range of set instructions were perceived as more appropriate to develop their musical creativity. For instance, as Elaine noted:

> For that [blues composition] unit, when they do their improvisation using the Blues scale...students...often get into a pattern, and they just repeat it over and over again. So, we have a checklist of things like 'have some short notes and

some long notes', 'use different pitches', 'repeat little patterns by sequence' and things like that.

In addition, Elaine observed that some of the students who felt more confident working with closed composition activities would do exactly what she 'asked them, and do it really well', and she commented they would be 'creative as well'. Emma, Laura, Elaine and Sarah observed, nevertheless, that the majority of their pupils were happily engaged with activities with different degrees of 'open' composition. Emma, commenting on video extracts of her pop song composition unit, noted that most of the pupils were 'involved in some way or other' and that only 'about ten per cent' did not fully engage with these activities. The issue for music teachers, then, is how to cope with the different learning styles in any given classroom. As Elaine observed, some pupils 'enjoy the freedom of improvising and others think it's too hard, because they don't know what to do'. She commented that the latter group of pupils just needs 'a few ideas feeding in'.

Teachers' views on the most appropriate environment to enhance creativity were coded under two broad categories: emotional environment and physical environment. Additional subcategories within these, such as *motivation* and *time requirements* illustrated practical issues in accordance with suggestions from previous studies. Three of the six teachers participating in the study observed that, in composition projects, added time pressures brought by examinations and a short time to finish the units affected the atmosphere for creativity. Therefore, the overall quality of the pupils' work suffered:

> [Students] liked they were free to come up with their own ideas, but they wanted more time. (Laura)

> We had such a short amount of time...there was that added pressure of having to learn the songs for the concert AND do the songwriting...I had to push, push, push, push the whole time...And now we've come back after half term, the concert is over...[and] they've stopped fighting me...it is just really relaxed and it wasn't relaxed before. (Emma)

James explained this happened particularly at the end of term:

> Ideally if we had enough time we could then go through each group and give them an idea of what they could have done to improve it. So I try to do that, if I've got time... But the Year 7s seemed very rushed at the end of last term.

The strain suffered by pupils under time restrictions during music activities was perceived by these teachers as detrimental for their compositions. These time pressures could be brought by exams, preparation for school concerts, increasing workload at the end of term or poor weekly timetabling for music that would limit the time allocated to composition projects.

Other subcategories were not found to be examined in the literature to the same extent. For instance, *school culture* contained comments on the schools' music activities and the status of the music department within the school, which included a case where the relations between the department and the school senior management were not positive (Laura). This school had a lack of space and severe budget restrictions, but 'offered valuable insights on how to counterbalance this situation by making use of the pupils' instruments, getting bids from outside agencies and sharing resources with other schools' (Odena et al., 2005, p. 15). Regarding the creative process, these teachers presented different views depending on the activities and the students, particularly Laura and Emma, who were more circumspect and were disinclined to describe a 'universal process' for all students. It seems from the variety of views found in the study that having a compulsory curriculum does not necessarily unify the views of the practitioners regarding creative musical products. All teachers, nevertheless, had criteria that they applied to assess the pupils' work, which were largely negotiated. Indeed, they observed that discussing the assessment with the students was essential to make them aware of the qualities of good work, a view that resonates with the students' views gathered in recent music education investigations (Berkley, 2004; Fautley, 2004) and in an inquiry on the introduction of 'Assessment for Learning' approaches in secondary schools (Leitch et al., 2008).

2.6 The influence of teachers' musical and professional experiences on their perceptions of creativity

A detailed examination of the Musical Career Paths and interview transcripts revealed that participants' experiences could be summarized as falling within three strands: *musical, teacher education* and *professional teaching* strands (Odena & Welch, 2007). Experiences in the *musical* strand included their own music education at school and at undergraduate level, as well as all their current and past musical activities out of school. The *teacher education* strand comprised the teachers' reflective explanations of their experiences during music education postgraduate courses. Finally, the *professional teaching* strand embodied all the anecdotes from their classrooms as well as the memories from previous schools. Participants' musical and professional experiences were summarized into strands for the purpose of making sense of the data; nevertheless the strands contain explanations of social activities that cannot be completely isolated. The significance of the strands on the teachers' perceptions of creativity seemed to relate proportionally to the level of variety in their experiences. These appear to have influenced their views of creative pupils, an environment that fosters creativity, the creative process and creative musical products. Both the *music* and *professional teaching* strands appear to have had a significant effect on the teachers' views of creative pupils. For example, the importance of the *professional teaching* strand is apparent in Patrick's and Laura's recollections from their current and previous schools: working in particular socio-economic school areas brought opposite perceptions of the importance of the students' home backgrounds on their creative potential. Patrick concluded that, from his teaching experiences, a musical family background was not necessarily a condition for creative students: 'I can think of students who are very musically able...who don't have musical backgrounds and others who do.' In contrast, Laura observed that: '[the pupils' home] background does have a very large effect on what they bring, and what they come out with'.

Furthermore, the schools and the day-to-day teaching experiences of Laura and Patrick were different too. Their comments regarding their school music culture underlined the differences between the two schools. Laura was teaching pupils with a wide range of family incomes and backgrounds from different cultures. Patrick was teaching pupils with more similar backgrounds in a relatively affluent city area – that is, in a girl's school where the status of music was far removed from that in Laura's school. While Patrick managed a well-resourced music department ('the instruments we have cost quite a lot of money'), Laura was the head of a small department with a shortage of staff and resources: 'It's a battle to find space in this school...We [have] got a bid from an outside agency to promote the music from certain cultural groups [but] we have no money FROM the school' (her emphasis).

As demonstrated above, at the time of data collection Patrick did not have the same perceptions as Laura regarding the home background influence on pupils' creativity. In addition, he had not experienced a school like Laura's in his own education, as can be seen from his Musical Career Path (Figure 2.2).

In contrast, Laura taught in a large multicultural comprehensive inner-city school in what is classified as an economically deprived area. Uniformed and undercover police could often be seen near the school gates, and she had to keep instruments locked in two large metal cages to prevent thefts. Before starting to teach at this school, she also had experience of working with hearing impaired children in another comprehensive urban school and at a children's camp in an Eastern European country. Figure 2.3 includes an extract of her Musical Career Path.

The *musical* strand also had an effect on how teachers perceived the students. For instance, Emma felt that, thanks to her musical experiences as an adolescent – finding school music restrictive and giving it up at 13, even though she continued to compose songs at home – she could now recognize and help the pupils more inclined to open composition activities and with a dislike for rules.

When about 5-6 years old I used to play around on the piano at a neighbours' – eventually I persuaded my parents to buy a piano and I started lessons […] I started the violin when I went to secondary school and after a year changed to the viola. I played in the orchestra and the wind band and performed in the regular concerts.

At 15 I joined the [County] Youth Orchestra - went on a tour to New England, USA - some of my happiest musical memories; the conductor's teaching style had a great influence on me. Studied A-level music at a specialist music course - lots of playing (especially piano accompanying) and concerts.

I studied for a music degree at [Oxbridge] - very academic course but I had an outstanding tutor who again influenced me as a teacher; lots of orchestral playing and opportunities to conduct which I really enjoyed.

After graduating I went to [university] to do a PGCE - I have always wanted to teach ever since I was about 6 years old! The course was excellent - introduced to many different styles of music - and I had two very contrasting but stimulating teaching practice schools. Both heads of department were very influential on my own teaching.

Started teaching in an inner-city boy's school - learnt a lot, mainly about how not to run a music department! After 18 months I went to be a head of department at another school. After 4 years I came to [this school] where I am now Head of Department. I really enjoy working here and am very proud of what we have achieved over the last four years. I find my teaching very creative and stimulating and my musical skills are continually being developed and stretched

Figure 2.2   Extract from Patrick's Musical Career Path response sheet

With a degree in Music and Drama, and composition being a strong interest, using music technology as an instrument was very exciting. Music making with youngsters at degree level led me to work with hearing impaired children in a [city] comprehensive school and at children's camp in [an Eastern country].

Living in [a North African country] was a strong link with teaching music at a school and playing Irish folk music at a regular venue.

Returning to get the PGCE at [an English university] and ending up running a secondary music department at a [city borough] comprehensive school (still there!!).

Travelling to South Africa on a music tour with youngsters has been an eye opener. Creativity in youngsters is alive and prospering […]

Figure 2.3   Extract from Laura's Musical Career Path response sheet

Regarding the teachers' views of an environment that fosters creativity, the *musical* strand experiences emerged as the most influential. Laura, Emma and Sarah, who had experience with different musical activities, including composition, and different music styles, were more articulate at describing such an environment. Moreover, they were able to detect disturbing factors (anxiety, lack of time) and facilitating features (motivation) and so work to improve the classroom conditions to maximize the musical development of all students. Other teachers with less contrasting experiences on the *musical* strand were more inclined to give the class a predetermined activity and expect creativity to 'grow' (Patrick). The *teacher education* experiences generally introduced participants to different music styles but did not go further into teaching them how to compose.

As mentioned earlier, Emma and Laura were more circumspect than other participants when describing the creative process. These two teachers, who had composing experience, acknowledged that although the creative process required time and effort for everybody, students would get to different composing stages in their own time, and that no general rule or rigid staging could be applied to all pupils.

Regarding the assessment of creative musical products, participants with contrasting experiences in their *musical* strand (different music styles) would consider as 'creative products' some compositions that did not follow the structure and instructions of the classroom activity. For instance, Sarah and Emma observed that they would discuss and agree an individual's assessment criteria with some students. Elaine acquired a similar broader approach from her *professional teaching* experiences, and an example of her teaching is discussed in the following section. The participants' *teacher education* experiences did not appear to affect their perceptions of creative products.

2.7 Discussion: towards a generative model of the teachers' thinking on musical creativity

The participating teachers acknowledged the effect of their musical expertise (e.g. when assessing the pupils' musical products) and the relative influence of their teacher education courses. In addition, their teaching experiences throughout their careers (*professional teaching* strand) appeared to shape their perceptions of musical creativity in the classroom in what might be described as a continuing feedback system (see Figure 2.4). These findings support Dogani's suggestion that teachers' choices regarding practice 'are constrained by their circumstances and their perceptions of those circumstances' and that 'in order to affect the quality of children's learning positively, teachers need to draw their teaching from a range of their previous experiences' as musicians and teachers (2004: 263). Figure 2.4 outlines the interactions between the Pupil-Environment-Process-Product framework 'at work' and the three strands, and how the interactions have the potential to modify the teachers' perceptions over time.

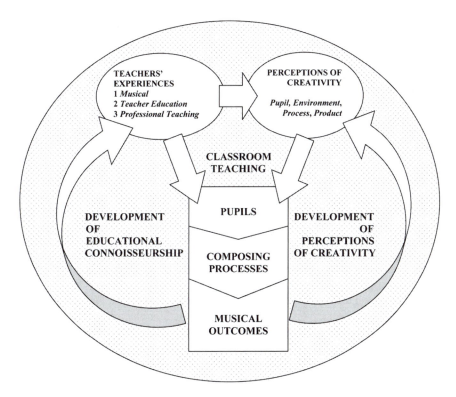

Figure 2.4   A generative model of the teachers' thinking on creativity in music education. Source: Odena & Welch (2009, p. 430)

Essentially, all the above elements are in constant interaction. When preparing the units of work and implementing them in the classroom, the teachers were drawing on their previous experiences (*musical, teacher education* and *professional teaching*), while simultaneously applying their preconceptions of creativity (*pupil, environment, process and product*). Depending on the teacher, their preconceptions had varying degrees of consciousness. For instance, Sarah and Elaine observed that they were not sure to what extent they were imposing their ideas of creativity when assessing the students' work:

[When marking] you are modifying pupils' work…taking away some of their creativity, because you are inherently working within norms. (Sarah)

By saying to them…'if you come back to this note your piece will sound finished off and more complete'…you are teaching a tradition…intervening in a way that makes the tune sound better, but at the same time you want them to be able to hear that it sounds better. So, in other words, I don't just accept their ideas, at face value...and I don't know if that's right or not. (Elaine)

In contrast, Patrick did not see a direct influence of his views on the students' creativity: 'I give [them] the instruments and space...and then creativity will grow.'

The left arrow in Figure 2.4, from bottom to top, shows how teachers develop *educational connoisseurship* (Eisner, 1991) through classroom teaching (e.g. observing the work of different pupils and their composing processes, and assessing musical outcomes). At the same time, their daily work slowly updates their preconceptions of creativity (right arrow), developing new Pupil-Environment-Process-Product perceptions. This includes, for instance, perceptions of the environment most appropriate to facilitate the development of musical creativity or, as discussed in the previous section, the influence of the students' home backgrounds on their potential.

It is apparent that the teachers with more experience of different music styles and composing activities were more aware of the different ways students can approach a composition assignment. They had learned from their own musical experiences, as well as from their teaching experiences. Some teachers were further in their learning journey than others: '[when teaching] my musical skills are continually being developed and stretched' (Patrick, Musical Career Path).

This learning journey carries with it plenty of opportunities for what has been defined by Schön (1983) as reflecting *in* and *on* practice. The first is the thinking and decision-making that goes on while teaching, in real time; whereas reflecting *on* practice is the type of thinking undertaken after the teaching has finished (something that was facilitated in the present study by the use of the video-eliciting technique). These reflecting processes, which have been represented as a cycle including planning, acting, observing and reflecting (Cain et al., 2007), require a fair amount of time and will from teachers, but ultimately, they are beneficial for practice. The generative model of the teachers' thinking presented here embodies the spirit of the reflective practice cycle and incorporates additional elements that interact and appear to generate changes in the teachers' thinking on musical creativity.

An illustrative example of how these interactions have the potential to modify perceptions and teaching practices over time concerns a student in Elaine's school who was initially described as 'conflictive', but towards the end of the school data collection was perceived more positively. This boy had had some behavioural problems in the past. During a unit on *blues* in which all students were asked to rehearse a blues melody at the keyboard and compose and record a solo part, he approached the activities in a different way. He adapted the original blues rhythm to a more contemporary *techno* style and quoted a melody from a dance song in his solo:

> He would just do exactly what he wants in any lesson…and he loves playing the keyboard, so I'd rather have him in the class doing something, than out of the class – which he has been during some of the year. So I try not to get too cross if he is not doing exactly what I've asked them to do. And what he was doing I felt was quite valid. (Elaine)

Elaine then gradually renegotiated the tasks and the assessment criteria with the student, allowing him an increased level of freedom. Watching the videotaped lessons during the final interview, she changed her initial description of the student, observing that he was also 'very creative' in a way that was 'out of the ordinary'. Commenting on one of the taped extracts, Elaine stated: 'he is very creative in a kind of anarchic way in that he would do things like listen to the tunes on his mobile phone, and reproduce them on the keyboard…and that's quite a skill'.

In fact, all the teachers had to adapt their composition/improvisation tasks to the different types of students, taking into account the limitations of the physical environment available (all participants wished they had more resources) and their own preferences (choosing a music style and activities they felt comfortable with). Their role in assessing all these factors, specially the unpredictable ones, and their role in acting upon them in real time was perceived as crucial to the success of the units of work and highlights the importance of the pedagogical expertise of these teachers, or what Eisner (1991) calls educational connoisseurship. This connoisseurship is gained through years of classroom practice, which would explain the relatively minimal influence of the *teacher education* strand on the teachers' perceptions when compared with the other two strands.

2.8 Conclusion: educational implications and issues for further inquiry

As we have shown in this chapter and in previous discussions of these teachers' thinking, the perceptions within the Pupil-Environment-Process-Product areas should not be generalized: teachers develop their own slightly different versions depending on their past experiences, current working context and teaching, and, potentially, any other musical activities undertaken outside school.

This study highlights the importance for music teachers of having practical knowledge of different music styles in order for the knowledge to impact on their teaching. It also supports suggestions that practitioners need appropriate composing experience if they are to both assess work from a range of styles (Pilsbury & Alston, 1996) and engage with the students' composing processes (Berkley, 2001). These processes are not homogenous and the results from this inquiry corroborate observations from other studies regarding the influence of the music style and the students' individual differences on the composing processes (Burnard & Younker, 2004; Seddon & O'Neill, 2003; Soares de Deus, 2006). All these recent studies exemplify the complexity of creativity in music education, which is not always reflected in teaching manuals and statutory guidelines. The generative model illustrates how this complexity is dealt with in the thinking of the participating teachers.

One educational implication that follows from this is the importance of newly qualified music teachers working alongside experienced practitioners to develop educational connoisseurship. Given that the generative model would work from the outset of each teacher's career and that participants presented different views that appear to be linked to different teaching and musical experiences, it would be advisable and beneficial for newly qualified teachers to undertake a mentoring scheme in order to have a sound start in the assessment and reflection of their teaching.

Implications for teacher education courses are, as mentioned earlier, the need for practical work using a variety of different music styles and activities. In a survey of teachers' perceptions and practices of musical improvisation in English primary classrooms, Koutsoupidou (2005) found that teachers were more likely to use improvisation if their higher education included this type of activity. Reflecting on the social worlds of children's musical creativity (see Burnard, 2006) could also be beneficial during development courses to allow teachers to go beyond collecting 'teaching recipes'. Both practical and reflective skills are needed to facilitate the engagement of pupils in composing/improvising experiences with a sense of musical flow (MacDonald et al., 2006). Finally, given the importance of the *musical strand* on the generation of these participants' thinking, further research is needed on the value for classroom teaching of providing opportunities for full-time music teachers to enjoy music-making activities with other musicians out of school.

The purpose of this study was to offer insights on the issues under inquiry. The video-eliciting interview technique and the Musical Career Paths helped to illustrate these teachers' cases with 'intense particularisations' rather than universal statements (Elliott, 2006). Further studies might include a longitudinal investigation, following a group of teachers from the beginning of their careers to a few years into their professional lives. A longitudinal design could reveal the progressive acquisition of the teachers' perceptions of creativity and their modification through interaction with their experiences, giving further support to the proposed generative model.

Acknowledgements

We are most grateful to the participants for their willingness to share their experiences and to Emeritus Reader Charles Plummeridge (Institute of Education) for his advice throughout the research process. The study was supported by the Catalan Government (*Batista i Roca* grants BBR-01-23 and 2002BBR00017). This chapter is a revised version of the article 'A generative model of teachers' thinking on musical creativity' published in *Psychology of Music*, Vol. 37(4), October 2009, by Sage Publications Ltd, All rights reserved. © SEMPRE, 2009.

An extended discussion of research literature and methodology is provided in the article.

References

Berkley, R. (2001). Why is teaching composing so challenging? A survey of classroom observation and teachers' opinions. *British Journal of Music Education*, 18(2), 119-138.

Berkley, R. (2004). Teaching composing as creative problem solving: Conceptualising composing pedagogy. *British Journal of Music Education*, 21(3), 239-263.

Boden, M. (1990). *The creative mind: Myths and mechanisms.* London: Weidenfeld & Nicolson.

Brinkman, D. J. (1999). Problem finding, creativity style and the musical compositions of high school students. *Journal of Creative Behavior*, 33(1), 62-68.

Burnard, P. (2000). How children ascribe meaning to improvisation and composition: Rethinking pedagogy in music education. *Music Education Research*, 2(1), 7-23.

Burnard, P. (2006). The individual and social worlds of children's musical creativity. In G. McPherson (Ed.), *The child as musician* (pp. 353-374). Oxford: Oxford University Press.

Burnard, P. (Ed.) (2007). Section 11 creativity. In L. Bresler (Ed.), *International handbook of research in arts education* (pp. 1173-1290). Dordrecht: Springer.

Burnard, P. & Younker, B. A. (2004). Problem-solving and creativity: Insights from students' individual composing pathways. *International Journal of Music Education*, 22(1), 59-76.

Byrne, Ch. & Sheridan, M. (2001). The SCARLATTI papers: Development of an action research project in music. *British Journal of Music Education*, 18(2), 173-185.

Cain, T., Holmes, M., Larrett, A. & Mattock, J. (2007). Literature-informed, one-turn action research: Three cases and a commentary. *British Educational Research Journal*, 33(1), 91-106.

Craft, A. (2001). Little c creativity. In A. Craft, B. Jeffrey & M. Leibling (Eds.), *Creativity in education* (pp. 45-61). London: Continuum.

Craft, A. & Jeffrey, B. (Eds.) (2008). Special issue: Creativity and performativity in teaching and learning. *British Educational Research Journal*, 34(5).

Creech, A., Papageorgi, I., Duffy, C., Morton, F., Haddon, E., Potter, J., de Bezenac, C., Whyton, T., Himonides, E. & Welch, G. F. (2008). Investigating musical performance: Commonality and diversity amongst classical and non-classical musicians. *Music Education Research*, 10(2), 215-234.

Department for Children Schools and Families & Qualifications and Curriculum Authority (2007). *The national curriculum. Statutory guidelines for Key Stages 3 and 4*. London: Department for Children Schools and Families & QCA.

Department for Culture Media and Sport (2006). *Nurturing creativity in young people: A report to government to inform future policy*. London: Department for Culture Media and Sport & Department for Education and Skills.

Department of Education Northern Ireland (2006). *Programmes of study and attainment targets* – see www.deni.gov.uk (accessed 28 July 2010).

Díaz, M. & Riaño, M. E. (Eds.) (2007). *Creatividad en educación musical [Creativity in music education]*. Santander: University of Cantabria.

Dogani, K. (2004). Teachers' understanding of composing in the primary classroom. *Music Education Research*, 6(3), 263-279.

Eisner, E. (1991). *The enlightened eye: Qualitative inquiry and the enhancement of educational practice*. New York: Macmillan.

Elliott, J. (2006). Navigating the winds of change: The voyage of the good ship action research. Keynote speech at the Collaborative Action Research Network 30th anniversary conference, University of Nottingham.

Elliott, R. K. (1971). Versions of creativity. *Proceedings of the Philosophy of Education Society of Great Britain*, 5(2), 139-152.

Entwistle, N. (1991). How students learn and why they fail. In J. Radford (Ed.), *Talent, teaching and achievement* (pp. 77-96). London: Jessica Kingsley.

Fautley, M. (2004). Teacher intervention strategies in the composing processes of lower secondary school students. *International Journal of Music Education*, 22(3), 201-218.

Fautley, M. (2005). A new model of the group composing process of lower secondary school students. *Music Education Research*, 7(1), 39-57.

Fryer, M. (1996). *Creative teaching and learning*. London: Paul Chapman.

Generalitat de Catalunya (1992). *Currículum. Educació primària [Primary school curriculum]*. Barcelona: Education Department of the Government of Catalonia.

Glover, J. (2000). *Children composing 4-14*. London: RoutledgeFalmer.

Goncy, E. A. & Waehler, C. A. (2006). An empirical investigation of creativity and musical experience. *Psychology of Music*, 34(3), 307-321.

Green, L. (2000). Music as a media art: Evaluation and assessment in the contemporary classroom. In J. Sefton-Green & R. Sinker (Eds.), *Evaluating creativity. Making and learning by young people* (pp. 89-106). London: Routledge.

Hargreaves, D. J. & Welch, G. F. (2003). *Effective teaching in secondary school music: Teacher and pupil identities*. End of award report, ESRC award R000223751.

Hickey, M. (2002). Creativity research in music, visual art, theatre, and dance. In R. Colwell & C. Richardson (Eds.), *The new handbook of research on music teaching and learning* (pp. 398-415). Oxford: MENC and Oxford University Press.

Kaufman, J. C., & Sternberg, R. J. (Eds.) (2010). *The Cambridge handbook of creativity*. Cambridge: Cambridge University Press.

Kennedy, M. A. (2002). Listening to the music: Compositional processes of high school composers. *Journal of Research in Music Education*, 50(2), 94-110.

Koutsoupidou, T. (2005). Improvisation in the English primary music classroom: Teachers' perceptions and practices. *Music Education Research*, 7(3), 363-381.

Leitch, R., Gardner, J., Lundy, L., Clough, P., Odena, O., Mitchell, S. & Galanouli, D. (2008). *Consulting pupils on the assessment of their learning – Teaching and Learning Research Programme, Research briefing 36*. London: TLRP.

Lincoln, Y. S. & Guba, E. G. (1985). *Naturalistic inquiry*. London: Sage.

MacDonald, R., Byrne, Ch. & Carlton, L. (2006). Creativity and flow in musical composition: An empirical investigation. *Psychology of Music*, 34(3), 292-306.

Mills, J. & Paynter, J. (Eds.) (2008). *Thinking and making: Selections from the writings of John Paynter on music education*. Oxford: Oxford University Press.

National Advisory Committee on Creative and Cultural Education (1999). *All our futures: Creativity, culture & education*. Sudbury, Suffolk: Department for Education and Employment.

Odam, G. (2000). Teaching composing in secondary schools: The creative dream. *British Journal of Music Education*, 17(2), 109-127.

Odena, O. (2001a). The construction of creativity: Using video to explore secondary school music teachers' views. *Educate~*, 1(1), 104-122.

Odena, O. (2001b). Developing a framework for the study of teachers' views of creativity in music education. *Goldsmiths Journal of Education*, 4(1), 59-67.

Odena, O. (2004). Some considerations on research dissemination with particular reference to the audience and the authorship of papers. *Music Education Research*, 6(1), 101-110.

Odena, O. (2005). Creatividad en la educación musical. Teoría y percepciones docentes [Creativity in music education. Literature and practitioners' views], *Eufonía. Didáctica de la Música*, 35(1), 82-94.

Odena, O. (2007a). Experiencias de un estudio del pensamiento del profesorado sobre creatividad musical en escuelas de Inglaterra. Implicaciones educativas [Learning from a study of teachers' thinking of musical creativity in England. Educational implications]. In M. Díaz & M. E. Riaño (Eds.), *Creatividad en educación musical* (pp. 61-70). Santander: University of Cantabria.

Odena, O. (2007b). Using specialist software for qualitative data analysis, *Education-line* – see www.leeds.ac.uk/educol/documents/165945.htm (accessed 30 December 2010).

Odena, O. (2010). Practitioners' views on cross-community music education projects in Northern Ireland: Alienation, socio-economic factors and educational potential. *British Educational Research Journal*, 36(1), 83-105.

Odena, O. (forthcoming). Creativity in the secondary music classroom. In G. McPherson & G. Welch (Eds.), *The Oxford handbook of music education*. Oxford: Oxford University Press.

Odena, O. & Welch, G. (2007). The influence of teachers' backgrounds on their perceptions of musical creativity: A qualitative study with secondary school music teachers. *Research Studies in Music Education*, 28(1), 71-81.

Odena, O., Plummeridge, Ch. & Welch, G. (2005). Towards an understanding of creativity in music education: A qualitative exploration of data from English secondary schools. *Bulletin of the Council for Research in Music Education*, 163, 9-18.

Pilsbury, Ch. & Alston, P. (1996). Too fine a net to catch the fish? An investigation of the assessment of composition in GCSE music. *British Journal of Music Education*, 13(3), 243-258.

Priest, T. (2006). Judges' assessments of creativity under three conditions. *Bulletin of the Council for Research in Music Education*, 167, 3-14.

Qualifications and Curriculum Authority (2006). *National curriculum online* – see http://curriculum.qca.org.uk (accessed 2 July 2010).

Qualifications and Curriculum Authority (2009). *How do we develop PLTS in music?* National curriculum online – see http://curriculum.qca.org.uk/key-stages-3-and-4/subjects/music (accessed 2 July 2010).

Savage, J. & Fautley, M. (2007). *Creativity in secondary education*. Exeter: Learning Matters.

Schön, D. A. (1983). *The reflective practitioner. How professionals think in action.* London: Basic Books.

Scottish Executive (2006). *Promoting creativity in education: Overview of key national policy developments across the UK*. Edinburgh: Scottish Executive Education Department.

Seddon, F. A. & O'Neill, S. A. (2003). Creative thinking processes in adolescent computer-based composition: An analysis of strategies adopted and the influence of instrumental music training. *Music Education Research*, 5(2), 125-137.

Soares de Deus, J. (2006). Adolescent's engagement in computer-based composition in Brazil. Unpublished PhD thesis, Institute of Education, University of London.

Webster, P. R. (2009). Children as creative thinkers in music. Focus on composition. In S. Hallam, I. Cross & M. Thaut (Eds.), *The Oxford handbook of music psychology* (pp. 421-428). Oxford: Oxford University Press.

Welch, G. F. (2006). What research into music teacher education tells us about the contexts and challenges for teacher education. In *Proceedings, Beijing international forum on music education 2006* (pp. 84-97) [Chinese version, pp. 98-113]. Beijing: NAMM/CSME/ISME/CNU.

Welch, G., Papageorgi, I., Creech, A., Himonides, E., Potter, J., Haddon, E., Whyton, T., de Bezenac, C., Duffy, C. & Morton, F. (2008). *Investigating musical performance: Performance anxiety across musical genres – Teaching and Learning Research Programme, Research briefing 57*. London: TLRP.

PART II
Examples from practice

Chapter 3

Preparing the mind for musical creativity: early music learning and engagement[1]

Margaret S. Barrett

3.1 Introduction

A common saying has it that creativity awaits the prepared mind. For music educators and music education researchers, the question 'how is the mind prepared for creativity?' is one of our central concerns. In one strand of my research interests I have pursued the investigation of the ways in which musical thought and practice develop in early life, with a particular focus on children's generative thought and activity, as composers, notators and song-makers (Barrett, 2003a, 2003b, 2005a, 2005b, 2005c, 2006, 2009, 2010, 2011, 2012a in press and 2012b in press). In this chapter I explore the ways in which creativity has been understood and defined, the ways in which creativity has been taken up in education and, through the interrogation of two young children's musical activity and engagement, examine the beginnings of creative thought and activity in music.

3.2 The research history

In 1950, J. P. Guilford proposed the concepts of divergent and convergent thinking in his address on creativity to the American Psychological Association (Guilford, 1950). This event has been credited with triggering the contemporary study of creativity in the field of psychology (Deliège & Wiggins, 2006; Runco, 2007a; Sawyer, 2006; Sternberg, 1999). Over the ensuing years psychologists have studied creativity from a range of theoretical perspectives including those of cognition, biology, health, social and organizational factors, personality and motivation, and history and historiometry (Runco, 2007a). In the contemporary world creativity and innovation have become culturally valued enterprises that provide potentially wide-ranging cultural, social and economic benefits (Florida, 2002; Howkins, 2009; Robinson, 2001).

---

[1]   Earlier versions of this chapter were presented to the 7th meeting of the Asia-Pacific Symposium for Music Education Research in Shanghai, June 2009, and the ideas seminar at The University of Queensland (March 2010).

Recent research in the field of creativity has encompassed the study of the characteristic features of creative individuals (Csikszentmihalyi, 1996; Gardner, 1993, 1995, 1997; John-Steiner, 1997), creative partnerships and collaborations (Farrell, 2003; John-Steiner, 2000; Moran & John-Steiner, 2003, 2004; Sawyer, 2003a, 2003b, 2008), creative processes (Bindeman, 1998; Sternberg, 1999), creative products (Runco, 2007a) and creative environments (Florida, 2002; Howkins, 2009). Creative thought and action as evidenced in people working individually or in collaboration, processes, products and environments have been theorized by some as a general capacity that applies across domains (Finke, 1995; Guilford, 1968) while others argue that creativity is a domain-specific capacity (Csikszentmihalyi, 1996; Gardner, 1993, 1997; Nakamura & Csikszentmihalyi, 2003; Sternberg & Lubart, 1995) requiring advanced skills, knowledge and techniques for its full development. Where creativity is viewed as a general capacity it is often conflated with thinking styles and processes, specifically problem-finding and problem-solving, a view that for some reduces creativity to a cognitive process and marginalizes the demands of particular domains of endeavour, and the role of the emotions and socio-cultural factors in the development of creativity (Deliège & Richelle, 2006). I shall return to the question of whether creativity should be considered a general capacity or a domain-specific capacity later in this chapter. A prior question asks us to consider how we define creativity.

3.3 Definitions of creativity

Over the last six decades of research a number of researchers have provided definitions of creativity. Torrance, for example, described creativity as 'the emergence of a novel relational product, growing out of the uniqueness of the individual on the one hand and materials, events, people and the circumstances of his life on the other' (1962, p. 139). Later definitions incorporated the notion of novelty identified by Torrance, but coupled this with the need for usefulness; in short, 'a product or response cannot merely be different for the sake of difference; it must also be appropriate, correct, useful, valuable, or expressive of meaning' (Amabile & Tighe, 1993, p. 9). By the late twentieth century these twin tenets of novelty and usefulness were well established in definitions of creativity as demonstrated by Sternberg and Lubart:

> Creativity is the ability to produce work that is both novel (i.e., original, unexpected) and appropriate (i.e., useful, adaptive concerning task constraints).
> (1999, p. 3)

Further work introduced the notion of social value to definitions of creativity, suggesting that 'creativity is reflected in the generation of novel, socially valued products' (Mumford et al., 1994, p. 3). The ways in which 'social value' has been understood is demonstrated in some 'systems' or 'confluence' views of creativity, particularly that of Csikszentmihalyi (1996), where that value is judged by the extent to which a *domain* of thought and practice is changed by the creative act or product, as judged by the *field* that supports the domain. For Csikszentmihalyi, 'creativity...is a process by which a symbolic domain in a culture is changed' (1996, p. 8).

The definition of 'creativity' as a process that produces novel, useful, socially valued *and* domain-changing products or acts limits creativity to the work of a very few individuals; in short, 'a person who regularly solves problems, or fashions products, or defines new questions in a domain in a way that is initially considered novel but that ultimately becomes accepted in a particular cultural setting' (Gardner, 1993, p. 35). Indeed Csikszentmihalyi initially put the view that 'children can show tremendous talent, but they cannot be creative because creativity involves changing a way of doing things, or a way of thinking, and that in turn requires having mastered the old ways of doing and thinking. No matter how precocious a child is, this he or she cannot do' (1996, p. 155). Writing more recently Csikszentmihalyi reinforces this view commenting that 'in my view, it is society that constitutes creativity; therefore you can't say that a child has any creativity...until a certain segment of society – the *field* – construes it as such' (in Sawyer et al., 2003, p. 220). Csikszentmihalyi does, however, admit the possibility of children's work being creative in some way in the following:

> children's spontaneous original productions are indeed socially valued, because the children's mothers and teachers value them. In this restricted sense, one could indeed say that children are *creative within the domain of children's arts* or what have you. But such domains are peripheral to every culture, except perhaps in developmental terms. (in Sawyer et al., 2003, p. 220)

This strong reading of a systems view of creativity is persistent, as evidenced in the following:

> What makes an effort potentially creative is the intention to change the world in some way, while what makes it creative is that it is judged to have done so...There are many possible ways to encourage the desire to change the world in small or large ways, but unless there is intent, and unless the outcome of the effort has produced worthwhile change, another term is probably more appropriate than creativity. (Feldman, 2008, p. xv)

To counter this somewhat restricted view of creativity, researchers have presented alternative views that admit of creativity occurring at different levels of sophistication and originality. Margaret Boden proposes that we distinguish between 'psychological creativity' and 'historical creativity', stating that 'P-creativity involves coming up with a surprising, valuable idea that's *new to the person who comes up with it*. It doesn't matter how many people have had that idea before. But if a new idea is H-creative, that means that (so far as we know) no one else has had it before: it has arisen for the first time in human history' ([1990] 2004, p. 2). Others propose the notion of Big 'C' and little 'c' creativity (Csikszentmihalyi, 1996; Sawyer, 2006), where Big 'C' creativity is evidenced in ideas and products that are culturally significant whereas little 'c' creativity pertains to those ideas and products that are individually significant. There are close parallels between these conceptions of creativity and that proposed by Feldman and colleagues (Feldman 2003; Morelock & Feldman, 1999) of 'High C', 'medium c' and 'low c' creativity. More recently, *mini-c* and *pro-c* creativity have been proposed (Kaufman & Beghetto, 2009) as a means of recognizing (1) creative thought and practice that encompasses the '*novel and personally meaningful interpretation of experience, actions, and events*' (Beghetto & Kaufman, 2007 in Kaufmann & Beghetto, 2009, p. 3) and (2) that creativity that 'represents the developmental and effortful progression beyond little-c' (Kaufman & Beghetto, 2009, p. 5). Such distinctions allow for the possibility that creativity may be novel for the individual, rather than society, useful at the local level and valued within the context in which the individual lives and works. Importantly, as intimated by Csikszentmihalyi (see above), for educators these conceptions of creativity as a process exercised at varying levels of originality, expertise and usefulness acknowledge that children are capable of creative thought and activity, where that thought and activity is judged within children's domains of practice. Young children's generative music-making constitutes one such domain of musical practice I suggest.

Psychologist Robert Sternberg has proposed a 'propulsion' theory of creativity that recognizes that 'creativity can be of different kinds, depending on how it propels existing ideas forward' (2003, p. 99). Sternberg (2003) identifies eight kinds of creative contributions that are categorized into three major types: (1) paradigm preserving contributions that leave the field where it is (involving replication and/or re-definition; (2) paradigm preserving contributions that move the field forward in the direction it is already going (involving forward incrementation and/or advanced forward incrementation); and (3) paradigm-rejecting contributions that move the field in a new direction from an existing or pre-existing starting point (including redirection, reconstruction/redirection, initiation and/or integration). Within this view, the need for 'novelty' as a defining feature is variable, depending on whether the creative contribution is more concerned with a 'minor replication' that 'confirms' an original creative endeavour in the field or a 'major redirection' in thought and action in the field. Importantly, when the need for novelty and usefulness as defined in various views of creativity is modified, creativity might well be seen as a more general capability than a domain-specific capability, drawing on general thinking styles and processes that might be acquired through instruction and schooling.

One of the most influential advocates for creativity in education, Sir Ken Robinson, highlights three principles when defining creativity: (1) creativity is about 'doing' something, in other words it happens within a particular domain. In this emphasis on doing something Robinson distinguishes between creativity and imagination, suggesting that the former becomes a means of 'applied imagination'; 2) creativity is original – at the personal, social, and/or the historic level; 3) creativity produces something that is valuable and/or worthwhile. In short, creativity is defined as 'imaginative processes with outcomes that are original and of value' (Robinson, 2001, p. 118).

Robinson's recognition of originality at varying levels – the personal, the social and/or the historic – admits the possibility of creative thought and action in day-to-day thought and activity across a range of domains, a concept that has come to be known as 'everyday' (Richards, 2007) or 'personal' creativity (Boden, [1990] 2004; Runco, 2007b). Importantly, in emphasizing that creativity is about 'doing something' in a particular domain Robinson returns us to the question of whether creativity is a general capability (individually located) or domain-specific (socially located as judged by the field). Creativity occurs in context, in a domain of creative performance (Runco, 2006). However, what might be understood as a domain of creative performance may vary from culture to culture, and within cultures when differing levels of experience and understanding are considered.

Each of the accounts of creativity provided above has arisen within the context of Western, largely Anglo-American, research communities. As such, these definitions and descriptions of creativity are shaped by the beliefs and values of the communities that support them. Modernist Western epistemologies value the notions of individualism, the novel, mastery and the socially useful (Barrett, 2011d), and it is perhaps not surprising that the accounts of creativity reviewed here converge in their emphasis on the individual creator producing works of originality and social usefulness. Lubart asserts that Eastern accounts of creativity are 'less focused on innovative products. Instead, creativity involves a state of personal fulfilment, a connection to a primordial realm, or the expression of an inner essence or ultimate reality' (1999, p. 340). Writing of Japanese notions of creativity in particular Matsunobu (2011) argues that 'imitation of a model' is central to artistic learning and highly valued within Japanese aesthetic practice. He writes 'creative impulse in the course of Japanese arts learning is geared more toward cultivating the inner richness – that is, cultivating the relationship with the tools, instruments, teachers, colleagues, and practitioner's own minds – than toward creating new objects' (Matsunobu, 2011, p. 50). These conceptions of creativity challenge the taken-for-granted notions that novelty and usefulness are the signal markers of creative output. In short, definitions of creativity are not fixed, and are subject to challenge.

3.4 Creativity in learning and education

Within the field of education researchers have turned their attention to creativity in endeavours to foster students' creative thinking (often defined in terms of divergent and convergent thinking and/or problem-finding and problem-solving), to provide alternatives to more 'traditional' teaching practices and to emphasize the generation of original work rather than the reproduction of ideas and materials

(Craft, 2005). Investigations have sought to identify the characteristic features of creative teaching, creative learning and teaching with and/or for creativity. This emphasis is founded perhaps in a largely unresearched view that creativity will raise standards and solve the manifest problems the world faces in terms of sustainable development. These are large claims for creativity in education.

Feldman suggests that there may be no such phenomenon as 'creative learning'; rather 'there is learning that may enable creative work and learning that may prevent creative work from occurring' (2008, p. xv). Jeffrey and Craft (2004), however, suggest that a focus on the relationship between creative learning and creative teaching may avoid what some see as a dichotomy between creative teaching and teaching for creativity. Craft and colleagues define creative learning as:

> Significant imaginative achievement as evidenced in the creation of new knowledge as determined by the imaginative insight of the person or persons responsible and judged by appropriate observers to be both original and of value as situated in different domain contexts. (Craft et al., 2008, p. xxi)

In this, we seem to be moving towards a domain-specific view of creativity.

Work arising from the Qualifications and Curriculum Development Agency in England identifies five behavioural elements of creativity, those of asking questions, making connections, imagining what might be, exploring options and reflecting critically (QCDA, 2010). There is strong resonance between these behaviours and 'creative skills' that others have identified as foundational to creativity, those of risk-taking, the capacity to improvise, resilience and collaboration (Craft et al., 2008), persistence, independence and self-reliance (Johnson, 2007, p. 281), the capacity to pay attention (Csikszentmihalyi, 1996, pp. 351-352), the capacity to tolerate ambiguity (Csikszentmihalyi, 1996, p. 346), and curiosity and drive (Csikszentmihalyi, 1996, p. 185).Others suggest that ideational fluency, or the capacity to 'improvise', to generate a range of responses and ideas, is another key skill that underpins creativity (Sawyer, 2003b).

These behaviours and skills emphasize a general capacity view of creativity. In contemporary views then, we might answer the question of whether creativity is domain-specific or general with the response that it is 'both'. Creativity appears to be located across a continuum that ranges from individually significant output in a 'local' domain through to socially recognized major domain changing activity and is underpinned by general behaviours, skills and dispositions.

When we turn to studies of learning and expertise other factors emerge as significant in the development of creative thought and practice in any domain. A supportive home environment, early and extensive exposure to the domain (not necessarily in a formal instructional mode) and focused and persistent practice are also identified as enabling factors in the development of expertise (Csikszentmihalyi & Csikszentmihalyi, 1993; Gardner, 1993; Howe, 1999; Johnson, 2007).

In a study of family influences on the development of giftedness Csikszentmihalyi and Csikszentmihalyi (1993) identified two key features as characteristic of those families in which young adolescents experienced high degrees of academic success: (1) a stimulating environment which provided opportunities for learning and in which there were high educational expectations; and (2) a highly supportive and coherent family structure.

Michael Howe further interrogates the role of early experience on learning through consideration of Hart and Risley's study of the effects of social class on 3-year-old American children's vocabulary and language development (1995). Howe suggests that the stark contrasts between the amount of words children in this study were exposed to in their home environments over the first three years of their lives (30 million words directed at children in professional class families, 20 million words in middle-class families and 10 million words in families on welfare) provides a compelling reason for differences in language performance. He comments:

> behind the observed variability in language performance were literally enormous variations in the children's actual experiences of language. In the light of the evidence that differences of that kind of magnitude in children's experiences lie behind differences in their capabilities, the investments of time that has been devoted to early intervention programmes have been so tiny as to make it seem highly unlikely that they would have large effects. (Howe, 1999, p. 198)

In short, more exposure to and experience of more varied language correlated positively with language performance. When one examines the original study, however, it is not just the amount of language that shapes the language outcomes for these children, but also the nature of that language. Hart and Risley point out that not only do families differ significantly in the number and quality of words provided to their children, they also differ in the uses of this language – that is, as an affirmative or a prohibition. They point out that the relative ratio of encouragements or discouragements per hour in a professional family was six encouragements to one discouragement, in a working class family two encouragements to one discouragement and in a welfare family one encouragement to two discouragements (Hart & Risley, 1995). The effect of such language use on children's subsequent engagement in interactions with others can only be imagined.

In thinking how we might prepare the musically creative mind, as teachers we are able to attend to two aspects beyond those encountered in the home environment: (1) the development of general behaviours, skills and dispositions that seem to support creative thought and action (general creativity) and (2) the development of domain specific knowledge, skills and understandings that prepare the child for work in that domain (domain-specific creativity). Both aspects are essential as 'access to a domain is essential to creativity. A person cannot be creative in the abstract, but only within the rules of some practice or idea system' (Nakamura & Csikszentmihalyi, 2003, p. 193).

There is nothing too surprising here. However, this leads me to the question 'how is the mind prepared for creativity prior to entering schooling?' I suggest that, more than any other art form, the extent to which children are exposed to music in their early life, and the ways in which they engage with music as a component of their interactions with self and others (Barrett, 2012a), plays a significant role in how the musically creative mind is prepared.

3.5 The beginnings of creativity

We are designed to learn through our interactions with people, culture and the physical worlds in which we live from the earliest moments of life (David et al., 2003). Our early interactions with others and the materials of our worlds are improvisatory, made-in-the moment and responsive, and play a central role in the developmental processes of young children. Communicative musicality (Malloch & Trevarthen, 2009), a key component of early communication and development, draws on the rhythms and modes of shared music and meaning-making between caregiver and infant in a process that builds mutuality, relationship and belongingness (Barrett, 2011c; Dissanayake, 2000). The processes of communicative musicality emphasize generative and playful music- and meaning-making between infant and caregiver. Runco argues that 'creativity is critical to children's development' as children's play and meaning-making 'provide children a grasp of what is possible' (2006, p. 121). For Runco, children's play is creative by nature and demonstrates 'originality and usefulness' for the child (2006, p. 122). Such views suggest that young children arrive at school with rich experience of creative thought and activity in a range of 'domains of creative performance'.

Exposure to and experience of music in use is perhaps one of the most ubiquitous features of young children's lives; yet, paradoxically, this dimension of the young child's early life has been largely unresearched. The exponential rise of music media and children's entertainment coupled with the use of these elements by many parents and child-carers as a major feature of parenting practice (Barrett, 2009) ensures that the majority of children have experienced significant amounts of music by the time they arrive at the classroom door. Research provides some insights into the nature of this engagement, including children participating as listeners, singers, song-makers and music-makers (Barrett, 2009, 2010). However, little is known of the extent of children's engagement in each of these activities and/or the genres of music with which they engage. Given the global popularity of such children's music groups as *The Wiggles*, we might speculate that such examples of children's music media are highly influential in children's early experience. Susan Young (2008) has suggested that an unresearched area of young children's music engagement lies in their interactions with toys in which sound and music are inbuilt features. These range from those toys that are intended to be viewed as musical instruments (toy electronic drum kits, guitars, harmonicas and so on) and those that incorporate music as part of the interaction of play (hand-held digital games, interactive story books, 'singing' dolls). As teachers, what do we know of young children's early engagement and how do we use this resource in our teaching? Recall the findings of the study that correlated high performance in 3-year-old American children's vocabulary and language development to their exposure to positive language use in the home environment. What might be the musical equivalent of 30 million words? Or 20 million? Or 10 million? In their musical encounters with others what is the proportion of encouragements to discouragements that young children receive?

3.6 Creativity and development in music

In a socio-cultural view of development, development occurs through a process of internalization, whereby the child appropriates and transforms experience encountered in interaction with others and the tools and signs of the domain in which learning and development occurs (Vygotsky, 1978, 1998). Moran and John-Steiner (2003) make the point that creativity is often viewed in the reverse – that is, as an internal process made external through cultural artefacts and creative products. They suggest that 'the two social processes, internalization and externalization, are in dialectical tension with each other. This tension provides fertile ground for new ideas and creative products' (Moran & John-Steiner, 2003, p. 63). They conclude that creativity 'depends on development and development depends on creativity' (Moran & John-Steiner, 2003, p. 63).

Central to the development of creativity is the development of the creative imagination, a process that occurs through children's play as they create, manipulate and assign meaning to the tools and signs at their disposal (Robinson, 2001). The individual pretend play of the child starts in social interaction (Smolucha & Smolucha, 1986). I have suggested elsewhere that children's independent invented song-making (an example of musical play) evolves from early musico-communicative interactions with others, is evidential of their capacity for 'elaboration' or 'ideational fluency', and is foundational in the development of creative thought and activity in music (Barrett, 2006). Invented song tends to draw on the musics to which children have access, and reflects their interests, both musical and extra-musical (Barrett, 2003a).[2] In what follows I shall introduce you to two young children for whom invented song and music-making is a significant feature of their daily life. Through an analysis of their invented song-making I shall explore the ways in which these children are building their knowledge of the domain of music and being supported in engaging in some of the behaviours that are foundational to creativity, including the capacity to improvise (Craft et al., 2008), persistence, independence and self-reliance (Johnson, 2007, p. 281), the capacity to pay attention (Csikszentmihalyi, 1996, pp. 351-352), curiosity and

---

[2] There is a growing literature on children's use and engagement with invented song. Summaries of this literature might be found in Barrett (2003a, 2006, 2010).

drive (Csikszentmihalyi, 1996, p. 185), and ideational fluency, or the capacity to 'improvise' (Sawyer, 2003b).

3.7 The research study

Beatrice and Jay were two of 18 children involved in a three-year longitudinal project investigating the role of invented song-making and music engagement in young children's (aged approximately 18-48 months) identity work and self-making.[3] Children in that study were recruited from two sites, a *Kindermusik* site (12 children) and a day-long childcare centre (6 children) in the major cities of Australia's Island State, Tasmania (Hobart and Launceston respectively).

The project drew on the participation of the children's parents to assist in data generation with parents maintaining a video diary of their child's music activity in the home environment and an accompanying paper diary that provided a weekly overview of musical activity, including the nature of the activity, the location of the activity, those present and the child's emotional state. Researcher observations also took place in the *Kindermusik* and childcare settings, and interviews were undertaken with parents, *Kindermusik* and childcare workers. These multiple forms of data and groups of participants ensured triangulation and the contribution of a range of perspectives concerning the children's engagement with and use of music. Both Beatrice and Jay were recruited from the *Kindermusik* site.

Beatrice was just 2 years of age at her commencement in the project and Jay was just 3.[4] Beatrice participated in the study for approximately 16 months, her withdrawal from the study coinciding with her withdrawal from the *Kindermusik* programme. Beatrice's mother, Barbara, cited a busy schedule of activities (including Gymbaroo, Learn to swim, dance classes) as the main reason for withdrawal from both *Kindermusik* and the study. While Jay only participated in the *Kindermusik* classes for one 15-week term, he and his family contributed data to the study for some two years. Over the course of the study Beatrice's mother, Barbara, submitted 14 weekly overview diaries and recorded 25 separate video diary episodes totalling 77 minutes of video footage. Erica, Jay's mother, submitted 13 weekly overview diaries and 47 separate video episodes totalling 216 minutes of video footage. Both mothers participated in two formal interviews and a number of informal interviews and exchanges through emails and chance meetings during *Kindermusik* observations. In the following section of the chapter I provide an overview of these children's engagement in music and examples of their generative music-making.

---

    [3]   This research was funded by the Australian Research Council through the Discovery Grants programme (Grant number DP0559050).

    [4]   The excerpts of Beatrice's and Jay's musical engagement have been extracted with permission from larger narrative accounts available in Barrett (2010) and Barrett (2012a) respectively.

3.8 Beatrice and Jay: lives storied in and through music

Both children are exposed to a diverse array of music in their home environment, predominately of the Western classical and/or popular music tradition. Both are familiar with a range of children's music media groups and products including *The Wiggles*, *The Hooley Dooleys*, *George* and *Hi-5*. Both children have developed an extensive repertoire of songs drawn from their varying experiences of and exposure to the *Kindermusik* repertoire, popular children's television programmes such as *Play School*, *Bob the Builder*, *Thomas the Tank Engine and Friends*, children's music media groups (as above) and children's films. In both families car transport is conducted to a soundtrack of music on CD and radio. This soundtrack includes the commercial products produced for the various levels of the *Kindermusik* programme, other examples of children's music media such as *The Hooley Dooley* CDs and the Tasmanian regional popular, classical and jazz radio stations. Both Barbara and Erica report these car journeys as opportunities to sing along to the music, to engage with their children in song performance and play.

Both children have access to music media products in the home and are encouraged to use these at their instigation. In both cases the children have a sound system in their bedroom and are in the habit of listening to a recorded story with music or music CD as part of their bedtime routine. Both children also possess a number of musical instruments. These include the *Kindermusik* hand percussion instruments (Beatrice), a number of 'toy' instruments including a 'toy' guitar and drum kit (Beatrice) and child-size Ukelele and hand-drums (Jay). In both cases much of the children's play (as recorded in video and overview diaries) revolves around use of these instruments and other found objects (e.g. in Jay's case, egg-cartons as drums) in music-making.

A key component of both children's engagement in music is the use of music as a form of communicative engagement between parent and child. For example, Barbara uses music as a means of modifying her daughter's behaviour:

> If I am trying to convince her to do something, I will make up a song about it and it seems more appealing…particularly in the bath. Max (Beatrice's brother) doesn't like his face and hair being washed so I will sing a song and make up a song as I am doing whatever it is at the time and he seems to be more accepting of it so that is why I will make up a song – to try and convince someone to do something…it seems sort of normal to me to think that it would make you more cheerful. There are occasions when I will say to Daniel (Beatrice's father) when he is struggling with the kids or something, and I say 'Sing a song. Make it happy' and as soon as you start singing, they get really excited and enjoy it. (mother interview 1)

Erica also engages in sung exchanges with her son Jay, a strategy that he has adopted and adapted to his own uses.

'It's a food song', announces Jay one morning as his mother switches on the video camera, and he begins to sing 'yes yes, yes yes, yes yes, yes yes, I like my food'. He sings at the top of his voice, dancing from leg to leg, only to stop suddenly. 'What's that music?' he asks, as a Bach Partita for solo violin plays in the background. 'It's a violin' Erica responds. 'What's that music?' he asks again, standing still, listening intently. 'That's just a piece of music for the violin, some-one's playing the violin.' His curiosity satisfied, Jay launches into a riff on 'Yes yes', alternating with a riff on 'No no'.

Breakfast and food are forgotten entirely as Jay jumps up and down on the spot singing the riffs in alternation. 'Would you eat your breakfast please?' Erica asks. Jay pauses briefly, looking at her, gauging the mood, before returning to a riff on No no. 'So that's a no, then?' inquires Erica. 'Yes yes, yes yes, yes yes, yes yes, no no, no no, no no, no no' responds Jay, dancing all the while. Erica follows up 'No, seriously, would you eat your vegemite bars please?' Jay, playful, a mischievous grin on his face, comes close to the camera singing his 'No, No' refrain. (video diary excerpt)

'No, no song motif'

'Yes, yes' song motif

Example 3.1   Jay's 'No, No – Yes, Yes'

Inventing song in order to communicate feelings to self and others is evident in Beatrice's music-making.

Barbara films Beatrice, seated at the breakfast bar with her brother Max and father one Saturday morning. Beatrice has been singing and is captured on film as she launches into a song about 'I love'. She sings to her brother: 'Me… you love me, I love you and we all love toast.' Waving her toast in the air she continues: 'And you know I love you, I love you, love Max.' She turns to her father, who nods along to the rhythm of her singing as she sings 'you love me, you love me, you all love me'…She sings the last phrase to the camera, her candour and confidence completely disarming as she announces the end of the song: 'finished'. The family applauds and Barbara exclaims: 'Very nice Beatrice! Very well done.'

Example 3.2 Beatrice's 'I Love Toast'

Both Beatrice and Jay use song as a means of commenting on their life and the people and objects that are close to them.

Early one morning Jay dressed in pyjamas is filmed swinging a length of tinsel suspended from the Christmas tree. Adam, his baby brother, is seated in a high chair, watching intermittently as he bangs a spoon against the table-top and grizzles. Unaware of his mother filming in the background Jay is singing phrases of 'Bob the builder' quietly to himself. He pauses and turns to see his mother. 'Hello' he says, and returns to swinging the tinsel. 'Baby crying' he muses aloud, then launches into song on the text Baby Crying.

This song finished he pauses momentarily, before starting to sing a song about a telephone ringing. The length of tinsel now becomes the phone as Jay holds the end up to his ears, alternating from side to side. His movements echo the beat of his singing. Adam is now transfixed by his brother, the tapping and grizzling silenced.

Bab-y cry- ing, bab y cry-ing bab y cry-ing now   Bab-y cry-ing bab y cry-ing

bab-y cry-ing now   Bab-y cry-ing bab-y cry-ing bab-y cry-ing now

Bab-y cry-ing bab-y cry-ing bab-y cry-ing now   Bab-y cry-ing bab-y cry-in

bab-y   cry   Bab-y cry-ing   yeah the bab-y cry -ing   oh the

ba - by   cry-ing   oh the   bab -y cry now oh the   ba - by cry there's a

bab-y cry there's a   bab-y cry there's a   ba-by cry there's a   ba-by cry there's a

ba-by cry there's a   ba-by cry there's a   ba-by cry there's a   ba-by cry-ing now!

Example 3.3 Jay's 'Baby Crying Now'

swing

Tel - e - phone ring - ing oh tel - e phone ring   Tel - e phone ring and I   say hell - o

5

tel - e - phone ring - ing   a   tel - e - phone ring - ing   tel - e - phone ring - ing   A

9

tel - e - phone ring - ing   a   tel - e - phone ringin - ing   tel - e - phone ring - ing   A

13

tel - e - phone   ring - ing   a   tel - e - phone   ring - ing

15

tel - e phone ring - ing   a   tel - e - phone a tel - e   tel - e -   phone

Example 3.4 Jay's 'Telephone Ringing'

Jay's song to his baby brother ('Baby Crying Now') may be viewed as a two-part structure of roughly equal length. The first ten bars comprise five two bar phrases characterized by repetition and minor elaboration on a rhythmic (a 4 beat bar of 8 quavers followed by a bar of 4 quavers, a crochet and a crochet rest) and melodic idea (a falling step-wise melody varied through an opening move of a fourth, and minor variations – rising or falling by leap or step – on the closing beats). The second ten bars shift the rhythmic focus through the introduction of shorter phrases and semi-quavers. The melodic direction is predominately rising, with a reference to the rhythmic and melodic structure of the first ten bars evident in the final two bars (bars 23/24). The structure of the song, its rhythmic repetition and regularity and simple melodic structure is reflective of many children's songs while not being a direct copy of any one song. By contrast, the song that immediately follows 'Baby Crying Now', 'Telephone Ringing', features wide intervals (5ths, 4ths) in the melody line and is sung with a swing feel. Jay's vocal performance reflects the jazz standards that he listens to and his ready appreciation of the characteristic features of the style including the swing feel and the closing 'lick' (see bar 17).

Beatrice's song about toast features a recurring melodic phrase to the words 'you love me'. Throughout the song this three note motif of a falling interval returning to the starting note anchors the rhythmic, melodic and textual structure of the song. The song is derived from the *Barney* children's television programme song 'I Love You, You Love Me' (sung to the melody of children's song 'This Old Man'). Yet Beatrice has made the song her own through extending the melodic shape of the phrase beyond that of the original (see bars 3 and 4 for example) and shaping the words of the *Barney* version to suit her needs in the moment. Beatrice's adaptation provides us with another example of the ways in which young children create musical structures that are 'original and useful for the child' (Runco, 2006, p. 122).

3.9 Concluding comments

What have we seen evidenced in the music-making of these two children? I suggest that we see the beginnings of an individual and personal style – note I describe this as individual, not original. We hear both children draw on the range of music resources at their disposal, their knowledge of the domain of music, in order to develop their own musical responses to the world and their experience of it. The extensiveness and volume of these responses indicate an 'ideational fluency' or capacity to improvise (Sawyer, 2003b). I suggest we see here not only the beginnings of the capacity to improvise, but also some persistence, independence and self-reliance (Johnson, 2007), coupled with a capacity to pay attention, be curious and exhibit 'drive' (Csikszentmihalyi, 1996). The 'general creativity' skills that underpin creativity are emergent in these children's adaptation of the musical materials of others, and their capacity to extend these in ways that are original for them. When we examine their music-making itself there is evidence of a growing vocabulary and repertoire of musical gestures, and the ways in which these might be related to each other. In short, the development of domain specific knowledge and skills necessary for creativity has begun. Where creativity is located across a continuum ranging from individually significant output in a 'local' domain (children's music-making) through to socially recognized major domain changing activity, underpinned by general behaviours, skills and dispositions, it is evident that these children are not only 'preparing' for creativity, they are engaging in creative thought and behaviour in and through their music-making.

When we examine the life experiences of these two children I am struck by the sheer volume and variety of music engagement in their daily lives. These children begin and end their days with music, and encounter music as audience members, co-performers and originators throughout much of their day in a variety of circumstances. Crucially, these children's efforts in music are encouraged, taken up and responded to positively by the key adults in their lives. For Beatrice and Jay it is not just the amount of music experience to which they are exposed, it is also the positive and supportive nature of that music experience. For too many young children their early encounters with music are ignored, dismissed as 'noise' or actively discouraged. Were we to afford children's early music-making the same attention that early positive language-making receives (those 30 million words in an encouraging environment) I wonder how accounts of music development, learning and engagement might change?

To what extent do we as educators acknowledge this rich reservoir of music experience and understanding that children bring to their schooling? How do we use this in our curriculum planning and development? How might we draw on these generative behaviours and evident disposition towards creative activity? These, I suggest, are the challenges we face in preparing musical minds for creativity.

References

Amabile, T. M. & Tighe, E. (1993). Questions of creativity. In J. Brockman (Ed.), *Creativity* (pp. 7-27). New York: Touchstone.

Barrett, M. S. (2003a). Invented notations and mediated memory: A case-study of two children's use of invented notations. *Bulletin of the Council for Research in Music Education*, 153/154, 55-62.

Barrett, M. S. (2003b). Meme engineers: Children as producers of musical culture. *International Journal of Early Years Education*, 11(3), 195-212.

Barrett, M. S. (2005a). Children's communities of musical practice: Some socio-cultural implications of a systems view of creativity in music education. In D. J. Elliott (Ed.), *Praxial music education: Reflections and dialogues* (pp. 177-195). New York: Oxford University Press.

Barrett, M. S. (2005b). Musical communication and children's communities of musical practice. In D. Miell, R. MacDonald & D. Hargreaves (Eds.), *Musical communication* (pp. 281-299). Oxford: Oxford University Press.

Barrett, M. S. (2005c). Representation, cognition, and communication: Invented notation in children's musical communication. In D. Miell, R. MacDonald & D. Hargreaves (Eds.), *Musical communication* (pp. 117-142). Oxford: Oxford University Press.

Barrett, M. S. (2006). Inventing songs, inventing worlds: The 'genesis' of creative thought and activity in young children's lives. *International Journal of Early Years Education*, 14(3), 201-220.

Barrett, M. S. (2009). Sounding lives in and through music: A narrative inquiry of the 'everyday' musical engagement of a young child. *Journal of Early Childhood Research*, 7(2), 115-134.

Barrett, M. S. (2010). Musical narratives: A study of a young child's identity work in and through music-making. *Psychology of Music* (published online 27 October 2010).

Barrett, M. S. (2011). On being and becoming a cathedral chorister: A cultural psychology account of the acquisition of early expertise. In M. S. Barrett (Ed.), *A cultural psychology of music education* (pp. 259-288). Oxford: Oxford University Press.

Barrett, M. S. (2012a in press). Mutuality, belonging, and meaning-making: Pathways to developing young boys' competence and creativity in singing and song-making. In S. D. Harrison, G. F. Welch & A. Adler (Eds.), *International perspectives on males and singing*. Dordrecht: Springer.

Barrett, M. S. (2012b in press). Troubling the creative imaginary: Some possibilities of ecological thinking for music and learning. In D. Hargreaves, D. Miell & R. MacDonald (Eds.), *Musical imaginations*. Oxford: Oxford University Press.

Bindeman, S. (1998). Echoes of silence: A phenomenological study of the creative process. *Creativity Research Journal*, 11(1), 69-77.

Boden, M. A. ([1990] 2004). *The creative mind: Myths and mechanisms* (2nd edition). London: Routledge.

Craft, A. (2005), *Creativity in schools: Tensions and dilemmas*. Abingdon: Routledge

Craft, A., Cremin, T. & Burnard, P. (2008). *Creative learning 3–11 and how we document it*. Stoke-on-Trent: Trentham Books.

Csikszentmihalyi, M. (1996). *Creativity: Flow and the psychology of discovery and invention*. New York: HarperCollins.

Csikszentmihalyi, M. & Csikszentmihalyi, I. (1993). Family influences on the development of giftedness. In G. R. Bock & K. Ackril (Eds.), *Ciba foundation symposium 178: The origins and development of high ability*. Chichester: Wiley.

David, T., Goouch, K., Powell, S. & Abbott, L. (2003). *Birth to three matters: A review of the literature*. London: Department for Education and Skills.

Deliège, I. & Richelle, M. (2006). Prelude: The spectrum of musical creativity. In I. Deliège & G. A. Wiggins (Eds.), *Musical creativity: Multidisciplinary research in theory and practice* (pp. 1-6). Hove: Psychology Press.

Deliège, I. & Wiggins, G. A. (Eds.) (2006). *Musical creativity: Multidisciplinary research in theory and practice*. Hove: Psychology Press.

Dissanayake, E. (2000). *Art and intimacy: How the arts began*. Seattle: University of Washington Press.

Farrell, M. P. (2003). *Collaborative circles: Friendship, dynamics, and creative work*. Chicago: University of Chicago Press.

Feldman, D. H. (2003). The creation of multiple intelligences theory: A study in high level thinking. In R. K. Sawyer, V. John-Steiner, S. Moran, R. J. Sternberg, D. H. Feldman, J. Nakamura & M. Csikszentmihalyi (Eds.), *Creativity and development* (pp. 139-185). New York, Oxford University Press.

Feldman, D. H. (2008). Foreword. In A. Craft, T. Cremin & P. Burnard (Eds.). *Creative learning 3–11 and how we document it* (pp. xiii-xvii). Stoke-on-Trent: Trentham Books.

Finke, R. A. (1995). Creative realism. In S. M. Smith, T. B. Ward & R. A. Finke (Eds.), *The creative cognition approach* (pp. 301-326). Cambridge, MA: MIT Press.

Florida, R. (2002). *The rise of the creative class*. New York: Basic Books.

Gardner, H. (1993). *Creating minds*. New York: Basic Books.

Gardner, H. (1995). *Leading minds*. New York: Basic Books.

Gardner, H. (1997). *Extraordinary minds*. New York: Basic Books.

Guilford, J. P. (1950). Creativity. *American Psychologist*, 5(9), 444-454.

Guilford, J. P. (1968). *Intelligence, creativity, and their educational implications.* San Diego, CA: Robert R. Knapp.

Hart, B. & Risley, T. (1995). *Meaningful differences in everyday parenting and intellectual development in young American children.* Baltimore: Paul H. Brookes.

Howe, M. J. A. (1999). *Genius explained.* Cambridge: Cambridge University Press.

Howkins, J. (2009). *Creative ecologies: Where thinking is a proper job.* St Lucia: University of Queensland Press.

Jeffrey, P. & Craft, A. (2004). Teaching creatively and teaching for creativity: Distinctions and relationships. *Educational Studies*, 30(1), 77-87.

Johnson, P. (2007). *Creators: From Chaucer to Walt Disney.* London: Phoenix/ Orion Books.

John-Steiner, V. (1997). *Notebooks of the mind: Explorations of thinking.* Oxford: Oxford University Press.

John-Steiner, V. (2000). *Creative collaboration.* New York: Oxford University Press.

Kaufman, J. C. & Beghetto, R. A. (2009). Beyond big and little: The four C model of creativity. *Review of General Psychology*, 13(1), 1-12.

Lubart, T. I. (1999). Creativity across culture. In R. J. Sternberg (Ed.), *Handbook of creativity* (pp. 339-350). Cambridge: Cambridge University Press.

Malloch, S. & Trevarthen, C. (2009). *Communicative musicality: Exploring the basis of human companionship.* Oxford: Oxford University Press.

Matsunobu, K. (2011). Creativity of formulaic learning: Pedagogy of imitation and repetition. In J. Sefton-Green, P. Thomson, K. Jones & L. Bresler (Eds.), *The Routledge international handbook of creative learning* (pp. 45-53). Abingdon: Routledge.

Moran, S. & John-Steiner, V. (2003). Creativity in the making: Vygotsky's contemporary contribution to the dialectic of development and creativity. In R. K. Sawyer, V. John-Steiner, S. Moran, R. J. Sternberg, D. H. Feldman, J. Nakamura & M. Csikszentmihalyi (Eds.), *Creativity and development* (pp. 61-90). New York: Oxford University Press.

Moran, S. & John-Steiner, V. (2004). How collaboration in creative work impacts identity and motivation. In D. Miell & K. Littleton (Eds.), *Collaborative creativity: Contemporary perspectives* (pp. 11-25). London: Free Association Books.

Morelock, M. J. F. & Feldman D. H. (1999). Prodigies. In M. A. Runco & S. R. Pritzker (Eds.), *Encyclopedia of creativity* (Vol. 2, pp. 449-456). San Diego, CA: Academic Press.

Mumford, M. D., Reiter-Palmer, R. & Redmond, M. R. (1994). Problem construction and cognition: Applying problem representations in ill-structured problems. In M. A. Runco (Ed.), *Problem finding, problem solving, and creativity* (pp. 3-39). Norwood, NJ: Ablex.

Nakamura, J. & Csikszentmihalyi, M. (2003). Creativity in later life. In R. K. Sawyer, V. John-Steiner, S. Moran, R. J. Sternberg, D. H. Feldman, J. Nakamura & M. Csikszentmihalyi (Eds.), *Creativity and development* (pp. 186-216). New York: Oxford University Press.

Qualifications and Curriculum Development Agency (2010). *The primary curriculum: Learning across the curriculum* – see http://curriculum.qcda.gov.uk/key-stages-1-and-2/learning-across-the-curriculum/index.aspx (accessed 30 September 2010).

Richards, R. (Ed.) (2007). *Everyday creativity and new views of human nature: Psychological, social, and spiritual perspectives*. Washington, DC: American Psychological Association.

Robinson, K. (2001). *Out of our minds: Learning to be creative*. Oxford: Capstone.

Runco, M. A. (2006). The development of children's creativity. In B. Spodek & O. N. Saracho (Eds.), *Handbook of research on the education of young children* (pp. 121-134). Mahwah, NJ: Lawrence Erlbaum Associates.

Runco, M. A. (2007a). *Creativity theories and themes: Research, development, and practice*. Burlington, MA: Elsevier Academic Press.

Runco, M. A. (2007b). To understand is to create: An epistemological perspective on human nature and personal creativity. In R. Richards (Ed.), *Everyday creativity and new views of human nature: Psychological, social, and spiritual perspectives* (pp. 91-108). Washington, DC: American Psychological Association.

Sawyer, R. K. (2003a). *Group creativity: Music, theatre, collaboration*. Mahwah, NJ: Lawrence Erlbaum Associates.

Sawyer, R. K. (2003b). *Improvised dialogues: Emergence and creativity in conversation*. Westport, CT: Greenwood.

Sawyer, R. K. (2006). *Explaining creativity: The science of human innovation*. Oxford: Oxford University Press.

Sawyer, R. K. (2008). *Group genius: The creative power of collaboration*. New York: Basic Books.

Sawyer, R. K., John-Steiner, V., Moran, S., Sternberg, R. J., Feldman, D. H., Nakamura, J. & Csikszentmihalyi, M. (2003). Key issues in creativity and development. In R. K. Sawyer, V. John-Steiner, S. Moran, R. J. Sternberg, D. H. Feldman, J. Nakamura & M. Csikszentmihalyi (Eds.), *Creativity and development* (pp. 217-242). New York: Oxford University Press.

Smolucha, L. W. & Smolucha, F. C. (1986). L. S. Vygotsky's theory of creative imagination. *Spiel*, 5(2), 299-308.

Sternberg, R. J. (1999) (Ed.). *Handbook of creativity*. Cambridge: Cambridge University Press.

Sternberg, R. J. (2003). The development of creativity as a decision-making process. In R. K. Sawyer, V. John-Steiner, S. Moran, R. J. Sternberg, D. H. Feldman, J. Nakamura & M. Csikszentmihalyi (Eds.), *Creativity and development* (pp. 91-138). New York: Oxford University Press.

Sternberg, R. J. & Lubart, T. I. (1995). *Defying the crowd: Cultivating creativity in a culture of conformity*. New York: Free Press.

Sternberg, R. J. & Lubart, T. I. (1999). The concepts of creativity: Prospects and paradigms. In R. J. Sternberg (Ed.), *Handbook of creativity* (pp. 3-15). Cambridge: Cambridge University Press.

Torrance, E. P. (1962). *Guiding creative talent*. Englewood Cliffs, NJ: Prentice-Hall.

Vygotsky, L. S. (1987). *Mind in society: The development of higher psychological processes*. Cambridge, MA: Harvard University Press.

Vygotsky, L. S. (1998). Imagination and creativity in childhood (1930/1998). *Soviet Psychology*, 28(10), 84-96.

Young, S. (2008). Lullaby light shows: Everyday musical experience among under-two-year-olds. *International Journal of Music Education*, 26(1), 33-46.

Chapter 4

Music composition as a way of learning: emotions and the situated self

Ana Luísa Veloso and Sara Carvalho

'Listen carefully when children are near'.

(Kaschub & Smith, 2009, p. 3)

4.1 Introduction

Listening to the spontaneous music-making of young children may be one of the best ways of understanding how and why children have the need to express themselves through sounds and music. In fact, it appears that the desire to make music is present since early childhood (Campbell, 1998; Glover, 2000; Kaschub, 2009; Kaschub & Smith, 2009; Young, 2002, 2003). Creating music seems to offer 'a unique and special way of experiencing what is to be alive' (Kaschub & Smith, 2009, p. 3). Music is something children do in order to structure, give meaning to and understand their daily experiences; young children invent their small songs, make sound effects while they are playing with toys, whistle invented melodic patterns; they do it in an attempt to express the relationships that they are beginning to establish with the world in which they live. In this sense, music becomes a different pathway to 'life-understanding, life-enhancement and life-wisdom' (Abbs, 2003, p. 67).

Based on the literature (Faulkner, 2003; Gromko, 2003; Wiggins 1999/2000, 2003, 2007) and on our own experiences it is our view that music composition in a classroom setting should emerge from all of these spontaneous musical creations, since they are based on the children's inner impulse to express themselves. Through creative engagement with music children can grow as individuals and as social beings who will gradually look at art not only as a means of expressing themselves, but also as a tool to help them make sense of the world by using their imagination. This can open a window for children to reflect on their actions, thoughts and feelings in the communicative process with the world and with others.

In this chapter we aim to make a contribution to the understanding of music composition as a powerful experience in children's lives: as a dialogic process (Barrett, 2003) and as a cognitive, emotional and social ground in which children develop their thoughts and understandings in music and about music, and also develop their identities as musicians and individuals (Abbs, 2003; Bresler & Thompson, 2002; De Nora, 1997; Greene, 1995). In the next section we discuss some lenses for the interpretation of the development of children's musical thinking when engaged in music composition projects. After the theoretical background, the findings and implications sections seek to make a contribution to the research area on children's music composition in naturalistic settings. We discuss a classroom-based study (Veloso, in preparation; Veloso et al., 2010) that might raise questions not only about the important role of the context in any musical activity, but also in respect to the 'tensions between the findings of research conducted in naturalistic settings and more contrived settings' (Burnard, 2006, p. 111). The children's comments on their own composing processes are taken into account, in an attempt to contribute to the understanding of the children's feelings and perspectives about their work, which is needed to create richer opportunities for them (Barrett, 2001; Burnard, 2006; Stauffer, 2003).

4.2 Theoretical background

4.2.1 Understanding through feeling and imagination

The 'paradigm of embodiment' (Borgo, 2007; Bresler, 2004; Csordas, 1990; Johnson, 2007; Pelinski, 2005) aims to clarify that human reason has its roots in the ways the body experiences the world. In advocating for this paradigm, several researchers (Bowman, 2004; Bowman & Powell, 2007; Damásio, 2000; Pelinsky, 2005) explain that the body is not only the foundation of everything we feel and interpret about what surrounds us, but also the first point of contact of the human experience, promoting a pre-reflection about our lives that will decisively influence everything we come to know about the world and about ourselves.

António Damásio (1998, 2000), in the work he developed about emotions, concluded that all our mental representations are embedded in an emotional context. Sounds, visual images and tactile sensations reach the brain as mental images, and are always marked or 'catalogued' by a certain emotional profile. An emotion arises with a set of changes in our body's activities. This new set of changes in the body is then transmitted to the brain in the form of another mental image. Feeling is the conscious state of being aware of these emotions and of the experience that caused them. In music, the process described by Damásio seems to determine the way we experience sounds, not only because music has structural characteristics that seem to resonate deeply in our bodies, but also because all body changes that emerge from this process induce a set of emotions that will shape the meaning we create from musical experiences. Therefore, musical meaning grows from sensations felt in the body. As stated by Johnson, 'emotion and feeling lie at the heart of our capacity to experience meaning' (2007, p. 53).

According to Damásio, imagination is the manipulation of mental images that are perceived at any moment of our experiences or that are stored in our memory. As this manipulation often connects ideas that are considerably different on a conceptual level, the process of imagination might lead to moments where creative ideas arise. Therefore, through imagination, those engaged in any artistic creative act have the opportunity to search for possibilities far beyond what is normally considered correct, or within the norm. As stated by Greene, 'imagination is required to disclose a different state of things; to open the windows of consciousness to what might be, what ought to be' (2008, p. 18). Therefore, we suggest that the development of imaginative possibilities, which give rise to creative actions, has its starting point in emotions and feelings. This starting point has also been mentioned in the literature in different ways. Some have simply called it the moment of 'inspiration' (Hagman, 2000), others 'immersion' (Strahl, 1990) or 'first insight' (Kneller, 1965). Peter Abbs, for example, has named this first moment of the artistic creative act 'the releasing of an impulse' (1991, p. 292). Focusing on this first moment of the artistic creative process, he observes: 'for art to be created there must be some primary impulse released in the art-maker... an unsolved impulse that demands articulation that requires amplification and completion through the labour of artistic shaping' (Abbs, 1991, p. 293).

In this chapter, we propose that this first moment of the creative act is marked and shaped by emotions, and that the primary impulse is the embodied, emotional event that is connected to the idea the artist wants to express. While seeing children as artists, Abbs explains that after this first impulse the child feels a need to work through an active medium towards the realization of a final form. In musical terms, the medium is constituted by sounds and the final form is the set of musical ideas that might lead to the development of a musical piece. On an emotional level, the creative impulse of the child is shaped in the musical idea that suddenly arises in their mind.

As the act of musical composition involves emotions and feelings, children will construct their musical knowledge through different paths, which will lead to a variety of directions when developing their understanding of music. However, we have to take into account another crucial factor with regard to musical meaning construction; according to Bresler (2004) the process of meaning-making from our musical experiences is inseparable from the context. This statement takes into account not only the musical material, as it is experienced by each child, but also the circumstances in which these materials are integrated and constructed in specific contexts with very specific dynamics. Emotions are influenced by a situated self and, consequently, by the context in which experiences are lived; this is a two-way process and, therefore, the interactions established inside the social context are also shaped by the emotions children feel during these experiences. As stated by Bresler and Thompson, 'the context and its relationships with musical material together create the fundamental cognitive and affective structure of musical learning, a complex structure which can be called the child's musical world' (2002, p. 12). Therefore, children's musical worlds are a mirror of their inner worlds; while composing children reconstruct themselves, their knowledge and their thinking, creating new meanings to their lives.

4.2.2 Learning with others

Studies of musical composition in the classroom have shown that group settings are a powerful means for promoting musical and reflexive thinking among pupils (Faulkner, 2003; Wiggins, 1999/2000, 2001, 2003, 2007). Despite this fact, there is a need for more enquiries on the interaction that is established among pupils, the 'horizontal interaction', and among pupils and teachers, the 'vertical interaction' (Olsson, 2007, p. 990). In this research area, one of the issues more frequently discussed is the question of shared understanding. Wiggins (1999/2000, 2003, 2007) has stated several times that the shared understanding that slowly emerges as musical composition evolves is what allows children to develop several insights about music and about ways to express their individual feelings and experiences. In a study by Faulkner (2003), shared understanding also appears as a crucial concept during the process of group composition. Faulkner states that shared understanding emerges during 'a continuous dynamic flow' (2003, p. 115) that is maintained by the group while they listen to each other's ideas; during this process, pupils test the ideas of others, approving or rejecting them. This may occur through verbal or musical comments, or by playing or singing something that they think is more suitable for a specific moment of their composition. Through these verbalizations, and musical observations, children begin to share a conceptual and emotional view of how the musical composition should sound. Slowly, as their ideas are accepted or rejected, children reflect on their own musical ideas and on possible ways to better express themselves, gaining personal confidence and growing as musicians.

The surrounding circumstances in which children compose have a profound influence on all of the actions and interactions that children engage in while composing in groups. In her book *Releasing the Imagination*, Maxine Greene explains that 'the classroom situation most provocative of thoughtfulness and critical conscious is the one in which teacher and learners find themselves conducting a kind of collaborative search, each from her or his lived situation' (1995, p. 23). Acknowledging this idea, it is our view that music teachers have a crucial role in helping children to develop their composition skills, not only through providing several opportunities for children to engage in musical composition activities, but also regarding the ways they interact with other children in the classroom. As children may be provoked through musical problems that involve musical composition tasks, they might be encouraged to work alone or with their classmates, to reflect on what their intentions are for the composition, on how they want the musical piece to sound, and to explore all the sounds available. Teachers can guide, give feedback and suggest possible paths to enable children to develop their own ideas. Using this kind of approach, teachers may provide a musical and learning environment in which pupils develop their individual paths to composing through an interactive dialogue between their own experience and the questions raised and suggestions given by the teacher (Reese, 2003). In this way, the shared understanding also embraces the teacher, who emerges not as an authority, but as a more skilful and experienced friend who can provide help in improving the children's compositions. In this kind of setting, where an emerging strong emotional link is the support for interactions between the teacher and pupil, they feel free to explore, to make mistakes, to reflect on those mistakes and to try new possibilities without fear, and as a result they further develop their musical strategies and knowledge. During this process, where children feel safe, they also develop self-confidence, and new ways of looking at themselves as musicians and composers.

4.3 The research context

4.3.1 Music education in Portuguese elementary schools

In Portugal, compulsory education is divided into three learning cycles. As shown in Table 4.1, music education is a compulsory subject only in the first and second cycle (Ministério da Educação, 2001).

Table 4.1   Music education in compulsory education in Portugal

	Number of academic years	Pupils' age	Music education as a curricular subject	Professional responsible for teaching music education
1st cycle	4	6-9	Compulsory	Primary teacher
2nd cycle	2	10-11	Compulsory	Specialist music teacher
3rd cycle	3	12-14	Optional	Specialist music teacher

In 2006, the Ministry of Education launched a programme that consisted of '10 weekly hours of extra-curricular activities (English, Music, Sports) taught by specialist teachers, where children attend on a voluntary basis' (Boal-Palheiros, 2008, p. 98). A music syllabus was created with specific guidelines intended to help teachers develop their work. The Portuguese Ministry of Education entitled these activities 'Curriculum Enrichment Activities' (Ministério da Educação, 2006). Even though music education is part of the official curriculum (Ministério da Educação, 2001) the implementation of the 'Curriculum Enrichment Activities' has been the cause of some ambiguity as there is repetition of music in both curriculums. Mota (2007) outlined some concerns about the implementation of music as an enrichment activity, explaining that with the new programme music education may be discarded from the elementary curriculum in some schools. Pupils not attending afterschool enrichment activities could be in danger of not receiving any music education. As a possible solution, Mota (2007; Mota & Costa, 2002) advocated for collaborative work between the primary teacher and a music specialist. This collaborative work could be done through the implementation of projects that, on the one hand, would have their focus on *making music*, through performance, composition or audition, and, on the other hand, would embrace a real interdisciplinary process relating music with other arts and also with other curriculum subjects. However, until now, this has not become general practice, and pupils receive music education in primary schools within the voluntary 'Curricular Enrichment Activities', while provision of musical activities in school hours depends on the particular primary teacher (Ministério da Educação, 2001).

4.3.2 Action research – a preliminary comment

The examples discussed in the following sections were part of an eight-month action research project carried out by the first author (Veloso, in preparation). The project, called 'Magic Sounds', was intended to foster an understanding of the ways musical composition activities in small and large groups might promote the development of musical thinking among children.

Action research was used in this study as a methodology inspired by the roots of artistic practice. This is partly due to the fact that a significant amount of the data analysed consisted of the music made and performed by the children, their original scores, their own comments about their music and the process of making meaning through music. Therefore, and following some of Bresler's ideas (2006, 2008, 2010), our intention in using action research was based on a parallel between understanding through musicianship and artistic practices in general and understanding through research. Both action research and artistic practice involve great self-commitment by the teacher-researcher and by the artist. In both procedures, artist and researcher are committed to expressing their interpretations of the world, reflecting on them through an inquiry based on imagination and on possible open solutions that are then re-interpreted by those that have access to the research or the work of art.

4.3.3 Research design

According to Stringer, action research is 'a collaborative approach to *inquiry* or *investigation* that provides people with the means to take systematic *action* to resolve specific problems' (2007, p. 8). For Kemmis and McTaggart (1998), action research means to plan, to act, to observe and to reflect, allowing for a deep analysis of the relationship between what is being done and what it is possible to do. In a classroom setting, this process should lead to a better understanding of the teacher-researcher's own practice, promoting new possibilities for improvement of the teacher's classroom activities through reflection and analysis (Bell, 2005).

The action research project, from which two examples of children composing will be described further, followed weekly small action research cycles and a big overall cycle (Table 4.2). The activities were monitored and evaluated through a sequence of 'plan-act-evaluate-reflect' (Cain, 2008, p. 284), in which the data collected were used as a source to reflect, evaluate and re-plan not only each individual music lesson but also the music project as a whole.

Table 4.2   Action research design of the 'Magic Sounds' project

Action research cycles	Plan	Data collection	Data analysis	Reflection and improvements for practice
Small cycles	Individual planning of each music session that occurred once a week	Participant observation Field notes, which included descriptions of immediate feedback given by children Video recordings	Definition of units of meaning within the data sources, organizing them into categories that could summarize relevant points for reflection	Data triangulation with research literature, in order to improve each music lesson
Big cycle	Planning of the entire music composition project in problematic moments of the research project, where the activities related to the musical composition project would be re-planned and refined	Participant observation Field notes Video recordings Self-reports Questionnaire	Analysing key experiences (Stringer, 2007): – looking for and interpreting problematic moments, turning-point experiences and events especially significant to participants (Denzin, 2001) Categorizing and coding with a critical friend: – categorizing and coding units of meaning from the identified key experiences – identifying significant themes – interpreting these themes	Organizing the findings and comparing them with the literature, in order to reflect and suggest other music composition classroom projects and the possible ways that these might help in understanding the feelings and musical thinking processes of pupils

4.3.4 Evidence from children composing – Prelude

In sections 4.3.6 and 4.3.7 we will describe two examples of children composing, the first with children in a small group and the second with children composing in a large group. These examples will serve as a base for the discussion section, in which more information from other pupils will be given in order to illustrate certain themes that emerged during data analysis.

4.3.5 Evidence from children composing – the 'Magic Sounds' project

The 'Magic Sounds' project had 72 participating children, aged 7, who were enrolled in the second grade of an elementary school from Northern Portugal. They belonged to the three existing second-grade classes in the school. Although each class was composed of 24 children, for research purposes the three classes were divided in half; therefore, pupils attended music classes in groups of 12. Music sessions occurred once a week, for a period of 45 minutes each during school hours. The previous year the children had been introduced to improvisation and composition activities, which gave them the baseline for them to grow further in the 'Magic Sounds' project. However, it was the first time that these children had been involved in a composition project of this length.

The implementation of the project was previously discussed and agreed upon with the school director, the primary teachers and the parents, who signed an agreement consenting to the audio and video recording of all sessions and to their use for research purposes. It was agreed that the real names of the children participating in the project would not be revealed; therefore, all of the children's names were altered.

The idea for the project was introduced by the theme the school had chosen for all first- and second-grade activities, 'Children around the world'. With this in mind, it was decided that the music sessions would involve the interaction with a community/school from a different country. The theme 'children around the world' was introduced in the music sessions through the reading and interpretation of the book *Banzo, the Magical Bird* (Miranda, 2002). It was Banzo, a beautiful and very colourful bird and the book's main character, who led these pupils on a journey to the far corners of the world. During this imaginary journey, the Portuguese pupils met their foreign friends: a class of pupils from St Louis, Missouri and another from Cabot, Vermont. As the pupils were reading and interpreting the book, several posts were left on the internet showing some musical pieces composed by the pupils in the previous academic year and asking for collaborators from other countries who would be interested in working with us. When these two groups of American pupils were found, children from both countries engaged in an intense exchange of photos, videos, letters and the children's music in audio files. Throughout this correspondence, pupils were sharing many ideas about their favourite things and it was noticed that, among these, pupils always mentioned their favourite colour. This led to the idea of a music composition project about favourite colours. Although it was planned that the children would also exchange their music compositions with their American friends and that these new friends would send their own compositions (created from the same music composition guide), this was not possible. Somehow, music teachers from Cabot and St Louis, despite their enthusiasm in the beginning, were unable to follow the project through to the end. This was mainly due to the fact that the school curriculum regarding compulsory musical activities and the many musical events the music teachers had to prepare did not leave enough time for this endeavour. As a result, the interaction with the American schools did not have a major influence on the project's final outcomes.

After this first phase of the project (sessions 1-10 – October-December 2008), the music composition activities were divided into the following stages:

- planning the music composition from the theme 'My favourite colour' using a music composition guide (Figure 4.1) previously prepared by the teacher-researcher, in groups of four/five elements (sessions 11 and 12 – January 2009)
- composing in small groups with the same pupils who had done the previous task (sessions 13 to 16 – January and February)
- presentation of the small group's composition and large group reflection's on the compositions presented (sessions 17-18 – March)
- large group composition, constructed, in part, by the ideas that had already been explored in the small groups (sessions 19- 22 – March and April)
- rehearsals (sessions 23-26 – April and May)
- final concert (May).

Student name	Favourite colour	What colours suggest to you sound, and what colours suggest to you silence?	Which dynamics suggest to you the colours that you marked as sound?	Make a correspondence between each one of the colours and a musical instrument/voice	If these three colours represented a musical piece, what colour would come first? And second? And third?

Figure 4.1   Music composition guide: *All about us*

The descriptions of the children's interactions provided in the following sections were gathered by the first author who was the teacher-researcher. Nevertheless, both authors of this chapter conducted the data analysis and interpretation.

4.3.6 Evidence from children composing – an illustration from Tiago, João and Filipe, session 13

In his composition guide Tiago stated that his favourite colour was dark blue. He also mentioned that dark blue reminded him of a sound in *forte* on the bass xylophone. So, now, he was searching for that sound. In just a few seconds he created a motive (Music example 4.1, first motive). His two colleagues began to follow this motive, one playing the maraca and the other the glockenspiel. On the table there were also bongo drums and a metalophone (instruments that were mentioned in the music composition guide). They spent one or two minutes exploring and scaffolding, without talking. They appeared to be intensely engaged in the music as if they had forgotten everything else. Their bodies moved and pulsed to the sound of the music they were playing. Body and mind seemed to be in motion with the music. Tiago was softly singing the motive he had created while he was playing the bass xylophone.

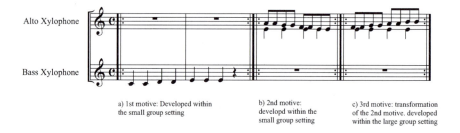

Example 4.1   Development of Tiago's musical motives

Before beginning the composition, and after finishing their music composition guide, the pupils from this group mentioned that in addition to expressing their favourite colours they also wanted to musically express 'a boy walking happily alone'. The motive that Tiago was playing really seemed to express that idea – a musical motive in *andante*, as if there was really someone walking through the music. As they continued playing, the teacher invited João, who was playing the glockenspiel, to play the bongo drums (he appeared to be a bit lost and considering what children had previously said about their composition, the bongo drums increased the possibility of sustaining what they were composing). Filipe, who was playing the maraca, switched to the metalophone. At this moment, Tiago was playing the bass xylophone, João was playing the bongo drums and Filipe was playing the metalophone. As they seemed to be deeply concentrated on their work, exploring and crafting, looking for ideas, they were left alone in the room in order to be given space and time to think on their own. As observed in the video recording, once alone Filipe adopted the role of the leader. He began to explain to his classmates who would play first and who would follow. João interrupted him, as there was something on his mind that he had to express right away; he had an idea to end the musical piece. Tiago and João discussed and presented ideas for the final section of the piece, and they seemed to reach an agreement: Tiago would scratch the xylophone from low to high sounds while João would beat on the bongo drums several times (like a drummer when making a 'break') and then would beat one last time in *fortissimo*, to signal the end of the piece. They began rehearsing. Tiago played his initial motive and Filipe, joining the group again, doubled the motive on the metalophone, by ear. At this moment, the teacher re-entered the room and moved closer to the students. Suddenly, Tiago had another idea: a phrase using E on his left hand as a pedal note accompanied by a descending movement from A to E on his right hand (Music example 4.1, second motive). He presented his idea to the group and was asked to teach it to the teacher. At that moment, the music teacher became another member of the group. While the music teacher was learning Tiago's motive the other two pupils changed instruments again. João began an improvisation on the metalophone and Filipe started playing the bongo drums. Filipe was encouraged to develop his musical idea on the bongo drums while the teacher picked up a maraca and played with them. All together the group began to play more and more *pianissimo*; silence emerged and they all stopped at the same time.

4.3.7 Evidence from children composing – chaos gives rise to a 'Beautiful Day', session 19

When the children began to work in a large group setting, the pupils were very excited and willing to participate. They all talked at the same time, they explored the instruments with intensity and they played and shared ideas in pairs. It was felt that the children needed guidance in their processes of communication. At that moment, the teacher interrupted them and organized the class.

After this brief pause the pupils began to share topics for discussion with their colleagues: How would the song begin? What instruments would be used? How many sections would our piece have? While always being monitored, pupils shared ideas by singing, playing or verbally explaining them. They decided that the piece would have two main sections. The first section, which for analysis purposes was later called section A, would begin with a motive in the bass xylophone and some percussion. After this decision was made, the pupils started to rehearse. The song was marked by the bass xylophone motive, while another student was improvising something he had been practising while working in the small group setting on the snare drum. Then, one of the metalophones joined them. As the music was growing, the children became increasingly concentrated on what they were doing. All their energy seemed to be concentrated on that moment and the music seemed to represent everything they were at that moment. They were embodied by the sounds they were creating. The teacher was also moved by the music and began to improvise with them using another metalophone. Some students had the idea to add some non-conventional instruments – a wind tube and a thunder drum. The music sounded fast and moved forward like free improvisation in a jazzy style until the end when the sound of the instruments slowly disappeared. During the group performance Tiago decided to change the second motive he had developed in the small group, playing it from the low to the upper notes. He maintained his pedal E note, but on his right hand he moved up from F to B (Music example 4.1, third motive). The other students listened, deeply engaged in what Tiago was playing. After this, both the pupil on the glockenspiel and the one on the metalophone invented a motive, to join Tiago. The bass xylophone joined the rest of the group, playing the same crochets in the right-hand rhythm as Tiago, with an ascending motive from E to G. In the end, the group decided to add the storm object and some tubes producing wind. They created a very rhythmic and energetic part (that later became section B) that led one of the pupils to say: 'when I play this part of the music I feel crazy with the music agitation'.

4.4 Discussion of findings

When Tiago stated that dark blue reminded him of a sound in *forte*, he was relating to concepts that are not semantically close. How can dark blue be related to a sound in *forte* played on the bass xylophone? If we go back to the creative phases mentioned by Abbs (1991), and to the ideas presented by Damásio (1998, 2000), we might suggest that the expressive impulse felt by Tiago was the feeling related to the image of dark blue. This same feeling led Tiago's mind into a musical quest for ideas which could then become another way of thinking in dark blue: a musical way of thinking and understanding. It is our view that when the same pupils mentioned that they also wanted to express 'a boy walking happily alone', they were talking about a global feeling of how they wanted their music to sound. The words they used worked as a metaphor, as they probably used their imagination to connect the feeling they wanted to express with their own life experiences. This feeling was shared by all three members of the group; as Wiggins observed (1999/2000), it was an emotional shared understanding of how they wanted the musical piece to sound. Again, this general feeling was transformed into music as children slowly found those musical ideas and conceptions that embodied the originating impulse. At the same time, this impulse, which was worked through the use of sounds, encouraged students to try different expressive possibilities, to look for and develop several techniques, to reflect on the possible ways they could arrange sounds in order to express themselves. In other words, this impulse enlarged and developed their understanding and knowledge of music. In these moments of exploration and craft, these pupils moved into a dialogic process with the musical materials; they brought their thoughts, their past experiences and knowledge to their music, until the moment they felt the music was a resonance of their inner selves. This is why we observed them deeply concentrated in what they were doing as if nothing else existed. The process of composing enabled these children to make sense of their experiences as 'boys walking happily in the world' and to share this small part of their identities with others. The above illustrations show how the process of music-making is a powerful means for children to extend and renew their experienced worlds, as it involves emotions and feelings that shape our imagination.

This same idea was also presented in self-reports that pupils were asked to write, drawing on their feelings and thoughts about the composition process and the final piece. One of the boys who improvised on the metalophone in the above large group example wrote: 'I feel as if I am climbing a step each time increasingly bigger.' Another pupil explained that he felt 'like a rock star, because the music is so powerful!' Both children seemed to have related some qualities of the musical piece with possible experiences sparked by their imagination. The music triggered something that transformed their daily routine. This new set of thoughts and feelings that emerged when they began their voyage from their selves into the music and from the music into themselves very likely came out through an emotional process grounded in the ways their bodies were moved by the music.

In addition to self-reports, all of the students answered a questionnaire that raised several issues related to the meaning and importance of the music composed by them. Luísa, a pupil from another class, wrote that when she played the music they had composed with her classmates she felt like 'a real musician'. Other answers to the questionnaire revealed that Luísa had created the concept of 'a real musician' by developing the awareness that in order to create music she had to develop several skills regarding musical composition and performance. The improvement of these skills, especially those regarding the performance of an instrument, required individual practice. Many pupils stressed the fact that, in the beginning, it was difficult for them to practice because they did not have any musical instruments at home. However, this obstacle was quickly overcome by some pupils who started using kitchen utensils and displayed on sheets of paper musical notes resembling a piano, a metalophone or a xylophone. Children were discovering how to learn. They solved their difficulties when they released their imaginative capacities and set themselves apart from what was given as certain. In our view, this was possible because they were highly committed and involved with the project: the interplay of music and emotions and the joy of expressing and transforming ideas, feelings and thoughts in musical terms (Illustration 4.1) became a platform for a deeper engagement with music that opened pupils' minds to foster new musical knowledge and new ways of thinking through and in music.

Illustration 4.1   Child playing in the final concert

This was also observed in the enhancement of several compositional skills. Pupils mentioned they made great effort when they were working with their groups in order to 'know what instruments would sound good with one another', to make the musical ideas in their 'head(s) come out of the instrument' or 'to know what the appropriate musical notes were'. As they presented and shared ideas on composing and learning together, they seemed to have acquired a clear understanding of the importance their classmates adopted in the process of questioning and growing as musicians and individuals. For example, Luísa revealed that her music was important to her because it was made with her colleagues, and she learned that when they worked together the music was 'better'.

Children composed their music without restrictive instructions or parameters, which resembles the ways in which young children engage in spontaneous musical creations. Creating music in groups in this kind of setting seemed to provide a strong emotional and conceptual context that empowered the development of individual musical thinking. In our view, pupils also learned that music-making was a possible base for creating meaning for their experienced worlds and, more importantly, to find their own individual voices. As André mentioned in his self-report: 'when I'm playing our composition, I feel I am inside the drum and that I am a lion playing with all my strength'.

4.5 Implications for practice

The experience lived in this project showed us the value of the role that teachers can play if they begin to see themselves and their pupils as musicians. Thus, when children are composing, it seems important that teachers play and sing with them in a musically collaborative way, looking at the pupils as musicians, as composers and as performers. When these moments occur, teachers have the opportunity to bring all their knowledge and energy as musicians into the music classroom. Acting like this, they may find themselves immersed in the music that is being made and played in the classroom; we believe in the importance of this aspect as often what is lacking in music composition classes is this kind of feeling through music.

If music teachers look at musical composition as a collaborative endeavour between teachers and pupils, it may lead them in new directions to learning and teaching composition. This particular way of being in the classroom influences how pupils see their music teachers, as they begin to see them as older friends with whom they can share their ideas, someone who will help them to find their own learning paths. In view of everything that happened during this project, two different issues emerge as possible strands for consideration. Firstly, it seems important that music teachers reflect on their role and their actions with regard to the already mentioned 'vertical interaction' (Olsson, 2007, p. 990) considering also the emphasis on the teacher's role that is embedded in the notion that 'the student has to learn to become the protagonist of his or her own knowledge' (Abbs, 2003, p. 15). The change in the teachers' role may start by allowing pupils to see teachers not as the ones with all the solutions, but rather as facilitators, promoting several opportunities and creating different settings in which children slowly construct their own musical world. Secondly, while planning these different opportunities, it seems important that teachers also take into consideration the environment where pupils will engage in the creative process. This environment should have scope for imaginative engagement with the world of sounds; children would need to explore and improvise with sounds that surround them, using instruments, sounding objects and their own voices and bodies, in both conventional and unconventional ways. They would need to relate to sounds as they relate to colours when they are painting, as this can open and shape their minds to a palette of sounds, textures, dynamics and gestures, which will become the building blocks of their composed music.

Our aim in this chapter was to open doors to possible paths, which may be reinterpreted by researchers and educators rather than be taken as fixed parameters. On the contrary, we invite the community of researchers and teachers to reflect on their own knowledge and experience, moving beyond findings from this particular study. We challenge readers to think about music education in a way that might foster possible answers to the individual's need to understand and interpret the world in a multiplicity of ways.

References

Abbs, P. (1991). From babble to rhapsody: On the nature of creativity. *British Journal of Aesthetics*, 31(4), 291-300.

Abbs, P. (2003). *Against the flow: Education, the arts and postmodern culture.* New York: Routledge.

Barrett, M. (2001). Constructing a view of children's meaning-making as notators: A case-study of a five-year-old's descriptions and explanations of invented notations. *Research Studies in Music Education*, 16(1), 33-45.

Barrett, M. (2003). Freedoms and constraints: Constructing musical words through the dialogue of composition. In M. Hickey (Ed.), *Why and how to teach music composition: A new horizon for music education* (pp. 3-27). Reston, VA: MENC.

Bell, J. (2005). *Doing your research project.* Maidenhead and Milton Keynes: Open University Press.

Boal-Palheiros, G. & Encarnação, M. (2008). Music Education as extra-curricular activity in Portuguese primary schools. In S. Malbrán & G. Mota (Eds.), *Proceedings of the 22nd international seminar on research in music education* (pp. 96-104). Porto: Research Commission of the International Society for Music Education.

Borgo, D. (2007). Free jazz in the classroom: An ecologic approach to music education. *Jazz Perspectives*, 1(1), 61-88.

Bowman, W. (2004). Cognition and the body: Perspectives from music education. In L. Bresler (Ed.), *Knowing bodies, moving minds: Towards embodied teaching and learning* (pp. 29-50). Dordrecht: Kluwer Academic.

Bowman, W. & Powell, K. (2007). The body in a state of music. In L. Bresler (Ed.), *International handbook of research in arts education* (pp. 1087-1108). Dordrecht: Springer.

Bresler, L. (2004). Prelude. In L. Bresler (Ed.), *Knowing bodies, moving minds: Towards embodied teaching and learning* (pp. 7-12). Dordrecht: Kluwer Academic.

Bresler, L. (2006). Towards connectedness: Aesthetically based research and its ethical implications. *Studies in Art Education: A Journal of Issues and Research in Art Education*, 48(1), 52-69.

Bresler, L. (2008). Research as experience and the experience of research: Mutual shaping in the arts and in qualitative inquiry. *LEARNing Landscapes*, 2(1), 267-280.

Bresler, L. (2010). What musicianship can teach educational research. *Music Education Research*, 7(2), 169-183.

Bresler, L. & Thompson, Ch. (2002). Context interlude. In L. Bresler & Ch. Thompson (Eds.), *The arts in children's lives: Context, culture, and curriculum* (pp. 9-13). Dordrecht: Kluwer Academic.

Burnard, P. (2006). Understanding children's meaning-making as composers. In I. Deliège & G. Wiggins (Eds.), *Musical creativity: Multidisciplinary research in theory and practice* (pp. 111-133). New York: Psychology Press.

Cain, T. (2008). The characteristics of action research in music education. *British Journal of Music Education*, 25(3), 283-313.

Campbell, P. S. (1998). *Songs in their heads: Music and its meaning in children's lives*. Oxford: Oxford University Press.

Csordas, T. (1990). Embodiment as a paradigm for anthropology. *Ethos*, 18(1), 5-47.

Damásio, A. R. (1998). *Descartes' error: Emotion, reason and the human brain*. New York: Harper Perennial.

Damásio, A. R. (2000). *The feeling of what happens*. New York: Mariner Books.

De Nora, T. (1997). Music as a technology of the self. *Poetics*, 27, 31–56.

Denzin, N. (2001). *Interpretive interactionism*. Thousand Oaks, CA: Sage.

Faulkner, R. (2003). Group composing: Pupil perceptions from a social psychological study. *Music Education Research*, 5(2), 101-124.

Glover, J. (2000). *Children composing 4-14*. London: Routledge.

Greene, M. (1995). *Releasing the imagination: Essays on education, the arts and social change*. San Francisco: Jossey-Bass.

Greene, M. (2008). Education and the arts: The windows of imagination. *LEARNing Landscapes*, 2(1), 17-20.

Gromko, J. E. (2003). Children composing: Inviting the artful narrative. In M. Hickey (Ed.), *Why and how to teach music composition: A new horizon for music education* (pp. 69-90). Reston, VA: MENC.

Hagman, G. (2000). The creative process. *Progress in Self Psychology*, 16, 277-297.

Johnson, M. (2007). *The meaning of the body: Aesthetics of human experience*. Chicago: University of Chicago Press.

Kaschub, M. (2009). A principled approach to teaching music composition to children. *Research & Issues in Music Education*, 7(1) – see www.stthomas. edu/rimeonline/vol7/kaschubSmith.htm (accessed 1 December 2010).

Kaschub, M. & Smith, J. (2009). *Minds on music: Composition for creative and critical thinking*. Plymouth, NH: MENC.

Kemmis, S. & McTaggart, R. (1998). *The action research planner*. Geelong, Vic.: Deakin University Press.

Kneller, G. (1965). *The art and science of creativity*. New York: Holt, Rinehart & Winston.

Ministério da Educação (2001). *Currículo Nacional do Ensino Básico* [*National Curriculum for Basic Education*]. Ministry of Education, Portugal – see www.

dgidc.min-edu.pt/recursos/Lists/Repositrio%20Recursos2/Attachments/84/ Curriculo_Nacional.pdf (accessed 1 December 2010).

Ministério da Educação (2006). Despacho nº 12590: 2ª Série [Order No. 12590: 2nd Series]. *Diário da República,* 1015, 8783-8787 – see http://min-edu.pt/ np3content/?newsId=1186&fileName=despacho_12591_2006.pdf (accessed 1 December 2010).

Miranda, R. (2002). *Banzo o pássaro mágico* [*Banzo, the magical bird*]. Vila nova de Gaia: Gailivro.

Mota, G. (2007). A música no 1º ciclo do ensino básico: O estado, a sociedade, a escola e a criança [Music in primary school: State, society, school and the child]. *Revista de Educação Musical,* 128-129, 16-21.

Mota, G. & Costa, J. (2002). Educação musical em contexto: À procura de uma nova praxis [Music education in context: Moving towards a new practice]. *Música Psicologia e Educação,* 4, 67-83.

Olsson, B. (2007). Social issues in music education. In L. Bresler (Ed.), *International handbook of research in arts education* (pp. 998-1006). Dordrecht: Springer.

Pelinski, R. (2005). Embodiment and musical experience. *Revista Transcultural de Música,* 9 – see www.sibetrans.com/trans/trans9/pelinski-en.htm (accessed 1 December 2010).

Reese, S. (2003). Responding to students compositions. In M. Hickey (Ed.), *Why and how to teach music composition: A new horizon for music education* (pp. 211-232). Reston, VA: MENC.

Stauffer, S. (2003). Identity and voice in young composers. In M. Hickey (Ed.), *Why and how to teach music composition: A new horizon for music education* (pp. 91-112). Reston, VA: MENC.

Strahl, M. O. (1990). On the artist and the creative process. *Journal of American Academy of Psychoanalysis,* 18, 669-673.

Stringer, E. (2007). *Action research* (3rd edition). Thousand Oaks, CA: Sage.

Veloso, A. (in preparation). Doctoral thesis.

Veloso, A., Carvalho, S. & Mota, G. (2010). Creating meaning through music composition: A contribution for understanding the development of children's musical thinking. In G. Mota & A. Yin (Eds.), *Proceedings of the ISME 23rd Research Commission Seminar 25-30 July, North East Normal University, Changchun* (pp. 18-22). Changchun, China: ISME Research Commission.

Wiggins, J. (1999/2000). The nature of shared meaning and its role in empowering independent musical thinking. *Bulletin of the Council for Research in Music Education,* 143(Winter), 65-90.

Wiggins, J. (2001). *Teaching for musical understanding.* New York: McGraw-Hill.

Wiggins, J. (2003). A frame for understanding children's compositional processes. In M. Hickey (Ed.), *Why and how to teach music composition: A new horizon for music education* (pp. 141-165). Reston, VA: MENC.

Wiggins, J. (2007). Compositional processes in music. In L. Bresler (Ed.), *International handbook of research in arts education* (pp. 453-470). Dordrecht: Springer.

Young, S. (2002). Young children's spontaneous vocalizations in free-play: Observations of two- to three-year-olds in a day-care setting. *Bulletin of the Council for Research in Music Education*, 152(Spring), 43-53.

Young, S. (2003). Time-space structuring in spontaneous play on educational percussion instruments among three- and four-year-olds. *British Journal of Music Education*, 20(1), 45-59.

Chapter 5

Towards pedagogies of revision: guiding a student's music composition

Peter R. Webster

I sit next to Carson[1] in his house as he demonstrates some of his music on the piano. Carson is a sixth-grade student in a suburban school near Chicago, Illinois, USA. He is 12 years old. Today is the first of many meetings that we will soon have and we are getting to know each other. 'Listen to this…' he says and he plays several measures of music on his somewhat out of tune baby grand in the front room. The music is large, full of big musical gestures growing from fast rhythmic patterns and tuneful melodies accompanied at times by block chords. He looks up at me with a great deal of pride and before I can say much, he heads into another piece that he is working on, much in the same style. Apparently he works on several pieces at the same time.

Moments before, I enter his beautiful home and meet his mother, father and little sister. All were excited about my visit and I could feel the positive energy flowing from this family almost immediately. 'Carson is really excited about your visit', says his mom and I thanked them all for putting up with my intrusion into their lives for my research.

Carson is now playing more music, some chords and some small fragments of new pieces. I am somewhat confused about how it all fits together. He explains that he has been playing piano for five years and studies with a local teacher. 'Do you study composition with her?' I ask. 'No', he replies, 'but I would like to take composition lessons.' I promise him that I will try to find a composition teacher for him if he wants and he seems excited about this prospect. I express a good deal of interest in his music and ask him what inspires him, what does he listen to? 'I like movie music, John Williams, like *Jaws*. Classical music and folk songs too.' 'Besides writing music for school assignments, what other occasions cause you to compose?' 'Christmas and holidays. I write a Christmas song each year,' he responds. 'Do you play other instruments?' I ask. 'Guitar and trumpet and I am starting to learn some music theory too from my piano teacher.'

Back to the piano again, perhaps less interested in talking with me and more intent on sharing the music in his head. This time, the music has very percussive bass lines occurring in the lower range of the piano. I marvel at the ease with which Carson plays and the excitement he exudes. 'I am working on this really long piece called *Time Machine*. It's in sections that go along with music history. It starts out with older sounds like Bach and stuff and moves to more modern.' He plays some from memory. 'Do you write out your music by hand?' I ask. 'No, I use the computer, Sibelius mostly with my

---

[1]   I have chosen to use pseudonyms for my informants in this chapter.

MIDI keyboard. It's a great program – do you have version 6? I like the sounds that come with that version.'

I am starting to understand Carson a little now. This is a fellow with good music keyboard skills who has come to find a home using the computer and standard notation software to help with recording his ideas. No looping software for this young man, no GarageBand scores with graphic notation – at least not right now in his musical journey. I marvel at how so many children have different starting places for composition and there is no one right way to begin.

We now move to his computer desk in a bedroom upstairs, far away from the baby grand piano in the front room. He has his own laptop but he shows me his music on this family's big-screen computer. A few of his compositions appear on the screen, all in various stages of completeness. 'How do you get your ideas?' I ask. 'I kind of improvise something and see if I like it – mostly melodies and stuff and then I add the harmony. I get the ideas down that I like and then I go back and sort of make it better, like adding dynamics and stuff. I like the different timbres in Sibelius. I figure out where the problems are and I fix them. I like lots of contrast, but I also like to make things kind of different but similar, you know?'

I assure Carson that I do understand what he means. The rest of our time this day is spent looking over some of his latest scores. Carson shows me pieces written for unusual groupings of instruments that might be considered an orchestra or a concert band. He clearly composes in real time with the computer and then goes back to edit. The music appears to be written in well-defined sections, is tonal with clearly defined key centres and moves rapidly with driving rhythms and clear melodies. There is much repetition, both in terms of a musical idea within a section and between sections as well. Carson is not afraid to use instruments sparingly and there is plenty of 'white space' in the music. There is musical thinking going on in the mind of this young man and I am anxious to study his music more. We transfer several digital files to my flash drive, including some past versions of pieces and I ask if I might come another time to interview him further. He laughs and quickly agrees and I leave our first meeting, after playing with the family dog, with a sense that I am likely to learn much from my time with Carson.

5.1 The teacher's role

Few question the wisdom of including composition as a musical experience for young people. Writers in this book, and many other scholars and practitioners over the last several decades, have argued persuasively for music teachers of all kinds to consider the benefits of engaging children in compositional work as a partner to other musical experiences such as improvisation, listening and the performance of other's music. From the days of early writings from Schafer (1979) and Paynter (1970) to the more recent contributions by Hickey (1999) and Kaschub and Smith (2009), the value to musical understanding of the personal journeys of children working and thinking in and with sound can hardly be questioned.

For my entire professional life, I have argued for the critical importance of creative thinking experiences in music (Webster, 1990). I have experimented with assessment approaches (Webster, 1987) and have put forth a model of creative thinking in music that was designed to encourage research and debate (Webster, 2002). On a somewhat separate dimension, I have also contributed to the application of music technology in music teaching and learning (Williams & Webster, 2008). The growing interest in music technology as an important partner for encouraging musical thought is related in obvious ways to creativity theory and composition by children and I will remain always grateful to be living and working in a time when these streams of interest are celebrated in our literature.

But a lingering wonderment in my mind over the years is just what this all means for how we, as teacher educators, advise professionals in their work with children in the composition context. What is the music teacher's role in encouraging the natural voices of children that Campbell (1998) speaks of so elegantly? This chapter is written to provide some small insight into how we, as music teachers, might improve one important aspect of our work with children: the encouragement of revision in compositional experiences.

For me, revision is the *active consideration of new material in the face of old with the idea of improving a final product*. It is based on the notion that the first gestures of musical ideas are worthy of change by expanding, extending or otherwise altering the musical ideas beyond the initial form. Revision can take many forms and can take place in countless ways.

It seems clear that children can generate initial musical ideas easily when encouraged to do so. When working in groups or independently, music can be created by using all sorts of instruments, by music notation-based programs such as Finale or Sibelius and by sequencer-like software such as GarageBand, or by the simple manipulation of previously created music with a recording device. We have many collections of such music and such work has helped us understand the musical processes and products of children's compositional output (e.g. Folkestad, 1996; Glover, 2000; Moorhead & Pond, 1978). Such work has led us to better understand the more naturally developing thinking processes of children at different ages and under different circumstances.

But what is *our* role as music teachers in the *development* of revision as a natural part of music-making? In the past, I have made the case for an active role by music teachers in the compositional experience without squelching the creative spirit of the young composer (Webster, 2003). This is a very difficult process in the student–teacher relationship and I continue to feel that a discussion about how to do this is needed for our profession. I see far too many occurrences of music teachers including composition in their curriculums simply to say that they encourage creative thinking to meet a standard (MENC, 1994) and employing no real strategies to use composition as a platform to teach about music and its meaning for each child. In short, there are no real pedagogies at play – no real consideration for how to structure growth in musical understanding through composition.

It is important to understand that I am not talking here about imagining new and unusual ways to prompt compositional thought with students, important as that is. We have outstanding examples of this in the writings of Wilkins (2006) and Kaschub and Smith (2009). What I have in mind is more of a style of interaction with children that, on the one hand, values their voice and, on the other hand, guides their thinking in ways that deepen and enrich their world of sonic possibilities so that the full impact of creative engagement with sound expressive of feeling is maximized. I have in mind not just encouraging the next composition, followed by the next and so forth. Rather, I would like to suggest that teachers have an obligation to help children realize that seeking assistance in compositional thinking is allowed and encouraged. We are able to do this far better in good music performance teaching, whether we are dealing with the preparation of music written by others or in improvisation instruction. We must find ways to do this effectively for music composition instruction.

5.2 Concerns about active engagement

For some, active engagement of the teacher in the compositional process may be detrimental, especially in group compositional work. Wiggins argues for the idea that revision is an extension of student work that happens naturally in group work and is a function of how the children interact with one another:

> When students work in an environment in which expressing and sharing musical ideas is an integral part of the whole experience, expressing and sharing ideas about compositional work is a natural part of that experience. Feedback and suggestions about students' compositional decisions occur quite naturally as an outgrowth of the normal patterns of classroom interaction that take place regardless of the musical activity in which students are engaged. (2005, p. 36)

I am sure that feedback and suggestions occur this way and this may well be an important approach to assist musical thinking as it might be found in a group setting; I would suggest, however, that group-think of this sort, especially among peers, is limited in offering the depth of experience that is evidenced when musical problems are solved with some nuanced guidance by experienced music teachers. I feel this is so for group work and certainly for individuals working on their own compositions.

Ruthmann (2008), in a thoughtful article based on his dissertation work, reminds us that agency matters. It does matter if a teacher interferes with or dominates unfairly the compositional intent of a young composer. Using an example of a teacher working with a student composer in the completion of a sound track, Ruthmann clearly shows how the intentions of a teacher to improve a composition might create negative consequences for creative thinking of a composer:

> Ellen's case illustrates the tightrope we walk as music teachers in our efforts to facilitate students' creativity. Ellen [student] invested a lot of herself in her

composition and viewed Mary's comments [teacher] as asking her to change something that she felt was really important in the composition. Teachers have their own personal agencies and educational goals for their students and have to negotiate their interactions with students. However, through adopting a pedagogy of composition that begins with the inclusive practice of seeking and understanding their students' musical intentions, teachers may be more successful at supporting their students' development as composers. (2008, p. 56)

Well said.

Carson was recommended to me as a subject for study by a highly regarded, middle school music teacher, Sally Johnson. Sally has won many awards for her creative teaching and is noted for use of technology in her music classroom. She won a teaching prize that brought her to my college campus to study with the faculty. In visiting her classroom, I discovered a brightly coloured teaching room with computer workstations with music keyboards arranged around the perimeter. There was plenty of room in the middle of the teaching space for movement activities and for sitting on comfortable carpeted areas for discussions. Sally's computer teaching station sat next to her desk and was used to project video images on the wall behind her. Down the hall from her classroom is the school's cafeteria and Sally has convinced her head of school to use a section of this large space for dramatic presentations for the school and for parents. She has a small stage constructed there with lighting appropriate for events. The school is a 'middle' school, serving grades 4 through 8 in a rather well-to-do suburb of Chicago. Sally does the 'general music' teaching and does so with a strong commitment to creative work in composition and improvisation with her students, far more than is common in American middle schools.

In each of her grade levels, Sally creates music projects for students that feature composition. Some projects are centred on video production, some around sound file creation using a program such as GarageBand. Still others involve music notation with Sibelius. Students often work in teams on collaborative composition. Poetry might be used for inspiration or perhaps artwork. Students do written projects on composers as well and create shared podcasts on music topics that are posted on the school's website. There is a constant hum of activity in Sally's room and there is much room for experimentation and creative thought. Sally encourages parents to be a part of her teaching. She does little with traditional performance groups and adheres to no one methodology in general music teaching such as Orff or Kodaly. She uses a point system for grading and students must complete projects to a stated criteria level before points are awarded. Students are given flexible ways to meet the point standard. Sally maintains the perspective of a 'guide on the side' in the manner of a true constructionist teacher.

As with many teachers who teach in such settings, Sally does very little with structured suggestions for change in students' own composition unless requested to do so by a student. There is no detailed composition pedagogy that asks students to move in stages through conceptual material as might be done while learning a musical instrument. My sense in talking with Sally is that her encouragement of collaborative work is similar to that described by Wiggins (1999).

It is in this rich and active environment that we find Carson, often working alone in a corner of the room, creating Sibelius compositions for projects in Sally's class and at home on his own, creating work to share with family and friends. When I ask Carson about whether he works with others in the class on projects, he says, 'Sometimes, I also like to work on my own.' Sally considers Carson to be one of her best students and shares with me many compositions from other students in Carson's class as well. One or two of the sets of scores I look at approach the depth and breadth of Carson's work, but most do not and are more typical of the musical gestures of sixth-grade music writers composing either by themselves or with others. I marvel yet again at the creative thinking that is exhibited by these middle school students, encouraged by a caring and thoughtful teacher who allows them great freedom. I leave my visit with Sally wondering what the music might be like in such an environment with more active engagement by the teacher with the music being constructed. Could the same creative energy be maintained while increasing the quality and depth of music understanding?

5.3 Why bother

So why take the trouble to walk the tightrope imagined by Ruthmann? Children clearly enjoy work on their own with little 'interference' from the teacher, as evidenced in classrooms like Sally's. It takes enormous time and energy for a teacher to consider a method of active engagement in group composition progress and in individual compositional decision-making. One might maintain that the children are learning by themselves and will construct their learning by simply doing more compositions each year under different circumstances. Some may indeed adopt this perspective, citing an aggressively postured constructionist approach (Webster, 2011).

As the reader might guess, I have some doubts – especially in light of the fact that we have no compelling empirical data that such an approach really leads to better musical understanding. My recent review of the major research on constructivist approaches to music learning yielded much conceptual and procedural support for such approaches but little hard evidence of long-term benefits (Webster, 2011). The difficult truth is that we have little credible evidence one way or the other about effective pedagogy for composition-based music education in schools.

What we do know is that revision is used in many other fields, including art education and writing (Bereiter & Scardamalia, 1987; Calkins, 1994; Fitzgerald, 1987; Gilmore, 2007). We know from this work that children may not naturally gravitate to revision, largely because they do not have proper diagnostic skills. Children can revise and can do so very well, but they must be taught to do it and to do it regularly. For example, better writing emerges when children are asked to compare different versions of work, find errors and attempt to correct problems. We also know from this literature that less experienced writers revise more 'surface' items and technical aspects, whereas more experienced creators tend to revise more meaningful material that requires more depth of thinking. In writing, Zellermayer and Cohen (1996) have suggested a system of question cues that teachers can use in encouraging children to carefully critique their writing.

For example, teachers might ask: 'Could you add more detail here?' 'Do you have any further thoughts on this issue?' 'What exactly do you mean when you write?' 'Why is this important?' Such questions can lead children to improve their writing.

In music, one might imagine analogous questions about music gestures. For example, 'Are you satisfied with the way this section sounds', 'Could you add other [instruments, rhythms, melodies, harmonies] to this section to make it sound more to your liking?' 'Consider this musical idea here. Do you think it would work in another section of your music?' 'What can you apply from our [listening/performing] work yesterday?' 'What are you thinking about here? What feeling in the listener would you like to convey? What are you hearing and is it different from what you have now?' A collection of questions of this sort might lead to some important insights about the musical workings of each child's mind (Reese, 2003; Younker, 2003) and 'ownership' of the idea of revision.

I have argued for additional reasons for consideration of revision based not on related disciplines, but on music itself (Webster, 2003). One reason is the central place that revision holds in the models of creative thinking in music that have been proposed; these models attempt to unpack the creative process as it seems to proceed in real music-making. Both Hickey (2003) and Sloboda (1985) have advanced models that include revision. In my own work, I have revised my creative thinking model to include a clearer role for revision as part of the movement beyond the initial gesture (Webster, 2002). I have included the 'working through' aspect in context with other steps in the creative process. Key here are the notions of revising, editing and new idea formation. Other researchers have included similar endorsements of revision in models that have flowed closely from actual observation of children's composition (Carlin, 1998). Another example includes the work done at Harvard's Project Zero (Gardner, 1989). The model of perception, production and reflection forms the theoretical heart of this important project. The 'reflection' piece, carried forth not only in music but in other arts as well, plays an important role in establishing an environment that might foster revision.

Another important reason to include revision as a priority in teaching strategy is its natural presence in children's actions. Empirical studies have focused on compositional process and most have reported something about periods of 'exploration' or 'reflection'. The well-known work by Kratus (1989) on the use of time during creative exercises demonstrated the presence of exploration and development. In more qualitatively based studies, Younker (1997) and Younker and Smith (1996) have shown how inexperienced and more experienced composers worked with musical ideas by naturally using revision techniques. Folkestad (1996) reported similar behaviours in his subjects when working with technology. In a study of high school students working in a flexible setting for composing, van Ernst (1993) reported some revision that occurred, but speculated on a different role by the teacher:

> The question is how the teacher might best engage students in a process of reflection, or metacognition, about their compositional work. The teacher in

the study encouraged the students to reflect on their own work and the work of others, especially after a performance. However, there was insufficient instruction in the process of reflecting and this suggests a possible variation to the role of the teacher. If the teacher adopted a conferencing approach to the process, it could involve choosing appropriate times during the composing of a piece and asking the student to reflect on the process itself, the choices made to date, the possible alternatives, and to focus on evaluating the work and making changes as necessary. (1993, p. 38)

We have some conceptual evidence that children do learn from revision. Kaschub (1997) profiles the processes of two composition projects, one with six sections of sixth-grade general music and one with a high school choir. In each project, a composer worked with the groups to create works cooperatively. The article is rich with examples of how the children gained a stronger understanding of music by participating in the composition project with revision and extension strategies. This is one example from the high school project:

Once the high school students began to gain confidence in their ability to generate melodic material, the guide [composer] challenged them to think in layers. He began by suggesting that the students sing the opening melody and then to try it as a canon. As students experimented with different compositional techniques they began to offer ideas that were developed beyond just the melodic frame. Students began to sing in duets and trios…and presented multiple ideas until idea generation had to be put on hold so that the ideas already offered could be explored. Several students mentioned that their confidence in their ability to generate musical material grew rapidly. (Kaschub, 1997, p. 21)

In the conclusion section of this study, Kaschub points to the great benefits that come from engagement in composition with revision in learning music. Studies by Christensen (1992) and Auker (1991) have provided additional evidence as well.

I am now back in Carson's house talking about his music some more. I have several sets of compositions. Each set has different files that represent the progress that he has made over several weeks. I have the ability to see his revision process after the fact and I regret that I have not been able to sit and watch him work for a long period of time. Perhaps that will come soon. Right now I study the scores.

I have come to know Carson and his family better over the last few weeks. Each time I visit, he shares new music with me and seeks my honest appraisal. I give him my ideas about the music and we exchange views on ways the music might sound if other choices were made. We talk about the Sibelius notation program and some of its features and I help him write some articulation marks. School has come to an end for the year and I have been able to see pieces develop that are not intended for class projects.

One new circumstance is that I have been able to find an accomplished private teacher for Carson. Elizabeth is a doctoral music composition student at my university with much experience teaching children. Carson explains some about what Elizabeth has been doing with him. 'She looks at music and asks me questions about it. When I tell her what I don't like or what I think kind of stinks about the music, she gives me a bunch of suggestions. She brings her cello and I love that,' says Carson. 'I am writing a cello piece for her right now.' I ask him how he likes her lessons and Carson is quite enthused. 'She helps me a lot – makes my music better. Look at these tympani parts for *Pirate Fears*!'

Pirate Fears is the latest long work that Carson is finishing and I have not seen this version yet. It is now 148 measures long, lasts over 5 minutes, and is scored for piccolo, flute, alto and baritone sax, three trumpets, two trombones and a bass trombone, timpani, vibraphone, two violins and a cello! The last time I saw it, prior to his work with Elizabeth, the work was half the size and had only the introduction and main section finished, no ending and a lot of repetitive ideas that did not seem to gel. Here was a greatly expanded piece with development sections, transitions and an ending. 'Elizabeth really helped me with the added cello part too and I have a key change, see?' Carson points to the portion in the middle of the score that changes key. This is new territory for Carson and for me. Home I go to figure out what this new version is all about.

5.4 Carson's *Pirate Fears*

Pirate Fears is vintage Carson. It is lively and up tempo with a kind of perpetual motion that I have come to expect in his music. I remember our first meeting when he talked of being inspired by film music – I can hear that here. The piece is built around a simple recurring, four-note melody in descending quarter notes. Music example 5.1(a)-(e) displays this pattern throughout the opening section of the music. In 5.1(a), the pattern is on the downbeat of each measure in Violin I. The eighth note pattern sets the rhythmic motion of the piece right from the start and serves as a foundation for the rhythms used in the entire piece. The vibraphone in 5.1(b) provides the descending pattern by itself in measure 13 and variations on this pattern occur throughout the piece, particularly in the lower brass. Measure 19, 5.1(c), reinforces the opening measures but this time in the woodwinds. Carson uses piccolo, flutes and the two saxophone parts in many of his scores and here they are used with lower brass as well. In earlier versions of this score, the articulations were not in place but now they are used effectively, especially measure 24, 5.1(d). His use of the staccato winds, still playing the jumping eighth note pattern that starts the composition, against the legato pattern of eighth notes in the brass has a marked effect on the listener. When the woodwinds enter in measure 28, just before the main theme, 5.1(e), the listener realizes that this is again the four-note pattern but this time varied.

Example 5.1 Carson's *Pirate Fears*, opening section

Music example 5.2(a)-(b), displays portions of the main theme which again follow the contour of the descending four-note pattern. This music dominates the next 34 measures, repeating in different instruments and accompanied by the lower brass, strings and tympani in different ways. In 5.2(a), measure 36 and continuing, the tune uses sixteenth notes and triplets in ways not heard before. In 5.2(b), of interest is the use of the violins and bass trombone playing a rising pattern that can be traced to the four-note pattern before and used as a counter melody of sorts. The tympani are now used as a key element in building tension and a feeling of growth in the music. Little of this was seen in previous drafts.

Example 5.2   Carson's *Pirate Fears*, main theme

Music example 5.3 represents a major tonal shift in the music. We now have only a cello and a vibraphone playing and we are clearly in a transition section. Up to this point, the piece has functioned traditionally in a minor, and the c minor tonality is a welcomed change. In the midst of this change is also the return of the four-note pattern played by the vibraphone. The cello is playing a challenging pattern of sixteenth notes, 5.3(a), that leads to the entry of the violin, 5.3(b), playing off of the cello and our four-note pattern. Of interest in this transition too is Carson's use of dynamic markings and crescendos and decrescendos. This transition lasts for 13 interesting measures which also move back to a minor tonality at measure 91. At this point, Carson brings back the opening staccato eighth note pattern in the strings that started the work and the listener is now back in familiar territory.

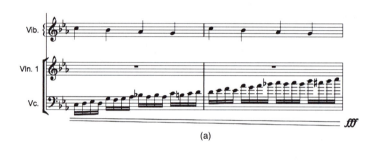

(a)

(b)

Example 5.3 Carson's *Pirate Fears*, transition

But there is a twist. Music example 5.4(a) displays a few measures of this transition but notice that the staccato eighth note pattern has a different set of pitches from the opening of the music. It is also not a continuous pattern and the last eighth note of the second measure of the pattern is replaced with a rest. This sets up the return of the main theme at measure 115, 5.4(b), at a quadruple forte.[2]

---

[2]   I note that the rhythm here is probably difficult to parse as a player and I make a mental note to tell Carson to be careful of this when he is using the automatic functions

(a)

(b)

Example 5.4 Carson's *Pirate Fears*, main theme redux

From this point forward, there are another 32 measures of music content similar to the main section but with clearly an attempt to vary rhythm and pitch content. Take a moment to study Music example 5.5(a) around measure 130. Here Carson is adding accidentals for colour not only in the main theme content but in

of notation software. This kind of information is what experienced teachers can do to help young composers ready their works for live performers.

the accompaniment patterns as well. At measure 140, we are treated to a dramatic return to the same eighth note patterns that started the music, this time with hardly any variations except for dynamics. The piece gets softer and softer until the final measures, 5.5(b), where the first violin only plays leading to a unison 'a' played by the full ensemble. We have an ending.

Example 5.5 Carson's *Pirate Fears*, ending

This is a level of sophistication that I have not seen in Carson's music before. Many of his longer pieces I have studied have similar vibrancy and tuneful melodies but many are quite repetitive. Few have counter melodies and none have the unity with variety that I see here. This is a piece that demonstrates what Carson wants in his music – something he was very clear about the first day I met him. What is exciting here is that Carson has composed a much finer piece as a direct result of some fine teaching. What did Elizabeth do with Carson, what was her secret in moving him forward musically as a composer? In preparation for this chapter, I wrote to Elizabeth to inquire about her approach to working with Carson. Here is her detailed response:

I have many thoughts regarding children and composition, and appreciate your inquiry very much. My husband teaches middle and high school orchestra and general music, so I am aware of the growing interest among educators in including creative work of various kinds in their curricula, and the relative lack of resources for doing so. My experience teaching pre-college composers comes both from private teaching and from teaching at the Walden School Young Musicians Program. Walden has its own musicianship curriculum,[3] adaptable for many age groups and institutional situations that incorporate composition and improvisation from the earliest to the most advanced levels. The curriculum is student-centered and activity-based and encourages students to improvise and compose using the music-theoretical materials they are studying, from simple acoustics, intervals, triads, etc. through complex functional harmony and atonal pitch structures. My own work extrapolating and expanding upon the elements of this curriculum that relate specifically to composition pedagogy provides the basis for my composition teaching.

On the subject of revision specifically, my first approach with young students (and many older ones) tends to be leading them through a process of discovery – *what details about the music are they hearing mentally, or playing for me, that have not yet made it onto the page?* Do they need more dynamics, articulations, etc. to make the page match what they hear? By posing revision first as the process of realizing their ideas more fully on paper, of making the work more individuated and more 'theirs', students realize that revision does not threaten the initial creation. From there I often ask students to imagine, play or sing various possible ways of changing certain elements of the piece. The process is playful and improvisatory rather than corrective. I always let the student be the final judge of which version they like best, but I find that by leading them through this exploratory process and posing multiple suggestions, they usually arrive at a revision that demonstrates greater musical sophistication and are able to articulate good reasons for their choices. Once a student is comfortable with this sort of process, I feel I can begin to use diagnostic language to identify

---

[3]   For more information about Walden, see www.waldenschool.org. The author of this chapter has no professional affiliation with this school.

possible weaknesses in their work or question larger assumptions about music that their work demonstrates. All this would of course take place over many lessons and be adapted to the experience level and musical interests of the student. (personal communication, 20 July 2010)

5.5 Pulling things together

Elizabeth and people who have years of experience working with young composers hold important insights to meeting the needs of young composers. Reese, in his thoughtful article on responding to student compositions, reviewed the writings of several such practitioners and summarized four 'lessons from the field' that may serve as a foundation to a pedagogy of revision:

> (1) Teachers of composition must always respond at first to the overall intent and expressive nature of the piece as a whole and not focus too quickly on technical aspects of the music.
>
> (2) Teachers must be conscious of and receptive to the readiness of a student to accept feedback. To determine this, asking 'how can I help you best' is a good start. We know that younger students may not be ready to revise a 'completed' composition but may choose to write something new. Older and more experienced students might be fine with revisiting a work.
>
> (3) A balance needs to be struck between too didactic an approach to feedback as opposed to a holistic one based on dialog and respect for student voice.
>
> (4) Teachers must recognize the nature of the original assignment to compose. If the purpose is to create a piece that has finite parameters as opposed to a more open assignment, the nature of feedback and calls for revision might be very different. (2003, pp. 217-219)

Gromko reinforces this:

> Even as I am promoting a student-centered orientation, I want to stress the profoundly important role played by a professional musician who is also a gifted teacher. Orienting education to the children's individual needs and interests requires the teacher not to do as much overt teaching in the traditional sense, but to be more keenly aware, socially astute, and musically flexible in response to the children's direction and ideas...Children need guidance and support in creative effective compositions. The teacher's primary role is to invite the artful narrative in such ways that children can trust they will be heard and understood, that is, to let children know they have something worthwhile to say and to help them find a way to say it. (2003, p. 89)

In closing, I propose below a few other building blocks for the design of pedagogies for revision.

- *Give ourselves agency.* We need to give ourselves permission to lead compositional activities with students. We must trust the fact that we understand music and bring great passion and knowledge to our teaching. We can prepare ourselves for this role by engaging in composition ourselves. Honing our own skills as composers allows us to bring our natural proclivities for music to bear as we guide children in developing and improving their musical thinking and feeling skills. We need to give ourselves permission to lead compositional activities with students and to offer guidance with understanding.
- *Encourage improvisational thinking as a partner with creating original music-making.* Burnard (2000) reminds us of the close relationship between composition and improvisation. A key way to increase the ability to think in sound ('audiate' if you choose this word) and to increase our musical vocabulary is to create experiences for our children that stress improvisation in tandem with compositional activity. Much more needs to be learned about the close relationship between these two key creative activities.
- *Listen, perform and discuss music.* It seems so obvious. The more we extend our sonic experiences and understand what a composer is doing to create what we hear, the greater the likelihood that revision will be considered as important during composition. The development of basic musicianship of the sort that comes from performing, listening and discussing music cannot be underestimated. Good composition pedagogy is based on a comprehensive approach to music teaching and learning.
- *Teach the formal properties of music at the appropriate time.* Theoretical understanding of music is not always necessary to create compositions for sure, but at some point it is worth doing. Understanding of acoustical and computer-based instruments is not always needed, but will be useful at some point. Notational understanding is sometimes optional but at some point will help. The simple fact is that the more children know about something, the more creative they can be. How and when this is done is a matter of personal preference and circumstance.
- *Establish a climate for revision.* Try to establish from the start that revision is a natural part of composing and that it is part of what we all do to make our work meaningful. Not all composition experiences need to have this as part of our expectations, but we need to begin to do it at some junction. I would recommend that strategies be formed to do this earlier as opposed to later in the compositional journey.
- *Ask children about how they are or have been revising.* Composition students may be revising as they go. We can never presume that when a composition is presented to us as teachers, that there has not been much thinking about

sound already. Try to establish what the process of composition has been in order to figure out how to help improve the work.

- *Have children discover on their own.* Ask the questions necessary for students to discover what might be profitable for revision. Let them be the final decision-maker, but be sure that as many sonic possibilities have been considered as makes sense. Feel comfortable with challenging ideas but never dictate.

- *Build over time.* Composition, like all meaningful musical experiences, has to be practised again and again. A variety of compositional experiences over years of music learning will result in the best solutions for meaningful revision. Know what each student has experienced and try to build on what has come before.

I think Carson would agree with all of this. I think his classmates in Sally's class would as well. A haunting question remains: how many more Carsons are there in our schools today who might be encouraged by our thoughtful teaching strategies?

References

Auker, P. (1991). Pupil talk, musical learning and creativity. *British Journal of Music Education*, 8(2), 161-166.

Bereiter, C. & Scardamalia, M. (1987). *The psychology of written composition.* Hillsdale, NJ: LEA.

Burnard, P. (2000). Examining experiential differences between improvisation and composition in children's music-making. *British Journal of Music Education*, 17(3), 227-245.

Calkins, L. (1994). *The art of teaching writing.* Exeter, NH: Heinemann Educational Press.

Campbell, P. (1998). *Songs in their heads.* New York: Oxford University Press.

Carlin, J. (1998). Can you think a little louder? A classroom-based ethnography of eight- and nine-year olds composing with music and language (eight year olds). Available from ProQuest Dissertations and Theses database (AAT NQ27143).

Christensen, C. (1992). Music composition, invented notation and reflection: Tools for music learning and assessment. Available from ProQuest Dissertations and Theses database (AAT 9231370).

Fitzgerald, J. (1987). Research on revision in writing. *Review of Educational Research*, 57(4), 481-506.

Folkestad, G. (1996). *Computer based creative music making.* Goteborg, Sweden: Acta Universitatis Gothoburgensis.

Gardner, H. (1989). Project Zero: An introduction to 'Arts Propel'. *Journal of Art and Design Education*, 8(2), 167-182.

Gilmore, B. (2007). *'Is it done yet?' Teaching adolescents the art of revision.* Portsmouth, NH: Heinemann.

Glover, J. (2000). *Children composing 4-14*. London: Routledge.

Gromko, J. (2003). Children composing: Inviting the artful narrative. In M. Hickey (Ed.), *Why and how to teach music composition: A new horizon for music education* (pp. 69-90). Reston, VA: MENC.

Hickey, M. (1999). Assessment rubrics for music composition. *Music Educators Journal*, 85(4), 26-33.

Hickey, M. (2003). Creative thinking in the context of music composition. In M. Hickey (Ed.), *Why and how to teach music composition: A new horizon for music education* (pp. 31-54). Reston, VA: MENC.

Kaschub, M. (1997). A comparison of two composer-guided large group composition projects. *Research Studies in Music Education*, 8(1), 15-28.

Kaschub, M. & Smith, J. (2009). *Minds on music*. Lanham, MD: Rowman & Littlefield Education.

Kratus, J. (1989). A time analysis of the compositional processes used by children ages 7 to 11. *Journal of Research in Music Education*, 37(1), 5-20.

MENC (1994). *National standards for arts education*. Reston, VA: MENC.

Moorhead, G. & Pond, D. (1978). *Music for young children* (reprinted from the 1941-1951 editions). Santa Barbara: Pillsbury Foundation for the Advancement of Music Education.

Paynter, J. (1992). *Sound and silence*. Cambridge: Cambridge University Press.

Reese, S. (2003). Responding to student compositions. In M. Hickey (Ed.), *Why and how to teach music composition: A new horizon for music education* (pp. 211-232). Reston, VA: MENC.

Ruthmann, S. A. (2008). Whose agency matters: Negotiating pedagogical and creative intent during composing experiences. *Research Studies in Music Education*, 30(1), 43-58.

Schafer, R. (1979). *Creative music education*. New York: Schirmer.

Sloboda, J. (1985). *The musical mind*. Oxford: Clarendon Press.

van Ernst, B. (1993). A study of the learning and teaching processes of non-native music students engaged in composition. *Research Studies in Music Education*, 1(1), 22-39.

Webster, P. (1987). Refinement of a measure of creative thinking in music. In C. Madsen & C. Prickett (Eds.), *Applications of research in music behavior* (pp. 257-271). Tuscaloosa: University of Alabama Press.

Webster, P. (1990). Creativity as creative thinking. *Music Educators Journal*, 76(9), 22-28.

Webster, P. (2002). Creative thinking in music: Advancing a model. In T. Sullivan & L. Willingham (Eds.), *Creativity and music education* (pp. 16-34). Toronto: Canadian Music Educators' Association.

Webster, P. (2003). 'What do you mean, make my music different?' Encouraging revision and extensions in children's music composition. In M. Hickey (Ed.), *Why and how to teach music composition: A new horizon for music education* (pp. 55-68). Reston, VA: MENC.

Webster, P. (2011). Constructivism and music learning. In R. Colwell. & P. Webster (Eds.), *MENC Handbook of Research on Music Learning*, Vol. 1: *Strategies*. New York: Oxford University Press.

Wiggins, J. (1999). Teacher control and creativity. *Music Educators Journal*, 85(5), 30-44.

Wiggins, J. (2005). Fostering revision and extension in student composing. *Music Educators Journal*, 91(3), 35-42.

Wilkins, M. (2006). *Creative music composition*. New York: Routledge.

Williams, D. & Webster, P. (2008). *Experiencing music technology* (3rd edition). New York: Cengage/Schirmer.

Younker, B. (1997). Thought processes and strategies of eight, eleven, and fourteen year old students while engaged in music composition. Available from ProQuest Dissertations and Theses database (AAT 9814345).

Younker, B. (2003). The nature of feedback in a community of composing. In M. Hickey (Ed.), *Why and how to teach music composition: A new horizon for music education* (pp. 233-242). Reston, VA: MENC.

Younker, B. & Smith, W. (1996). Comparing and modeling musical thought processes of expert and novice composers. *Bulletin of the Council of Research for Music Education*, 128(Spring), 25-36.

Zellermayer, M. & Cohen, J. (1996). Varying paths for learning to revise. *Instructional Science*, 24(3), 177-195.

Chapter 6

The nature of the engagement of Brazilian adolescents in composing activities

José Soares

6.1 Introduction

The aim of this chapter is to outline the theoretical and empirical basis of the links between socio-cultural and technological factors, musical behaviour and the nature of the engagements of adolescents in composing activities, with particular reference to two specialist music schools in the Brazilian state of Minas Gerais. The chapter begins by offering a brief overview of the research findings in this area and examines some aspects of creativity as reflected in the literature – how it can be defined and the range of elements that influence the composing process and the resultant musical product. After this, the Brazilian context is examined, focusing on the structure of the specialist music schools system in Minas Gerais State, which is followed by a description of the mixed-methods research design used in the study. The chapter concludes with a discussion of the results. Activity theory (Engeström, 1999) is employed as a theoretical framework to consider what is involved in computer-based composition work. Findings suggest that the computer software represented a powerful tool, which had the potential to enable adolescents to express their musical ideas and intentions, that the composing product was influenced by the design of the curriculum and that their previous technological experiences had a positive effect when composing within the school context.

6.2 Theoretical underpinnings

6.2.1 Musical behaviour

Researchers of musical behaviour tend to lay emphasis on the context (social and cultural) in which it occurs (Hargreaves & North, 1997; Hargreaves et al., 2002; Welch, 2000). In addressing this question, the main concern is to identify factors that affect (both directly and indirectly) how someone experiences music within a particular socio-cultural context.

Welch (2001) points out that both individual and group musical behaviour may be conceived as products of the interaction of individual neuropsychobiological development, a particular socio-cultural context (and thus contextualized) and a specific music genre. When one of these three generative elements is changed, the resultant musical behaviour changes too.

There are two interesting positions arising from this conceptualization. One is a direct effect of the socio-cultural context on the developing neuropsychobiological history of the individual and on how music is produced and valued. This means that individual actions might be determined by independent variables operating at a higher level of analysis, which, in turn, influence processes at a lower level. The second position is methodological. Musical behaviour cannot be fully explained without taking into consideration the way all three generative elements operate together.

With regard to technology, its pervasiveness and significance have led some researchers to attempt to explain its impact on societies, cultures, education and people's behaviour in general (Lievrouw & Livingstone, 2002; Slack & Wise, 2002). However, technology forms a constituent part of society (Livingstone, 2002). Technology and culture are not separate worlds, and there is no cause and effect relationship between them (Slack & Wise, 2002).

Arguably, the musical experiences that adolescents encounter in socio-cultural and technological contexts are transferred to their educational context, and these experiences might create a tension in their musical behaviour inside school as the educational context redefines and reshapes the students' behaviour. Within this educational context, music technology (particularly computers) has been used to support the teaching and learning of music (Kwami, 2001; Odam, 2000; Pitts & Kwami, 2002). This study particularly focuses on investigating how adolescents react to their specialist music school context when composing with computers.

6.2.2 Creativity

The literature suggests that social and environmental factors play a major role in creative performance (Hennessey & Amabile, 1988). The term 'creativity' derives from the Latin word *creare*, which means 'to produce, to foster, to raise and to create'. It has been described as a systemic phenomenon that denotes a continuous process (Vieira, 2003) and reflects the interaction that occurs between a person's thoughts and a socio-cultural context.

Csikszentmihalyi (1988, 1997) argues that creativity is a phenomenon that results from the interaction of three systems. The first is domain, which consists of a set of symbolic rules and procedures. The second, the field, comprises expert individuals who decide whether or not a new idea or product should be included in the domain. The third is the person who uses the symbols of a given domain (e.g. music) to form new ideas; if these symbols are selected by the experts, both as a novelty and in the appropriate field, they can be included in the domain. This active model suggests how, where and when creativity occurs.

The role of the person in this model is to assimilate and modify the cultural information that has been acquired. As a result, the field selects variations that can be incorporated within the domain. Thus, a person who has no access to (musical) information may not be capable of a creative act, no matter how able or skilled s/he is. In other words, Csikszentmihalyi suggests that 'one needs to know music to write a creative symphony' (1988, p. 330). Nevertheless, his model is usually applied to professional adults rather than school-age pupils.

A large number of studies, which involve psychometric and cognitive approaches (North & Hargreaves, 2008), have been conducted into understanding different aspects of creativity, and this suggests that composing conforms to the creative act discussed in the psychological literature (Fautley, 2004). Guilford (1967) set out a model that entailed two kinds of productive skills: convergent and divergent thinking. The former moves towards a fixed response; in the latter case there is no fixed answer and the thinker can move freely.

Much of the literature on both general and musical creativity regards the generation of ideas as a form of exploration (divergent thinking), which is an important phase in truly creative behaviour. Moreover, Getzels and Csikszentmihalyi (1976) found that the most successful outcomes arose when longer periods of exploration occurred during the creative process. Early in the twentieth century, Wallas (1926) divided the creative process into four stages: preparation, incubation, illumination and verification. The ideas of Guilford and Wallas influenced the model for creative thinking in music put forward by Webster (1988), which considers how the novice composes. The central part of Webster's model includes four key elements that are linked to two domains (enabling skills and enabling conditions). The 'enabling skills' possessed by the pupils include musical aptitudes, understanding of musical materials, craftsmanship and aesthetic sensitivity. The 'enabling conditions' that stem from the individual or the environment consist of motivation, subconscious imagery, the environment and personality (Webster, 1988). Webster's model is useful because it has close affinities with the creative act theory of Wallas and attempts to explain creative processes by examining alternative sources (Fautley, 2004).

Other research studies have investigated creativity in general, and composing in particular, as an interaction between the person, the process, the product and the environment (Hennessey & Amabile, 1988; Odena & Welch, 2007). This perspective is consistent with the systemic approach of Csikszentmihalyi (1997). There has also been research into the strategies adopted by adolescents when engaged in creative computer-based composition (Folkestad, 1998).

Two contrasting research approaches to computer-based composition can be found in the literature: (a) studies concerned with those who use the computer as a medium through which issues such as the cognitive processes of learning and composing can be examined (whether on an individual or collaborative basis) (e.g. Folkestad, 1998; Seddon, 2001) and (b) studies concerned with those who use the computer as a tool that affects musical behaviour when composing (e.g. Purves, 2001).

It can be argued that some technological tools encourage students to conjure up musical ideas (or create), while others impose constraints on the creative act, since the freedom of creation and interpretation is exercised in a context of restrictions and resistance (Canclini, 1990). For this reason, composition here is analysed primarily as the product of socio-cultural experiences, as well as a form of technology (or medium) used to create musical ideas.

6.3 Socio-cultural and technological contexts for learning music in Brazil

The range of socio-cultural and technological contexts available for musical development and learning, where social groups engage in musical practices and attach different meanings to a variety of forms, are characterized in Brazil by their rich musical diversity.

This diversity is partly the result of the encounter of three musical traditions: (1) written/classical, transposed from European music; (2) aural-oral/popular indigenous music; and (3) aural-oral/popular, transposed from African music (Wisnik, 2002). It is exemplified by a variety of musical forms such as bossa nova, *pagode*, *forró*, regional, samba, *axé* and *sertanejo* (Albin, 2002).

As far as the involvement of the Brazilian people with music is concerned, in 2009 20.3 million CDs and 5.4 million DVDs were sold in Brazil (Brazilian Association of Phonographic Producers, 2009). This is 9.32 per cent fewer CDs and 3.98 per cent more DVDs than in 2008. The problem of piracy (both physical and online) is probably the key factor that explains the decline of CD sales in Brazil, with the rise of DVDs, Blu-ray and MP3 downloads. Of the total number of music sales, 66 per cent of CDs and 65 per cent of DVDs were of music from the national repertoire, while 31 per cent of CDs and 30 per cent of DVDs were from the international repertoire and 3 per cent of CDs and 5 per cent of DVDs made up the classical repertoire.

The above statistics show that CD and DVD buyers prefer Brazilian music to international and classical music. Assuming that the large volume of sales reflects a considerable degree of interest in music among the public, this suggests that Brazilian music probably plays an important role in the lives of these buyers.

These issues are particularly significant in the case of Minas Gerais, where this study was carried out. An examination of the socio-cultural context of Minas Gerais must take into account its cultural diversity and the fact that it borders on several other states. For instance, the eastern region is linked to São Paulo State, the south is integrated with the society of Rio de Janeiro State and the North is connected to Bahia State. One effect of this proximity is the emergence of different regional identities associated with musical preferences. For example, in the north, *axé* is one of the most popular musical styles among the young people. In contrast, in the east, one of the most popular musical styles is a regional type of country music called *sertanejo*.

Three related issues arise from an analysis of the cultural diversity of Minas Gerais: first of all, the key role played by transposed musical forms in the construction of regional identities within the state; secondly, the implications of these different musical forms in shaping people's musical behaviour; and, thirdly, the influence of the socio-cultural background on education.

6.4 The specialist music schools system in Minas Gerais

Despite the great exposure to music in Brazil, there is limited access to formal music lessons in the basic educational system. Music instruction is usually available in private lessons or at music schools. However, the Federal Government has passed a new Law No. 11.769/08 (Brazilian Ministry of Education, 2008), which stipulates that music should be a compulsory part of the syllabus (though not a subject) in the school curriculum at all levels of basic education.

The new Law 11.769/08 made some alterations to Art. 26 of the Law 9394/96 (National Education Guidelines and Framework Act), which established Arts (music, visual arts, drama or dance) as a compulsory subject, and meant that regular schools did not have to offer music as a separate subject in their curricula. In fact, the schools had the right to choose which form of art should be taught at each level of basic education. As a result, some students completed their education without learning any music in a formal way. Thus, before 2008, only some schools offered music as part of their curriculum, while others offered it as an optional extra-curricular activity.

It should be stressed that Brazil has no national curriculum; rather, there are national curricular parameters (PCN) or guidelines for all areas. Schools have the autonomy to plan their own curricula.

In the light of this, Minas Gerais, the fourth largest of the Brazilian states, with a population of approximately 20 million inhabitants, has implemented its own state system of education, called the 'sistema mineiro de educação' (Minas Gerais system of education). The state specialist music schools form a part of this system and Minas Gerais is the only Brazilian state with this provision (SEE-MG, 2001). The schools provide specialist music education for a part of each day/week and the students attend a regular school for the rest of the day/week.

The state specialist music schools (12 altogether) came into existence in the second half of the twentieth century. The institutions are autonomous and adopt a model of teaching and learning music that lays emphasis on both classical and popular music. The structure of the music school system has two levels, which are outlined in Table 6.1. The first level (primary education) is divided into two phases and lasts for nine years. In Phase I the music curriculum is more general, while in Phase II it is more specialist and advanced. The secondary level lasts for three years. It seeks to help students enhance their critical thinking, musical knowledge, musical understanding and creativity so as to be able to adapt to changing social conditions. Students attend classes on their chosen instrument for two hours a week and these lessons usually lay a strong emphasis on classical music.

Table 6.1   Structure of the music schools system in Minas Gerais, Brazil

Levels and subdivisions		Duration	Age range
Primary education	Phase I	5 years	6-10 years
	Phase II	4 years	11-14 years
Secondary education		3 years	15-17 years

The majority of students are aged between 7 and 17 years old. They have to undergo a selective entrance procedure as there are not enough places for all the students enrolled in the regular schools (whether private or state). Before enrolling in the specialist music schools, students are required to provide evidence that they are attending the equivalent or sometimes a higher year/level in their regular school.

Illustration 6.1   Using music software in a specialist music school

Two of these 12 schools introduced computers in their music curriculum in 1997 and 2002, respectively (see Illustration 6.1). Sonar, Finale and Encore are the most common forms of music software available. There are a number of different underlying reasons for using computers in schools. These include reducing the cost of education, giving support to the computer industry, preparing students to work and live in a society permeated with technology and enhancing the quality of their learning process and outcomes (e.g. Bliss, 1999; Bottino, 2004; Hodges, 2001; Pitts & Kwami, 2002). However, the above reasons are not always supported by evidence to corroborate all the benefits that their supporters claim, and the literature suggests that in terms of both quantity and quality, until recently there has been limited use of computers in schools in Brazil (Poppovic, 2002).

The research discussed in this chapter was conducted in these special circumstances. The design of the study was structured in a multilayered framework, recognizing that actions are determined, at least in part, by what individuals have embarked on in various situations.

6.5 Research design

6.5.1 Methods of data generation

A sequential mixed-methods design was adopted, in which the quantitative phase preceded the qualitative phase. The two types of data were analysed separately and were only integrated during the interpretation stage (Creswell, 2003).

The quantitative phase was aimed at identifying factors that could explain the students' listening preferences. It included a survey that involved setting a self-administered questionnaire to collect data from a sample of 210 students aged 13-16 years (114 in School A and 96 in School B). The schools were located in two contrasting geographical regions, in the north (School A) and east (School B). The purpose of the survey was to discover possible socio-cultural and technological similarities and differences between the regions. In the total sample, 53.3 per cent of the students were female and 46.7 per cent were male. The data were related to the students' backgrounds (including their experience of computer-based composition), leisure activities undertaken outside school, listening activities and use of technology at home and elsewhere. The students were also asked to state, by means of a seven-point rating scale, how often they listened to 17 different musical styles selected on the basis of their representativeness in the two regions, including Brazilian rock, dance, Brazilian popular music, classical instrumental, *forró*, samba, regional, *pagode* and folk music. An explanation of some of these styles is provided in the Appendix.

In the second (qualitative) phase of the study, 12 students were selected by means of purposive sampling from a group of 28 who had volunteered to take part in a computer-based composition activity. Their names have been changed to protect their anonymity. All of them had access to a computer and the internet, outside school. The criteria applied for selecting them were based on (1) their listening preferences with regard to three main categories/scales (Brazilian music, classical music and rock music) that were identified after carrying out a factor analysis of the 17 musical styles. Six students were selected from each school and these comprised the four who scored highest on the 'Brazilian music' scale, the four who scored highest on the 'classical music' scale and the four who scored highest on the 'rock music' scale. The aim was to cover the range of musical styles so that it would be possible to find out in what ways their influence on the process of computer-based composition differed; (2) gender: six boys and six girls; (3) age: all the students were aged 14 to 15; (4) whether or not they had composed with a computer before; and (5) if they were familiar with music software. The aim was to have two balanced groups of students of varying degrees of familiarity and competence and to control for the effects of factors in the process, such as gender and age. The participant students were free to drop out at any time, but none of them did so before the end of the project.

Seven students, aged 14, were from school A. Four students (Felipe, Carolina, Talitha and Cristina) played acoustic guitar and two students (Marco and Lucas) played the keyboard, and their curricular paths were oriented to popular music. One student (Luciana) played the piano and her studies were oriented to classical music. Luciana and Cristina were the only students who were familiar with commercial music software (Finale and Encore). None of them had had any composition experience with computers.

Five students, aged 14 and 15, were from school B. Two students (Henrique and Juliana) played the recorder and two students (Eduardo and Débora) played the piano in a curriculum oriented to classical music. One student (Vinícius) played the acoustic guitar in a curriculum oriented to popular music. Henrique, Juliana and Eduardo were familiar with commercial music software (Finale, Encore and Sibelius). Vinícius was familiar with Finale, Encore, Band-in-a-box and Sonar. Vinícius and Eduardo were the only students who had come from a composition with computers background.

The students worked individually on a PC that had a version of Sonar 2.01 installed. They did not receive feedback or discuss ideas among themselves. A keyboard was provided and the students could use their own musical instrument if they preferred. In the end, seven out of the 12 students composed their piece of music with the keyboard and five with their own musical instrument (which was then transferred to the computer).

The computer-based composition process was conducted in three steps. Firstly, the students were asked to complete a task that involved composing a free piece of music lasting between one and two minutes, using computer software (Sonar 2.0). The task was open-ended to allow for creative freedom and was carried out in three sessions of 30 minutes each. Before carrying out the task, the students had a 30-minute instruction session, which enabled them to use the computer software effectively. They all attended this session regardless of their prior experience with computers.

Following this, the researcher provided the students with a friendly environment to compose in. At this stage, the students could either compose directly on a keyboard connected to the computer or use their main instrument (such as an acoustic guitar) to generate musical ideas and transfer them to the PC.

The process was recorded by means of a video card installed in the computer. Finally, there was a third stage when the researcher was able to capture the screen manipulation and observe the activities undertaken when the students were not using the music software.

After carrying out the composition task, semi-structured interviews over the internet (instant messenger) were conducted. The purpose of these was to examine the students' views about the composing process and product. The transcripts of the interviews were produced automatically while the interviews were being conducted over the internet.

6.5.2 Analysis

The findings outlined in this chapter emerged from three main analytical stages. The first involved the use of a range of techniques for analysing the questionnaire data, including Person's chi-square to test for significant differences between different sets of responses, factor analysis and multiple regression analysis.

In stage two, the data gathered during the computer-based composition processes were examined in an attempt to find common themes. All of the 12 compositions were transcribed together with full descriptions of the activities that the students had carried out during the computer-based composition process. Two key activities were identified: (1) on-task (when the students were engaged in the composition task) and (2) off-task (when the students were not engaged in the composition task but followed a different agenda). As Seddon (2001) points out, students can engage in on-task activities with or without an aural reference. The episodic coding of the composing process was adapted from Seddon (2001). Each episode constituted a unit of analysis or coding unit.

The frequency, sequence and duration of the on-task and off-task activities revealed a number of patterns and themes in the data, which reflected the different composition strategies adopted by the participants. The strategies were interpreted in accordance with the five basic phases of the composition process outlined by Fautley (2004): *exploration* or *generation* of ideas, *organization, revision, editing* and *off-task*. The *generation* of musical ideas may take only a few minutes or last a long time. Quite often, the musical ideas are extended, transformed or rejected. Once the musical idea has been generated, the composition process starts to flow (Csikszentmihalyi, 1997). Sometimes various ideas are played several times on the instrument to give coherence and form to the composition. This period of improvisation, which involves carrying out random explorations on a musical instrument, plays an important role in generating musical ideas. When the musical ideas are 'grasped', they are reworded, tried out and extended as appropriate (*organization* and *revision* phases). The composition process usually concludes with the completion of the musical product and a period of listening to allow the effect of the performance to be assessed (*editing*).

Stage three of the analytical process involved examining the content of the students' semi-structured interviews after they had completed their composing task. Both manifest and latent content were coded, as instant messenger does not allow for the expression of emotion through the use of visual aids such as smiling faces. The punctuation was carefully analysed to complement the interpretation of the interview transcripts (Robson, 2002).

6.6 Findings

6.6.1 Quantitative phase – survey

The findings showed that 106 of the students (50.5 per cent) regarded themselves as white, 90 of them (42.9 per cent) regarded themselves as mixed and only 14 (6.7 per cent) saw themselves as black. As has been confirmed by previous research results, black people do not have the same access to formal education as white or mixed people in Brazilian society (Schwartzman, 2003). A chi-square test demonstrated that the distribution of students by ethnic background differs statistically between the two schools ($c^2 = 20.444$, $df = 2$, $p<0.001$). School B was predominantly made up of white students (65.6 per cent) and School A mainly consisted of students from a mixed background (57 per cent).

Guitar, piano and keyboard were the most popular instruments, accounting for 81.4 per cent of the total number of participants. Although there were several other instruments, each had relatively few players compared with these three main groups.

As far as access to technology is concerned, 60 per cent of the students had a computer at home – 33.8 per cent of the boys and 26.2 per cent of the girls. The gender difference is not statistically significant. However, a larger proportion of students in School B had a computer at home compared with students in School A. The association was statistically significant beyond the .01 level ($c^2 = 10.391$, $df = 1$, $p=0.001$). This result is in line with the socio-economic differences between regions within Minas Gerais State; in other words, the per-capita GDP where School B is located is higher than the respective figure for School A.

The students were asked to report their familiarity with the following musical packages, which were divided into four categories: (1) score writing (Finale, Encore and Sibelius); (2) sequence (Voyetra, Cubase and Sonar); (3) accompaniment (Band-in-a-box); and (4) digital audio editor (Sound Forge). The students in School B tended to be more familiar with these musical packages than their counterparts in School A. This can be explained by the fact that School B has a longer tradition of using computers in its music curriculum than School A. In particular, the students were more familiar with Encore (39.6 per cent in School B and 21.1 per cent in School A). It is not a surprising result as the schools have adopted a policy of encouraging musical literacy.

The internet was accessed at home or elsewhere. The boys spent on average 2.73 hours and the girls 3.10 hours per week on the internet. The internet was used for a wide range of purposes: 78 per cent used it to look up information, 64.7 per cent to download music, 50.3 per cent to read/send emails, 47.4 per cent to chat and 46.2 per cent to visit websites. Girls tended to chat, look for information and use email more than boys.

The amount of time spent listening to music on a daily basis was also investigated. On average, the students stated that they listened to music for 2.38 hours per day. The girls tended to listen to music on the radio more than the boys ($c^2 = 4.60$, df = 1, p<0.03). These findings are consistent with earlier studies that have shown the importance of music to young people (North et al., 2004; Tarrant, North & Hargreaves, 2002). The musical style more often listened to by students was Brazilian rock. The mean rating assigned to this style was 4.71 on a seven-point scale ranging from 'not at all' to 'very much'. Brazilian rock was followed by dance music (M = 4.01) and Brazilian popular music (M = 3.77). The least popular styles were folk music, *pagode* and regional (detailed statistics for the study are available in Soares, 2006). A factor analysis found that listening preferences were in one of three main scales: Brazilian music scale, classical music scale and Brazilian rock scale. The regression results demonstrated that one of the most important determinants of listening preference was the choice of instrument and the curriculum-orientation of the school syllabus, grounded in either a classical or a popular repertoire.

6.6.2 Qualitative phase – case studies

The analysis of the case studies revealed the complex route that the students followed during the computer-based composition process. Several multiple pathways were identified. This illustrates how the students went through various phases, and moved back and forth throughout the process of composition.

A comparison of the time spent on each composition phase revealed that students with a background of composing with computers spent more time on the *generation* phase than their counterparts who spent more time on the *revision* phase. A tentative explanation for this is that students who are familiar with music software are not constrained by the computer and are thus able to focus on the development of musical ideas.

The data generated from the semi-structured interviews with the students just after they had completed their composition task showed that in the initial phase of the composition process the students attributed the generation of their musical ideas to various factors such as a melodic theme, a rhythm, a progression of chords and emotional motivation. Comments such as the following illustrate this point:

> I chose the chords on the guitar. I checked to see if it sounded right and then I began to record. After that, I started to arrange it but I didn't spend much time on this (Cristina)

Most of the students believed that computers helped them to compose, particularly in correcting mistakes and enabling them to listen to the work in progress. The students regarded this as a benefit but pointed out some drawbacks in using the computer during the composing activity (e.g. the fact that the sound of the computer is artificial). Four students expressed their satisfaction with computers, two for technical reasons:

> A little bit – it helped because it was faster and had some tools. But I played and composed myself and not with the aid of the computer. (Vinicius)

> It helped to remove tiny errors…you can do several things at the same time and play one piece of music together with another. It helps you to make your own band. (Luciana)

Eduardo, interestingly, claimed that the computer was both a stimulus and an aid to creativity:

> When you use a computer, you have a clearer notion of what you are doing because while you are composing, you can hear what you are composing…when you compose on paper, you know more or less what you are doing because you don't hear the notes you are playing, you don't listen to the rhythm, or melody…I don't know if you understand what I mean. But using a computer, the composer can work with an exact knowledge of what he is doing because he can listen to what he is composing. (Eduardo)

However, this view was directly contradicted by the remarks of Henrique: 'I don't think there are any advantages apart from being able to hear what you are doing.' The students also made comments about the musical style they had chosen to compose in. Five students mentioned they had chosen a classical style, while two students had chosen Brazilian rock, one student gospel and one dance music. Significantly, only two students composed their piece of music in the style that they preferred (Brazilian rock and classical).

The students also carried out a self-assessment of their composition product. Most of them (eight) did not appear to be happy with it and gave it a low valuation. Comments such as the following illustrate this point: 'My music was pretty dreadful' (Felipe); 'On a scale of 1 to 10, I put it at 5 or 6' (Vinicius).

Overall, there was little anxiety among the respondents about the use of computers. In fact, the students had positive feelings about their computer-based composition experiences; however, the results do not appear to show that their aims when composing were fulfilled. Further investigations with larger samples of students should shed light on this issue.

6.7 Discussion

The results of both the quantitative and qualitative parts of this study – in particular the information about the students and the evidence of their attitudes obtained from the interviews and questionnaires – can be combined to obtain a fuller understanding of their preferences and musical behaviour during the computer-based composition activity.

If the musical behaviour of adolescents within the specialist music schools is partly shaped by factors outside school, the socio-cultural and technological contexts should be taken into account to understand the ways they engage in musical activities (such as computer-based composition). The process of computer-based composition and the resulting products are not confined to technological resources and teaching strategies, but may also include external factors (such as listening to music) and internal factors (such as the nature and scope of the school curriculum).

A useful analytical framework that may be employed to explain the multifaceted phenomenon of computer-based composition is provided by activity theory (see Engeström, 1999). This theory allows the researcher to integrate the macro and micro perspectives. One of the principal contributions of activity theory is that it enables a psychological account of individual development to be integrated with a socio-historical account of the evolution of culture. At any given time and space, the actors, motives and mediational tools that constitute an activity can be taken to originate from two sources: (1) the cultural history of the mediational tools, together with the social resources through which the outcomes can be sought and (2) the evolving history of individual agents, which allows desires (or intentions) and dissatisfactions to be embedded in a set of personal techniques and tools (Engeström, 1987; Welch & Ockelford, 2009). The combination of actions and outcomes is called an activity. It should be noted that as well as embodying physical tools the cultural history of a device like a computer includes the social system that underpins it. The idea of an activity system is shown in Figure 6.1.

According to activity theory, each activity is directly governed by the outcome that shapes it (a single outcome for one activity). It views human phenomena as dynamic and active (Mwanza & Engeström, 2005). Manmade artefacts should not be understood as objects in themselves, but as existing within the activities that give rise to their use.

Activity theory requires us to understand how a tool is built upon the users' prior tools, responds to their desires and dissatisfactions, and, through its affordances (Gibson, 1979), extends the capacity of the user in unexpected directions. We may see all of these factors at work in computer-based composition activities within a school context. Within the structure of an activity system, a mediational tool may become the object of the system at certain moments of the activity. For example, this may include the introduction of computers and educational software that are designed and developed by engineers, programmers and instructional designers for use in learning activities in school. In developing this technology, computers and educational software are initially the *object* in the activity system, while the team of engineers/programmers is the *subject*. However, when these technologies are integrated into the music curriculum of the school, they become tools that mediate teaching and learning activities and are designed to bring about higher-order thinking skills (the *object*), with students and/or teachers as the *subject*. Technology may nevertheless become an *object* rather than a tool for the student or teacher when the subject encounters problems in using the hardware or software (Lim & Hang, 2003).

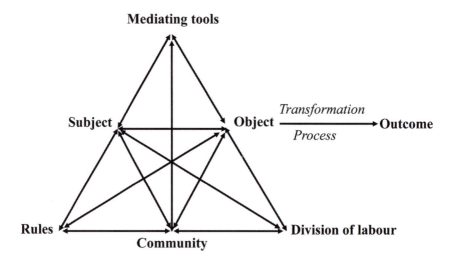

Figure 6.1   The mediational structure of an activity system. Adapted from Engeström (1987, p. 178)

The compositional process of the participating Brazilian adolescents can be modelled within the activity system in Figure 6.2. The proposed model illustrates a system in which the activity of the subject (the adolescents) is directed towards the object (the creation of music) and is transformed into outcomes with the help of a physical tool (a computer). The subject accepts or appropriates rules (codes of musical styles and conventions in the music curriculum, as well as conventions established by programmers) to work in a community (a school located within a socio-cultural context). In the community, there is a division of labour (between adults and adolescents) with tasks being allocated, and power and responsibilities being shared between the participants of the activity system after a process of negotiation.

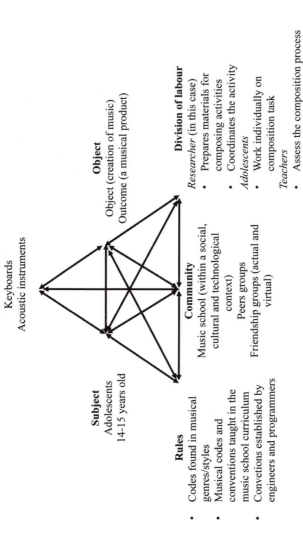

Mediating tools
Music software
Keyboards
Acoustic instruments

Object
Object (creation of music)
Outcome (a musical product)

Division of labour
Researcher (in this case)
• Prepares materials for composing activities
• Coordinates the activity
Adolescents
• Work individually on composition task
Teachers
• Assess the composition process and product
• Teaching the curriculum content
Parents
• Making technology available

Subject
Adolescents
14-15 years old

Community
Music school (within a social, cultural and technological context)
Peers groups
Friendship groups (actual and virtual)

Rules
• Codes found in musical genres/styles
• Musical codes and conventions taught in the music school curriculum
• Convetions established by engineers and programmers

Figure 6.2   Adolescents' engagement in a computer-based composition activity

Thus, the application of the activity system is useful in understanding the interrelated external elements that influenced the musical behaviour of the adolescents during the computer-based composition activity and the internal elements that influenced its outcome (the musical product). An example is the influence of the community (music school) and the rules (in the curriculum) that governed the students' choices when composing. Although the preferences of two students were for the Brazilian rock category/scale, the musical instruments that they played in their music curriculum were oriented towards classical music and so might have influenced their decision to compose in a classical style. The school curriculum and the school ethos appeared to be a transformative force which led the students to develop their own musical ideas, by using computers as tools.

In the study reported here, there was no clear evidence that listening preferences and gender had any decisive influence on the composing process and product. Furthermore, adolescents with a background in composition with computers tended to spend more time on the generation of musical ideas than those who did not. Thus the computer and the educational software were not viewed as tools that impeded the students' heuristic way of thinking. These results support other studies and suggestions that previous experiences are an important part of any musical activity within the school (Fautley, 2004; Folkestad, 1998; Nilsson & Folkestad, 2005). Overall, this study suggests that the way the composition task is carried out depends on how adolescents (the subjects) approach the computer (the tool) and the extent to which they appropriate codes and conventions (rules), both inside and outside of the school. It is important to understand what takes place inside the activity system so that teachers can make a broader assessment of the composition process and product.

Acknowledgements

This study was supported by the National Council for Scientific and Technological Development (CNPq). I am grateful to the students and teachers of the two specialist music schools in Minas Gerais, Brazil. I also acknowledge the valuable contribution to the research of Paulo Amauri, André Campos, Fábio Carvalho, Maria Cowen, Colin Durrant, Marina Giannakaki, Frank Hanson, Robert Kwami, Marília Mazzaro and Graham Welch.

Appendix

Some representative musical styles from the two regions[1]

1. *Brazilian rock* – this style became popular in Brazil in the 1980s. It is characterized by the use of several rhythms. One of its leading exponents is

---

[1]   A discussion of the 17 representative styles is available in Soares (2006).

Paralamas do Sucesso, one of the most popular Brazilian musical groups, well known in Brazil for its incorporation of reggae, ska and traditional rhythms in its compositions (Ferreira, 2004).

2. *Brazilian Popular Music* (MPB) – this arose in Brazil in the late 1960s and early 1970s as an undergraduate protest movement during the period of military dictatorship. This explains why the lyrics often include criticism of social injustice and dictatorial repression (Albin, 2004). Owing to the complexity of its melodies and harmony, MPB is regarded as highly intellectual music (Ulhôa, 2004).

3. *Forró* – this is a form of dance and music that is popular in the north-east of Brazil. The musical instruments used to play the *forró* are the accordion, triangle and zabumba (a drum) (Ferreira, 2004).

4. *Samba* – this has been recognized as the most typically Brazilian form of musical expression. It is characterized by strong syncopation and rhythmic patterns. Samba is directly linked to carnival and samba schools; however, there are other samba styles such as samba *canção*, a slower and more sentimental samba, samba *do morro*, which is heavily percussive, and samba reggae, which takes on the reggae backbeat (Sandroni, 2004).

5. *Regional* – in Minas Gerais State this style is understood as being music composed by local musicians for acoustic instruments such as the viola (a small instrument with 5 double-strings and shaped like an acoustic guitar). The lyrics usually dwell on environmental issues and the socio-cultural conditions of the local community (Reily, 1992).

6. *Pagode* – this originates from the mid-1970s and is a gathering of musicians from Rio's carnival. Currently, *pagode* musical groups have a pop flavour and rely on keyboards, electric guitars and bass instruments. The style is generally associated with lower-class and black people (Albin, 2002).

References

Albin, R. C. (2002). *Brazilian popular music: History of a century*. Culture session, Brazilian Embassy – see www.brazil.org.uk/mpb/naven.htm (accessed 20 June 2005).

Albin, R. C. (2004). MPB: Provocation of integration. In E. B. Laranjeira, I. N. Freitas & T. C. Costa (Eds.), *Brazilian popular music* (pp. 22-37). Brasilia: UNDP.

Bliss, J. (1999). Learning with and by machines. In J. Bliss, R. Säljö & P. Light (Eds.), *Learning sites: Social and technological resources for learning* (pp. 165-170). New York: Earli.

Bottino, R. M. (2004). The evolution of ICT-based learning environments: Which perspectives for the school of the future? *British Journal of Educational Technology*, 35(5), 553-567.

Brazilian Association of Phonographic Producers (2009). *Mercado Brasileiro de música 2009* – See www.abpd.org.br/downloads/Final_Publicacao_09_2010_ CB.pdf (accessed 10 May 2010).

Brazilian Ministry of Education (2008). *Lei 11.769/08* [*Law 11.769/08*] – see www.mec.gov.br (accessed 15 July 2009).

Canclini, N. G. (1990). *Culturas híbridas: Estrategias para entrar y salir de la modernidad* [Hybrid cultures: Strategies for entering and leaving modernity]. México: Grijalbo.

Creswell, J. W. (2003). *Research design: Qualitative, quantitative and mixed methods approaches* (2nd edition). London: Sage.

Csikszentmihalyi, M. (1988). Society, culture, and person: A systems view of creativity. In R. J. Sternberg (Ed.), *The nature of creativity: Contemporary psychological perspectives* (pp. 325-339). Cambridge: Cambridge University Press.

Csikszentmihalyi, M. (1997). *Creativity: Flow and the psychology of discovery and invention.* New York: Harper Perennial.

Engeström, Y. (1987). *Learning by expanding: An activity theoretical approach to developmental research.* Helsinki: Orienta-Konsultit.

Engeström, Y. (1999). Activity theory and individual and social transformation. In Y. Engeström, M. Reijo & P. Raija-Leena (Eds.), *Perspectives on activity theory* (pp. 19-38). Cambridge: Cambridge University Press.

Fautley, M. (2004). Teacher intervention strategies in the composing processes of lower secondary school students. *International Journal of Music Education,* 22(3), 201-217.

Ferreira, M. (2004). The contemporaneousness of Brazilian music. In E. B. Laranjeira, I. N. Freitas & T. C. Costa (Eds.), *Brazilian popular music* (pp.130-133). Brasilia: UNDP.

Folkestad, G. (1998). Musical learning as cultural practice: As exemplified in computer-based creative music-making. In B. Sundin, G. E. McPherson & G. Folkestad (Eds.), *Children composing: Research in music education* (pp. 97-134). Lund, Sweden: Lund University.

Getzels, J. W. & Csikszentmihalyi, M. (1976). *The creative vision: Longitudinal study of problem finding in art.* New York: McGraw-Hill.

Gibson, J. J. (1979). *The ecological approach to visual perception.* Boston: Houghton Mifflin.

Guilford, J. P. (1967). *The nature of human intelligence.* San Francisco: John Wiley & Sons.

Hargreaves, D. J. & North, A. C. (1997). The social psychology of music. In D. J. Hargreaves & A. C. North (Eds.), *The social psychology of music* (pp. 1-21). Oxford: Oxford University Press.

Hargreaves, D. J., Miell, D. & Macdonald, R. A. R. (2002). What are musical identities, and why are they important? In R. A. R. Macdonald, D. J. Hargreaves & D. Miell (Eds.), *Musical identities* (pp. 1-20). Oxford: Oxford University Press.

Hennessey, B. A. & Amabile, T. M. (1988). The conditions of creativity. In R. J. Sternberg (Ed.), *The nature of creativity: Contemporary psychological perspectives* (pp. 11-38). Cambridge: Cambridge University Press.

Hodges, R. (2001). Using ICT in music teaching. In C. Philpott & C. Plummeridge (Eds.), *Issues in music teaching* (pp. 170-181). London: Routledge.

Kwami, R. (2001). Music education in a new millennium. In A. Loveless & V. Ellis (Eds.), *ICT, pedagogy and the curriculum: Subject to change* (pp. 216-228). London: Routledge.

Lievrouw, L. A. & Livingstone, S. (2002). The social shaping and consequences of ICTs. In L. A. Lievrouw & S. Livingstone (Eds.), *Handbook of new media: Social shaping and consequences of ICTs* (pp. 1-15). London: Sage.

Lim, C. P. & Hang, D. (2003) An activity theory approach to research of ICT integration in Singapore schools. *Computers & Education*, 41(1), 49-63.

Livingstone, S. (2002). The changing social landscape. In L. A. Lievrouw & S. Livingstone (Eds.), *Handbook of new media: Social shaping and consequences of ICTs* (pp. 17-21). London: Sage.

Mwanza, D. & Engeström, Y. (2005). Managing content in e-learning environments. *British Journal of Educational Technology*, 36(3), 453-463.

Nilsson, B. & Folkestad, G. (2005). Children's practice of computer-based composition. *Music Education Research*, 7(1), 21-37.

North, A. C. & Hargreaves, D. J. (2008). *The social and applied psychology of music*. New York: Oxford University Press.

North, A. C., Hargreaves, D. J. & Hargreaves, J. J. (2004). Uses of music in everyday life. *Music Perception*, 22(1), 41-77.

Odam, G. (2000). Teaching composing in secondary schools: The creative dream. *British Journal of Music Education*, 17(2), 109-127.

Odena, O. & Welch, G. (2007). The influence of teachers' backgrounds on their perceptions of musical creativity: A qualitative study with secondary school music teachers. *Research Studies in Music Education*, 28(1), 71-81.

Pitts, A. & Kwami, R. (2002). Raising students' performance in music composition through the use of information and communication technology (ICT): A survey of secondary schools in England. *British Journal of Music Education*, 19(1), 61-71.

Poppovic, P. P. (2002). *Relatório de atividades 1996/2002 proinfo* [*Report 1996/2002 proinfo*]. Brasilia: Brazilian Ministry of Education.

Purves, R. M. (2001). A computer program for investigating transformation geometry concepts in musical and visual form: From theory to realisation. Unpublished master's dissertation, University of London.

Reily, S. A. (1992). *Música sertaneja* and migrant identity: The stylistic development of a Brazilian genre. *Popular Music*, 11(3), 337-358.

Robson, C. (2002). *Real world research: A resource for social scientists and practitioner* (2nd edition). Malden, MA: Blackwell.

Sandroni, C. (2004). Transformations of the Carioca samba in the twentieth century. In E. B. Laranjeira, I. N. Freitas & T. C. Costa (Eds.), *Brazilian popular music* (pp. 78-83). Brasilia: UNDP.

Schwartzman, S. (2003). *The challenge of education in Brazil* – see www. schwartzman.org.br/simon/challenges.pdf (accessed 25 May 2005).

Seddon, F. A. (2001). Adolescent engagement in computer-based composition: Analysing the process and product in relation to instrumental experience. Unpublished doctoral dissertation, University of Keele.

SEE-MG (2001). *Legislação pertinente às escolas estaduais de música de Minas Gerais* [*Legislation applicable to the specialist music schools in Minas Gerais state*]. Belo Horizonte: SEE.

Slack, J. D. & Wise, J. M. (2002). Cultural studies and technology. In L. A. Lievrouw & S. Livingstone (Eds.), *Handbook of new media: Social shaping and consequences of ICTs* (pp. 485-501). London: Sage.

Soares, J. (2006). Adolescents' engagement in computer-based composition in Brazil. Unpublished doctoral dissertation, Institute of Education, University of London.

Tarrant, M., North, A. C. & Hargreaves, D. J. (2002). Youth identity and music. In R. A. R. Macdonald, D. J. Hargreaves & D. Miell (Eds.), *Musical identities* (pp. 134-150). Oxford: Oxford University Press.

Ulhôa, M. T. (2004). New rhythms and names: Marisa Monte, Carlinhos Brown, manguebeat, rap. In E. B. Laranjeira, I. N. Freitas & T. C. Costa (Eds.), *Brazilian popular music* (pp. 121-129). Brasilia: UNDP.

Vieira, W. (2003). *Homo sapiens reurbanisatus*. Foz do Iguaçu: CEAC.

Wallas, G. (1926). *The art of thought*. London: Watts.

Webster, P. R. (1988). Creative thinking in music: Approaches to research. In J. Gates (Ed.), *Music education in the United States: Contemporary issues* (pp. 66-81). Tuscaloosa: University of Alabama Press.

Welch, G. F. (2000). The ontogenesis of musical behaviour: A sociological perspective. *Research Studies in Music Education*, 14(1), 1-13.

Welch, G. F. (2001). *The misunderstanding of music*. London: University of London.

Welch, G. F. & Ockelford, A. (2009). The role of the institution and teachers in supporting learning. In S. Hallam, I. Cross & M. Thaut (Eds.) *The Oxford handbook of music psychology* (pp. 307-319). Oxford: Oxford University Press.

Wisnik, J. M. (2002). *Music: An overview* – see www.brazil.org.uk/page. php?cid=167 (accessed 25 June 2009).

Chapter 7

Empathetic creativity in music-making

Frederick A. Seddon

7.1 Introduction

This chapter reports two exploratory research studies that were designed to examine the communication that took place between the musicians in two small musical ensembles. The ensembles represented music-making in two different musical genres and were a jazz sextet and a string quartet. The same research method and analysis procedures were employed to examine the communication that took place between the musicians in these musically diverse ensembles as they engaged in a variety of music-making activities in their respective musical genres.

The chapter begins by providing an outline of the concepts of empathetic intelligence (Arnold, 2003, 2004) and empathetic creativity (Seddon, 2005), and how the latter concept emerged from the former. The chapter continues by providing an overview of the two research studies that support the concept of empathetic creativity (Seddon, 2005; Seddon & Biasutti, 2009). Differences between the communications employed by the musicians, potentially related to their genre specific music-making activities, are examined in the discussion section. The chapter concludes with an overview of how the adaptation of the Constant Comparative Method (Seddon & O'Neill, 2003) as an analysis tool for the qualitative analysis of creative musical actions and dialogue has facilitated research into musical creativity over the last decade and how this research could influence future music education research and practice.

7.2 Theoretical underpinnings

7.2.1 Empathetic intelligence

Empathetic creativity is based on the concept of empathetic intelligence proposed by Roslyn Arnold (2003, 2004). Arnold argues a case for empathetic intelligence from a pedagogical perspective. She maintains that effective learning can take place when an educator creates a dynamic between thinking and feeling and that empathetic intelligence articulates aspects of the intersubjective (i.e. between subjects) and intrasubjective (i.e. within subjects) (Arnold, 2003, 2004). Empathetic intelligence is the fluid and dynamic engagement between individuals who observe, feel, intuit, think, introspect, imagine and evaluate their own data gathering of phenomenological moments while being aware that their attitude influences their subjective objectivity. According to Arnold, empathy is achieved by understanding the thoughts and feelings of self and others through attunement, decentring and introspection, engaging in an act of 'thoughtful, heartfelt imagination' (2003, p. 15). Attunement prepares individuals for exploration, risk-taking, concentration and rapport. In this context it goes beyond mere concentration and aesthetically pleasing self-absorption to include cognitive distancing or the awareness of self-engaging in the experience, resulting in the phenomenon of aesthetic judgement. Attunement is often conveyed through 'mirroring', during this process the 'other' is recognized and validated but the 'self' is also validated. Mirroring can be unconscious or deliberate, for example when people choose to dress alike. In pedagogy, mirroring can be verbal, for example echoing or elaborating words used in an exchange. Decentring serves to distinguish between sympathy and empathy because sympathy suggests we share common experiences but empathy encourages us to decentre and see things from another's point of view, experiencing layers of thought and feeling beyond what might be immediately accessible. Introspection requires the capacity to reflect on past experience to guide future action by working through stored, embodied and often unconscious memories to select significant ones. Empathy is a complex condition requiring objectivity, self-understanding and complex cognitive and affective functioning. Empathetic intelligence in teaching and learning requires collaborating individuals to interact empathetically through mirroring and attunement, creating preparedness for exploration, risk-taking, concentration and rapport, taking into account shifts in intrasubjective and intersubjective experiences resulting in a creative act.

7.2.2 Empathetic creativity

Arnold's pedagogically oriented intersubjective engagement resonates with musicians' intersubjective creativity if we consider the following. Musicians engage in a mutual creative learning experience when they play together. They have to be able to trust the musical abilities of the other players during performance especially if they are taking musical risks. By listening and responding to other musicians a collaborative and intersubjectively generated performance is produced. No one acts as a leader directing the performance; instead the performance emerges out of the actions of everyone working together (Sawyer, 1999).

Empathetic musicians are sensitive to 'attunement' in order to signal attention and 'mirroring' to affirm and modulate musical responses. Empathetic attunement between musicians goes beyond mere concentration and aesthetically pleasing self-absorption to cognitive distancing coupled with self-engagement and aesthetic judgement. Musical attunement can occur at both a sympathetic and an empathetic level. At a sympathetic level of attunement there can be musical cohesion but clashes of musical styles, interpretation of rhythms or accommodating a weaker player can prevent musicians reaching an empathetic level of attunement. In order to reach empathetic attunement musicians must decentre and see things from the other musicians' musical points of view. During decentring, musicians are not only concerned with their collective time-keeping role but strive also to achieve a collective transparency of sound where each part is discernible. This requires them to musically occupy a complementary space in horizontal and vertical planes. The process of decentring facilitates empathetic attunement and can lead to performers hearing things from the other musicians' points of view and, as a consequence, thinking of and feeling phrases beyond what had been immediately accessible to them. Introspection plays a part in empathetic attunement as either consciously or subconsciously musicians draw upon past experience to negotiate the many possibilities from multiple associations of their ideas. By going over old ground in search of the new, musicians constantly strive to put their thoughts together in different ways. During performance, a distinction may be drawn between the interplay of 'stocks of musical knowledge' and truly 'spontaneous musical *utterances*' (Davidson & Good, 2002) or 'spontaneous musical *variations*' (Seddon & Biasutti, 2009). For example, musicians describe how they listen to recordings they have made and hear themselves playing novel phrases or employing novel interpretations of pre-existing phrases in ways they have never previously practised that have emerged as a result of what the other musicians were playing at the time. Attunement can only occur through communication so in order to reveal attunement it is necessary to investigate the communication processes employed by musicians during music-making.

7.3 The jazz sextet study (Seddon, 2005)

7.3.1 Aims of the research

The aim of the research in this study was to reveal the modes of communication the student jazz musicians employed while rehearsing and performing jazz music, which included improvised instrumental solos.

7.3.2 Participants

The participants were six adult students (5 male, 1 female) pursuing an undergraduate jazz course at a university situated in the south of England. Names have been changed to protect anonymity.

7.3.3 Method and analysis

In order to reveal their modes of communication the students agreed to be observed and videotaped during six, one-hour group rehearsals and the forty-minute performance gig. The analysis of the videotapes was adapted from a procedure used for the qualitative analysis of text. This method of analysis is based upon 'grounded theory' (Glaser & Strauss, 1967) where categories emerge through a process of inductive reasoning rather than being specified in advance with the data allocated to predetermined categories. The adaptation was based on the Constant Comparative Method (Glaser & Strauss, 1967; Lincoln & Guba, 1985) which involves five main stages: immersion, categorization, phenomenological reduction, triangulation and interpretation (McLeod, 1994). In stage one, *immersion*, a detailed descriptive transcript was made of the videotaped data. This transcript aimed to capture the rich descriptive nature of the process observed. In stage two, *categorization*, systematic and repeated readings through the data assigning communication categories to the observed participant interaction led to the emergence of different types of communication. During stage three, *phenomenological reduction*, similar types of communication were grouped together revealing 'themes'. When a type of communication emerged that could not be included in an existing group, a new group was formed to accommodate it, leaving room for a continuous refinement in the grouping. Six different types of communication were revealed through this process, which were subsequently interpreted by the researcher as verbal and non-verbal types of communication that were related to the activities of instruction, cooperation and collaboration. In stage four, *triangulation*, videotaped examples of the six types of communication were presented to participants along with researcher interpretations of each type of communication. In a process known as *member checks*, the participants were then asked to comment on the researcher interpretations. Stage five, *interpretation*, involves making sense of the data from a wider perspective, constructing a model or using an established theory to explain the findings of the study.

7.3.4 Results

Table 7.1   Modes of communication during jazz ensemble playing

Mode of communication	Verbal	Non-verbal
Instruction	Musicians are told what and when to play in pre-composed sections (the head)	Musicians learn a pre-composed part by ear or read from music notation
Cooperation	Musicians discuss and plan the organization of the piece prior to performance in order to achieve a cohesive performance	Musicians achieve sympathetic attunement and exchange stocks of musical knowledge, producing cohesive performance, employing body language, facial expression, eye contact, musical cues and gesticulation
Collaboration	Musicians discuss and evaluate their performance of the music in order to develop the content and/or style of the piece	Musicians achieve empathetic attunement; take creative risks which can result in spontaneous musical utterances. When they do, this signals empathetic creativity

Source: developed from Seddon (2005).

The six modes of communication revealed in the analysis were verbal/non-verbal instruction, verbal/non-verbal cooperation and verbal/non-verbal collaboration (see Table 7.1). A *verbal* communication was interpreted as *instruction* when a member of the group gave the other members specific verbal instructions on how a pre-composed section of the piece should be performed without requiring any discussion. For example, during a rehearsal Laura gives the rest of the band clear instructions on the structure of her piece.

Laura: 'Right, it's Pete and Chris playing what they just played...'

Keith: 'Twice or...'

Laura: 'Just once.'

A *verbal* communication was interpreted as *cooperation* when discussion between the musicians regarding possible organizational changes (e.g. the form, sequence of solos and possible endings) took place in a democratic way. These organizational changes to the form of the piece were agreed to enable the musicians to cooperate in order to achieve a cohesive performance by agreeing the basic form of the piece beforehand. For example, during rehearsal after playing a piece through, the following group discussion evaluating the organization of the piece took place.

(Chris): It worked

(Pete): It wasn't too bad was it?

(Anthony): So what does it do... You know, when it gets into the solos?

(Pete): Yeah...in between each solo you nod when you get to the last one.

(Anthony): Yeah, yeah, yeah but I mean it goes erm...der...der...der...der...der...der [sings phrase]...and you're straight in there aren't you?

(Pete): That's on the top that der...der...der...is at the top of the solo, yeah.

A *verbal* communication was interpreted as *collaborative* when discussion regarding possible creative changes took place in a democratic way. During verbal collaboration creative changes were discussed, developed and implemented following group evaluation of both the piece and the musicians' individual and combined performances. For example, during rehearsal after playing a piece through, the following group discussion evaluating the 'feel' of the piece took place:

(Paul): I didn't think the feel worked for me in the solo…it doesn't really happen…

(Chris): The blow [improvised solo playing] over it?

(Paul): Well just the whole feel of it…the whole…

(Laura): I think maybe we could try it a bit quicker

(Chris): Yeah.

(Anthony): Yeah.

(Paul): You didn't want to swing it…did you? Or did you?

(Keith): I don't think you would be able to swing it anyway. It would sound like a completely different tune.

A *non-verbal* communication was interpreted as *instruction* when there was a musical dialogue consisting mainly of one musician demonstrating how a pre-composed section of the piece should sound by playing it on an instrument or vocalizing the tune. For example, during a rehearsal the group wanted to learn a new piece but they had no written copy of it so one of the musicians who knew the piece played it for the others to learn by ear.

A *non-verbal* communication was interpreted as *cooperation* when the musicians became sympathetically attuned displaying non-verbal communication (e.g. body language, facial expression, eye contact, musical cues and gesticulations). This mode of communication facilitated a cohesive performance and at times contained sympathetically attuned musical cues that focused on cohesive issues rather than creative issues.

A *non-verbal* communication was interpreted as *collaboration* when communication was conveyed exclusively through musical interaction and focused on creative exchanges. This non-verbal collaborative form of interactive creative musical communication requires empathetic attunement to occur and provides the potential vehicle for empathetic creativity to emerge through spontaneous musical utterances.

Researcher judgements of sympathetic vs. empathetic attunement were made based upon comparisons of observed participant communication, both visual and musical, produced during videotaped observation sessions. When sympathetically attuned, the musicians were perceived to be drawing on their musical knowledge base, improvising without taking risks or challenging their individual or collective creativity. Sympathetic attunement was visually evident in expressions of relative disinterest (e.g. no smiles, affirmative nods or energetic body movements). Sympathetic attunement was musically evident in comparatively predictable, complementary musical responses providing musical cohesion without creative risk through sharing stocks of musical knowledge. When empathetically attuned, the musicians seemed to respond to each other in an atmosphere of risk-taking and challenge, which extended their knowledge base. They took risks with musical phrases and timing and in so doing challenged each other's musical creativity. Empathetic attunement was visually evident in expressions of interest (e.g. smiles, collective affirmative nodding and animated body movements). Empathetic attunement was musically evident in the production of unpredictable musical 'invitation' or 'response' when participants engaged each other in challenging musical interaction. Researcher interpretations indicated that responses went beyond cohesive modes of communication to creative modes of communication.

To provide validation of researcher interpretations of the data participants were shown video clip examples of each of the modes of communication, sympathetic and empathetic attunement, and they were asked to review and critique the research of which they were the focus. This procedure is known as *member checks*, where participants are asked to tell researchers if they have accurately described their experience and produced a 'recognizable reality' (Brown & Gilligan, 1992; Lincoln & Guba, 1985).

Researcher identification and interpretation of the six modes of communication and sympathetic and empathetic attunement were supported by participant *member checks*. These six modes of communication and attunement provide support for the theoretical concept of empathetic creativity being the production of spontaneous musical utterances that can emerge from empathetically attuned collaborative musical communication. There was agreement between the researcher and some participants about the occurrence of periods of empathetic attunement during both rehearsal and performance. The researcher and all participants were in agreement that no spontaneous musical utterances were produced during the period of the study. A link was observed between the activity engaged in and the mode of communication adopted. Instructional modes were adopted during initiation of the rehearsal of a piece. Cooperational modes were adopted when developing the cohesive nature of a piece. Collaborative modes were adopted for developing creative aspects of the piece.

7.4 The string quartet study (Seddon & Biasutti, 2009)

Seddon & Biasutti (2009) investigated the communication between members of a renowned professional string quartet as they rehearsed for and delivered a concert performance. Adopting Seddon's research approach (2005), they reported how the musicians 'invited the researchers to videotape three rehearsals prior to the concert, a pre-concert rehearsal, which took place immediately before the performance and the concert performance' (Seddon & Biasutti, 2009, p. 400). The video recordings were made by Michele Biasutti. Analysis of the videotaped rehearsals and performance revealed six modes of communication between the members of the string quartet that were directly related to musical aspects of rehearsal and performance. These modes of communication formed two main categories, verbal and non-verbal, each containing three distinct modes of communication that were subsequently interpreted as instruction, cooperation and collaboration. *Verbal* communication was analysed and described as *instructional* 'when a member of the group gave another member specific verbal instructions on when to start playing, members verified notes in the score with each other or instructed each other how a section of the piece should be performed' (Seddon & Biasutti, 2009, p. 404). These verbal exchanges did not require any discussion, for instance the first violinist clearly instructed the other members of the quartet to begin playing at bar 22 from the second time bar: 'Let's go from bar 22 the second time.' Verbal instruction emerged mainly when the musicians were beginning rehearsal of a score and was distinguished by an absence of discussion between them.

A *verbal* communication was interpreted as *cooperative* when discussion between the musicians regarding possible organizational or technical changes, for example repeats or bowing, took place. These changes were agreed to enable the group members to cooperate in order to achieve a cohesive performance by agreeing the technical aspects of the piece beforehand. Verbal cooperation emerged when musical communication was suspended. It provided a verbal medium for the musicians to clarify and adapt organizational issues or technical problems, which did not directly involve creative issues.

A *verbal* communication was interpreted as *collaborative* when discussion regarding possible creative changes took place. During verbal collaboration changes in interpretation were discussed, developed and implemented following group members' evaluation of both the piece and the musician's individual and combined performances. For instance, an evaluation of a section of a piece was made and discussed as follows:

> (2nd Violin): Take care that it is not too much at bar 17 [singing demonstration] but I'm not sure of that.

> (1st Violin): As you were saying before, playing the downward slurs? Perhaps it is true? I exaggerated.

> (Cello): Usually, when it is a bridge passage it is better, if you slur downwards, after you can do whatever you want. It could happen in many places of the piece, it is never regular but it is a change of accent and you must not change it. (Seddon & Biasutti, 2009, p. 405)

Verbal collaboration also emerged when musical communication was suspended. It involved the musicians' descriptions of their creative preferences, such as interpretation of phrasing, dynamics and tempo. This gave a sense of the creative development of the score belonging to the group rather than the individual.

A *non-verbal* communication was interpreted as *instructional* when (a) the group members focused on reading the music notation to the extent that it could be argued that the notation was instructing them on what to play and (b) when there was a musical dialogue consisting mainly of one or more of the musicians demonstrating for another how a particular section of the piece should sound by playing it on an instrument or vocalizing it. For example, the members of the quartet were observed focusing intently on reading the notation. Essentially, in this mode of communication, often found in the early stages of rehearsing a new piece, the notation instructs the musicians' playing.

A *non-verbal* communication was analysed and described as *cooperative* when the musicians became sympathetically attuned, displaying non-verbal communication such as facial expressions, eye contact, musical cues and gesticulations. This mode of communication facilitated a cohesive performance and at times contained sympathetically attuned musical cues that focused on cohesive issues, for example staying in time and generally playing together. When cohesive performance became problematic, playing would cease and verbal communication would address these problems. Depending upon the nature of the problem this would involve either verbal cooperation or verbal collaboration.

A *non-verbal* communication was interpreted as *collaborative* when communication was conveyed directly through musical interaction that focused on creative exchanges. This required empathetic attunement between the musicians to occur. In this mode of communication the music itself acts to communicate along with body language, which tends to be more exaggerated, expressing enjoyment and positive evaluation of their combined playing. When this phenomenon occurs it provides the vehicle for empathetic creativity to emerge in the form of spontaneous musical variations.

Seddon & Biasutti (2009) argued that, as with the jazz musicians in Seddon (2005), the main differences between non-verbal cooperative and non-verbal collaborative modes of communication lay in the levels of attunement (sympathetic or empathetic) between the musicians and the focus of their communication (cohesion or interpretation). *Non-verbal cooperative* modes are related to sympathetic levels of attunement and group cohesive issues and *non-verbal collaborative* modes are related to empathetic levels of attunement and group creative issues as exemplified through visual and musical communication between the musicians. When sympathetically attuned, the musicians were perceived to be drawing on their musical knowledge base, playing without taking risks or challenging their individual or collective creativity. Sympathetic attunement was visually evident in expressions of relative disinterest, such as affirmative nods, energetic body movements and no smiles. Sympathetic attunement was musically evident in comparatively predictable performance providing musical cohesion without creative risk through adhering to previously rehearsed interpretations. When empathetically attuned, the musicians seemed to respond to each other in an atmosphere of risk-taking and challenge, which extended their joint creativity.

They took risks with musical phrasing, timing and dynamics, and in so doing, they challenged each other's musical creativity.

Seddon & Biasutti (2009) proposed that empathetic attunement was visually evident in expressions of interest, for example smiles, collective affirmative nodding and animated body movements, which resulted in a more animated performance. This more animated and 'risk-taking' performance 'could result in the production of unpredictable musical variations on interpretation when participants engaged each other in challenging musical interaction' (Seddon & Biasutti, 2009, p. 407). These responses appeared to go beyond cohesive modes of communication to creative modes of communication. Empathetic creativity was interpreted to have emerged when the ensemble was empathetically attuned and a novel spontaneous musical variation was produced. Two of the modes of communication, *cooperative verbal* and *non-verbal*, were revealed to be related to activities facilitating cohesive performance of the music. Another two of the modes, *collaborative verbal* and *non-verbal*, were revealed to be related to activities facilitating creative developments in the interpretation of the music. Although it was possible to identify six distinctly different modes of communication the musicians seldom used these modes separately; they often employed them simultaneously. For example, the musicians often illustrated verbal instruction, cooperation and collaboration with their non-verbal counterparts. Evaluation of the performances produced was based upon researcher judgements of the production of spontaneous musical variations, which are examples of empathetic creativity as distinct from adherence to stylistic convention (Seddon, 2005).

To provide validation of researcher interpretations of the six modes of communication, sympathetic and empathetic attunement and empathetic creativity, participants took part in the *member checks* procedure described in the previous jazz study. All members of the string quartet individually concurred with and confirmed researcher interpretations of the six modes of communication, concepts of sympathetic and empathetic attunement and empathetic creativity. Results of the string quartet study (Seddon & Biasutti, 2009) also reported that the musicians were able to collectively create spontaneous musical variations while empathetically attuned during the concert performance. It was proposed that the examples of spontaneous musical variations perceived by the researchers and confirmed by the musicians during the *member checks* procedure were examples of empathetic creativity and constituted novel musical performances.

7.5 Discussion: comparing the musicians' modes of communication

Taking an overview across both studies presented above provided an opportunity to examine differences in communication between musicians during group music-making based upon the experience of the specific ensemble, the traditions of the genre of music and the particular music-making activity being undertaken in relation to the genre of music played.

There was an extraordinary degree of similarity between the modes of communication that took place between the musicians in the jazz sextet and the string quartet. Both of these ensembles employed verbal and non-verbal modes of communication that were related to the particular focus of the activity they were engaged in (i.e. instruction, cooperation and collaboration) and both were engaged in rehearsal as a preparation for performance. The main difference between these two ensembles was grounded in the musical genre. In the jazz sextet the lack of prescriptive precision in the pre-composed sections of the piece and the inclusion of improvised solos allowed the musicians the freedom to create spontaneous musical utterances. This meant that the rehearsal process provided the jazz musicians with the opportunity to develop their communication skills to an empathetic level of attunement, which could provide opportunities for the emergence of empathetic creativity.

It is important to note that during the course of the study with the student jazz musicians, they were able to achieve empathetic attunement but no spontaneous musical utterances emerged. One explanation for this could be that they were student musicians who had not been playing together for a long period of time. Perhaps the amount of time spent in developing instrumental and collaborative communication skills is directly related to the potential emergence of spontaneous musical utterances? Some support for this proposition can be found in the results of the string quartet study. The musicians in the string quartet were more experienced than the student jazz musicians and had played together for a considerable period of time. In the string quartet study, the classical musicians were able to achieve empathetic attunement that resulted in spontaneous musical variations, which were examples of empathetic creativity. This suggests that more instrumental experience and greater amounts of time spent playing together are related to improved communication between musicians, which can facilitate empathetic creativity. However, this argument is not supported by reports of professional jazz musicians, who have no prior experience of playing together and are able to meet for impromptu sessions and still produce spontaneous musical utterances.

Differences between both groups of musicians relating to the function of rehearsal emerged across the two studies. For the student jazz musicians, rehearsal provided an opportunity to develop empathetic attunement in a relaxed environment where the possibility of the emergence of a spontaneous musical utterance was enhanced. They felt that the added pressure of performance could inhibit their willingness to take the musical risks that are necessary in the production of spontaneous musical utterances. In contrast, the classical musicians felt that rehearsal was an opportunity to coordinate their timing and expression and that spontaneous musical variations would occur during the performance. The viola player exemplified this by saying 'You don't worry if it doesn't happen during the rehearsals because it costs effort and psychophysical stress and during the rehearsal it is not necessary to do that because we know that all four of us will do that during the concert'. More research is required to determine if the difference in approach to rehearsal between jazz and classical musicians revealed in these studies is related to musical experience or is genre specific.

Examining communication between musicians during music-making is an under-researched area. The studies described above present researchers with opportunities to explore such communication and how it impacts upon issues of group rehearsal and performance. It is proposed that the studies support the concept of empathetic creativity, which is multifaceted, but additional studies would be required to clarify the concept. Empathetic creativity is something that musicians intuitively recognize but is difficult to measure empirically. It is hoped that these studies provide a rationale for the concept of empathetic creativity that can be tested by researchers in future investigations.

The data analysis procedure employed in the two studies described above was based on a procedure known as the Constant Comparative Method, which I first adopted and adapted for use in a musical context in a study conducted by Seddon and O'Neill (2003) and further developed in Seddon (2006). These enquiries examined the impact of formal instrumental musical training on the composition strategies of and communication between adolescent pupils. They are outlined in the next two sections, before discussing implications for music education in the final section.

7.6 The Constant Comparative Method

7.6.1 Exploring students' individual creative thinking processes (Seddon & O'Neill, 2003)

Seddon and O'Neill (2003) examined the creative thinking processes employed by 48 adolescent pupils as they engaged in computer-based composition. Participant pupils were divided into two groups, those who had or had not received prior formal instrumental musical training (FIMT). The data collected was continuous videotaped screen manipulations made by the participants as they individually composed their musical pieces using a music sequencing program. The application of the Constant Comparative Method as an analysis tool allowed for the emergence of composition strategies adopted by the participants while composing. Comparison of the participant pupils with and without prior experience of FIMT revealed differences in composition strategies adopted related to the participant's prior musical experience. Results revealed that pupils without prior experience of FIMT spent more time 'exploring' during computer-based composition than pupils with prior experience of FIMT. Seddon and O'Neill (2003) proposed that participant pupils with prior experience of FIMT brought preconceived ideas about musical composition to the task, which limited their perception of the need to 'explore' options during the composition process.

7.6.2 Exploring students' collaborative compositions (Seddon, 2006)

Seddon (2006) extended the work of Seddon and O'Neill (2003) by introducing collaborative computer-based composition as a component of the research investigation. The collaboration was conducted between pupils from two different schools, one in the UK and the other in Norway. Collaborative computer-based composition took place via email between composing pairs, one based in each country and balanced for prior experience of FIMT. By introducing collaboration into the research process, Seddon (2006) aimed to reveal communication processes and composition strategies adopted in this email environment. Prior musical experience in the study was based on whether or not the participants had received a minimum of four years FIMT. Eight participants (4 Norwegian, 4 English) aged 13-14 years formed four composition pairs, one from each country. Pair 1 was both non-FIMT, Pair 2 was both FIMT, Pair 3 was one FIMT (UK) one non-FIMT (Norway) and Pair 4 was one FIMT (Norway) one non-FIMT (UK).

After a brief period of technology training each composing pair had six composition sessions. After each composition session the evolving compositions were saved in separate files and emailed between UK and Norway until completion. This process produced six music files for each composing pair. Music files were subjected to repeated listening and categorization by the researcher based on an adaptation of the Constant Comparative Method validated in the previous study (Seddon & O'Neill, 2003). This process revealed the musical dialogue and different composition strategies adopted by the composing pairs.

Pair 1 (both non-FIMT)
The musical material produced by this non-FIMT composing pair was produced in the form of consecutive musical extensions that followed on from what had been previously stated. There was very little evidence of interaction between the musical parts until the last changes made by the Norwegian participant and even then the musical dialogue consisted of 'filling in the gaps/silences' left by previous musical statements. Researcher interpretation of the musical dialogue between this pair was that there was little creative collaboration between the pair and their musical dialogue represented a cooperation to complete the task without conflict. When compared to the other pairs' dialogue, Pair 1's initial musical statement was very short and the piece was short overall.

Pair 2 (both FIMT)
The musical material produced by this FIMT composing pair overlapped with their partner's previously stated material immediately after the collaborative composing process began. This provided evidence that the pair were engaging with each other's musical material in an interactive way. Comparisons between pairs revealed that the musical dialogue between Pair 2 was considerably more complex when compared with Pair 1's musical dialogue. The initial musical statement is relatively long and complex when compared with Pair 1, and the overall length

also is much longer than Pair 1's composition. The complexity of the musical dialogue indicated that they could communicate through the music itself.

Pair 3 (UK FIMT, Norway non-FIMT)
The musical material produced by this mixed musical experience composing pair displayed an interactive component through the overlapping of musical material (as with Pair 2). When the researcher (a trained musician and psychologist) listened to the musical material, the concluding sound of each participant's composition session was interpreted as 'invitational'.

Pair 4 (UK non-FIMT, Norway FIMT)
The musical material produced by this mixed musical experience composing pair displayed an interactive component through the overlapping of musical material (as with Pairs 2 and 3). However, when listened to by the researcher the musical material was found to be disjointed and culminated in the Norwegian participant more than doubling the length of the piece in the final composition session, which left the UK participant no opportunity for response.

Overall, results from Seddon (2006) revealed prior experience of FIMT was associated with extended and complex musical dialogues, critical engagement with musical ideas and increased levels of exploratory behaviours, which resulted in a more 'exploratory' environment. No prior experience of FIMT was associated with uncritical musical dialogues and a 'cumulative' environment. This outcome contradicted the results of Seddon & O'Neill (2003) which reported higher levels of 'exploratory' behaviour linked to untrained individuals. More research would be required, nevertheless, to examine whether or not musical communication or the email environment was influential in this result.

7.7 Implications for music education

All the research reported above employed the adaptation of the Constant Comparative Method, described in Section 7.3.3, as a qualitative analysis procedure for investigating creative processes such as musical composition, improvisation, rehearsal and performance. These inquiries, undertaken during the last decade, revealed strategies of composition for individuals engaged in computer-based composition, as well as the communication processes employed during collaborative creative music-making. The results of this research could help to guide developments in music education because they reveal important aspects of the creative process. Music education that focuses on engagement in the creative process both individually and collaboratively may ultimately provide the stimulus for lifetime engagement with music for all regardless of the extent of formal instrumental musical training. Although the acquisition of instrumental skills is of primary importance to those who aspire to a professional career in music, most individuals do not wish to commit the time required to fulfil these aspirations. Many people would prefer to experience the exhilaration of musical creativity without having to dedicate themselves to hours of daily instrumental practice in order to do so. Understanding the communication processes behind empathetic creativity and the application of music technology to enable musical novices to engage in this communication might provide the knowledge to realize this possibility through future music education. Further research in the areas discussed in this chapter might help to inform the development of innovative music education that delivers the experience of empathetic creativity during group music-making regardless of prior musical experience.

References

Arnold, R. (2003). Empathetic intelligence: The phenomenon of intersubjective engagement. Presentation to the first international conference on pedagogies and learning, University of Southern Queensland (Proceedings in CD).

Arnold, R. (2004). *Empathic intelligence: Relating, educating, transforming.* Sydney: University of New South Wales Press.

Brown, L. M. & Gilligan, C. (1992). *Meeting at the crossroads: Women's psychology and girl's development.* Cambridge, MA: Harvard University Press.

Davidson, J. W. & Good, J. M. M. (2002). Social and musical co-ordination between members of a string quartet: An exploratory study. *Psychology of Music*, 30(2), 186-201.

Glaser, B. G. & Strauss, A. L. (1967). *The discovery of grounded theory.* Chicago, IL: Aldine.

Lincoln, Y. & Guba, E. (1985). *Naturalistic inquiry.* Beverly Hills, CA: Sage.

McLeod, J. (1994). *Doing counselling research.* London: Sage.

Sawyer, R. K. (1999). Improvised conversations: Music collaboration, and development. *Psychology of Music*, 27(2), 192-204.

Seddon, F. A. (2005). Modes of communication during jazz improvisation. *British Journal of Music Education*, 22(1), 47-61.

Seddon, F. A. (2006). Collaborative computer-mediated music composition in cyberspace. *British Journal of Music Education*, 23(3), 273-283.

Seddon, F. A. & Biasutti, M. A. (2009). Comparison of modes of communication between members of a string quartet and a jazz sextet. *Psychology of Music*, 37(4), 395-415.

Seddon, F. A. & O'Neill, S. A. (2003). Creative thinking processes in adolescent computer-based composition: An analysis of strategies adopted and the influence of formal instrumental musical training. *Music Education Research*, 5(2), 125-138.

Chapter 8

Cognition and musical improvisation in individual and group contexts

Su-Ching Hsieh

8.1 Introduction

There are several assumptions surrounding the art of improvisation. The first deals with the definition of improvisation concerning the implications of its perceived rules, including whether improvisatory knowledge is pre-learned or spontaneous and to what extent a particular musical genre dictates and influences the nature of improvisation. The second focuses on the development of skills and knowledge involved in learning to improvise – that is, does a learner need pre-knowledge and skill acquisition to improvise to a high level? Furthermore, how do we make explicit any similarities and differences in 'how we think we do it' and 'what we actually do' during the process of learning to improvise individually and in teams?

This chapter examines the development and practice of improvisation skills in individual and group contexts. I begin with a review of the literature on the process of musical improvisation, including its development, the notion of creative cognition and a number of factors influencing group improvisation. I then discuss the findings of a recent inquiry on improvisation in three contexts: (1) a learner self-study; (2) a duo between a novice and an expert; and (3) a group of novices playing in an expert group. I then consider the findings from the three contexts in the light of the literature review and outline some implications for music education in the concluding section.

8.2 Background to improvisation

Improvisation has been studied from different perspectives and knowledge areas, including organization theory, communication and music. Researchers of organizations have looked into musical improvisation, particularly jazz practices, for the development of organizational theories (Barrett, 2002; Weick, 1999) and music educators have explored organizational theories when developing ensemble leadership models (e.g. Leck, 2009). The notion of improvisation has been linked with planning as a first stage, followed by implementation. Weick (1999) comments that during the process of improvisation the time gap between planning and implementation narrows, therefore composition generates from execution. The more flexible the design and execution of an activity in time, the more improvisational the activity is (Moorman & Miner, 1998). Several bodies of literature support this definition of improvisation. For instance, improvisation is described as 'thinking in the midst of action' in education and it takes place when 'acts of composing and performing are inseparable' in communication (Bastien & Hostager, 1992, p. 95). In music it is also referred to as 'real-time composition' (Pressing, 1988, p. 142) and as 'making decisions affecting the composition of music during its performance' (Solomon, 1986, p. 226).

8.2.1 The process of musical improvisation

Improvisations in jazz and many world music traditions are rule governed, providing constraints for the musicians, for instance related to a specific song, harmonic structure and characteristic rhythmic patterns (Pressing, 1998). These consequently draw a boundary around the musicians' creative choices, while giving them a licence to operate between several available and appropriate alternatives. Pressing (1998) suggests that the process of improvisation depends extensively on long-term memory and the simulated activations of unconscious automatic processes with conscious cognitive processes.

Johnson-Laird (1988) believes that in order to be able to improvise effectively in a particular genre the subconscious knowledge base processes need to be automated so that the performer can access these at the moment of creation. If the knowledge base is effectively internalized in long-term memory from sufficient practice and performance experience, the resources used to create surface melody are free to concentrate on developing coherent and structural unity. The improviser must have sufficient motor programmes to have access to patterns and sequences from style specific knowledge. The nature of the movement sequence is structured from particular notes imposed by the physical constraint of the instrument. Johnson-Laird (1994, 2002) observes that at the deepest level improvisers activate basic structures in memory, at a middle level they make feedback decisions in relation to the structure of the referent and at the surface level improvised melody is produced. Once the improvisers become more experienced, more complex actions involved during the process of improvising become automated. However, in the early stages of learning to improvise, more simple processes through the application of short-term memory can produce acceptable improvisations of a more mechanical nature. Processes such as feedback generate new ideas through ongoing monitoring of performance, allowing some initial unintended wrong notes to become incorporated intentionally into future performances (Kenny & Gellrich, 2002). In addition, an important part of creativity and improvisation is believed to be the interaction with fellow musicians, the audience and the environment, which is seen to make each improvisatory performance distinctive (Johnson-Laird, 1994).

8.2.2 The development of improvisation skills

Within jazz practices, accomplished musicians develop their improvising skills by learning example solos of the masters from older generations (Berliner, 1994). They practise such solos until these can be imitated note by note. These then subsequently become the basic forms of reference for the development of related abilities in order to push the limits of what musicians have learned into the creation of new music. This new music has elements that are similar in characteristics to the imitated models that the musicians have internalized. The listeners can often identify the source of the influences, but sometimes the developments happen in dramatic and radical ways.

A number of studies have been undertaken on the differences between expert and novice improvisers (e.g. Kratus, 1996). The ability of knowing how a melody will sound before it is played on an instrument is reported as being essential to the development of expertise among improvisers. It has been marked as an ability to create a mental image of the sound through 'audiation' (Gordon, 1993). Other skills that expert adult improvisers develop include:

- the skill to internalize music in a short space of time during real-time improvisatory performance
- sufficient knowledge in analysing musical structures
- the skill to manipulate an instrument or the voice to achieve musical intentions convincingly and fluently
- sufficient knowledge of strategies for formulating an improvisation and the flexibility to change strategies if necessary
- sufficient knowledge of stylistic conventions for improvising
- the skill to transform the stylistic convention to the development of a personal style (Kratus, 1996).

The development of expertise in musical improvising is believed to involve a series of stages (Hallam, 2005; Kratus, 1996). In Stage 1, the learner develops their skills through explorations in their playing. Stage 2 is focused on process – that is, musical doodling without any overall structure. Stage 3 is about product-oriented improvisation where the learner incorporates musical techniques into the playing. During Stage 4, the learner is seen to become more fluid in producing improvisation and executes more controls on the technical aspects of performance. In Stage 5, the nature of the improvisation becomes more structured. And in the final Stage 6, the learner develops their personal style in improvisation as well as being fluent in improvisation and in adopting appropriate musical styles.

Sudnow (1978) reported that acquiring jazz improvisation skills as an adult classical musician was tedious, effortful and frustrating. During his learning to improvise, he had difficulties in acquiring knowledge from aural sources, applying the technical constraints imposed by particular instruments, which impacted on the improvised response and in recognizing the differences between spontaneously created material and improvised fillers. Sudnow (1978) also documented one of his more successful strategies in learning to improvise. As the development of his skills progressed, he developed a strategy called 'frantic playing' for applying the internalized knowledge. In order to achieve this, he had to give up cognitive control and let his hands find the notes instead. This risk-taking strategy led to a sense of more 'right' notes and Sudnow's improvisation reportedly started to sound more like that of an experienced improviser. Performances that combine flow states (Csikszentmihalyi, 1991) with a degree of risk-taking could hold the key in achieving optimal levels of musical communication in improvisation. Berliner comments on the attainment of this level of performance as being 'within the groove' (1994, p. 389). In some performances, when improvisers experience a peak experience or flow state, it assists them to move beyond their own earlier cognitive limits. There are several significant factors reported in facilitating the development of improvising skills in jazz, including creativity in early musical environments, assisting jazz communities as part of an education system, developing jazz languages and repertoire, encouraging musical interactions, and commitment (Berliner, 1994; Sudnow, 1978).

8.2.3 Factors influencing the quality of group improvisation

Cunha et al. (2002) found a number of factors that influence the quality of organizational improvisation, some of which seem relevant when examining improvisation in music groups. These factors include leadership, member characteristics, information flow and organizational configuration. *Leadership* is seen to be significant in affecting the quality of organizational improvisation. Researchers have referred to the most appropriate style as a 'servant' leadership (Greenleaf, 1977) and as a rotating leadership (Bastien & Hostager, 1988). The theory of a rotating leadership links to the increasing level of complexity and the interdisciplinary nature of the opportunities or problems that organizations potentially face, which require different competencies and knowledge at different times. Within group improvisation, the role of each individual member could constantly switch from being a counsellor, the leader or part of the supporting system. The leadership style of the group's formal leader can act as a moderator of improvisation (Cunha et al., 2002). A directive leader could have a negative impact on improvisation if he or she imposes visible and obtrusive control upon the group. The style of a 'servant' leadership could provide a positive impact on the effectiveness of organizational improvisation. This style is conceptualized as holding stewardship for followers and for the purposes of the organization (Greenleaf, 1977).

In jazz practices, the *member characteristics* suggest that the level of performance experiences and skills that each individual has determines the group's ability to pursue improvisational activities (Crossan et al., 1996; Weick, 1999). Further, it seems that group improvisational performance could be limited by the skills of the least able member (Bastien & Hostager, 1988; Hatch, 1999). The degree of diversity of the group membership can also affect the degree and quality of group improvisation (Cunha et al., 2002). Homogeneous groups could compromise the 'novel' element of organization improvisation. Therefore, their potential for the production of improvisation might be limited to small variations that are based on current ideas, products, practices and routines (Hatch, 1997; Weick, 1998, 1999). An additional membership characteristic is the ability to manage explicit emotional states in both the group and the improvisation performance context (Cunha et al., 2002). The management of the state of an individual's performance anxiety is crucial. Improvisation performers could experience quite a high level of anxiety due to the perception of working with no structure (Barrett, 2002; Hatch, 1999). This level of anxiety seems to require an explicit and effective treatment, as it can rarely be resolved implicitly. The ability to recognize and deal with the emotional state of performance positively is believed to be essential to the process of improvisational performance (Cunha et al., 2002).

Information flow is another determining factor in the quality of improvisation. It is divided into categories of factors relating to the organization and its environment and the intra-organizational information flow (Cunha et al., 2002). Information flow is an essential factor in producing effective improvisation as it can act as the centre of communication within the organizational improvisation. This communication is the effective link between individual and group performance within the organization (Bastien & Hostager, 1988). If there is no communication present during the performance, the improvisation could break into ineffective responses from within the group (Moorman & Miner, 1998).

Finally, *organizational configuration* is a factor that relates to the effectiveness of improvisation. Some researchers observe that it is necessary to build a close and trusting relationship between members to develop a safe environment for the occurrence of improvisation (Crossan et al., 1996; Weick, 1999). In doing this, group size has the potential to influence the group's ability to improvise. Considerably larger size groups can reduce the distinction between routine behaviour and improvised behaviour. This might be caused by the fact that, within a large group of people, the notion of coordination could not occur based only on mutual adjustment, and this type of control would have a negative effect on the ability to improvise. Further, the larger the group becomes, the higher the probability of information distortion becomes and the speed of communication of real time information decreases, reducing the incidence of improvisation (Moorman & Miner, 1995).

8.3 Creative cognition

Creative cognition has been developed from experimental cognitive psychology and often makes reference to basic laboratory studies of 'normative creativity' (Ward et al., 1999). Additionally, it carries a firm belief in the continuity of cognitive functioning between mundane and exceptional creative performance.

Creative cognition includes a range of factors – other than cognitive processes such as working memory and flexibility of stored structures – in the development of creativity, including intrinsic motivation, situational contingencies, the timeliness of an idea and the value that different cultures place on innovation (Amabile, 1983). Creative cognition emphasizes mental operations due to that fact that it assumes that many non-cognitive factors develop their impact by way of their influence on cognitive functioning (Ward et al., 1999). For instance, it is argued that increased motivation would have an impact on the tendency to engage in particular processes, such as the application of analogical reasoning, mental model simulation or conceptual combination. However, the variations in the processes themselves would cause differences in the quality of creative ideas that different thinkers would produce (Ward et al., 1999).

8.3.1 Geneplore model

One of the early influential frameworks of the creative cognition approach was the 'Geneplore model' (generative and exploratory) of creative functioning (Finke et al., 1992). This framework was proposed as a heuristic model rather than an explanatory theory of creativity. It suggested that:

> Many creative activities can be marked as an initial generation of candidate ideas or solutions, followed by extensive exploration of those ideas. The initial ideas are sometimes described as 'pre-inventive' in the sense that they are not complete plans for some new product, tested solutions to vexing problems, or accurate answers to difficult puzzles. Rather they may be an untested proposal or even a mere germ of an idea, but they hold some promise of yielding outcomes bearing the crucial birthmarks of creativity: originality and appropriateness. (Ward et al., 1999, p. 191)

Overall, the model assumes that an individual would alternate between generative and exploratory processes, developing the structures according to the constraints of a specific task. Exploratory processes in creative cognition could involve the searching for desired attributions in the mental structures, metaphorical implications of the structures, potential functions of the structures, the evaluation of structures from different perspectives, the interpretation of structures as representing possible solutions to problems and various conceptual limitations that are suggested by the structures (Finke et al., 1992). Creative thinking then can be subscribed through the ways in which these processes are combined. For instance, a writer might start the beginnings of a new plot line by mentally combining familiar and new concepts, and then develop the ramifications of their combination in fleshing out the details of the story (Ward et al., 1999).

8.3.2 The pre-inventive structure

The Geneplore model can also distinguish between the cognitive processes that are used in creative cognition and the types of mental structures they operate on. Finke et al. (1992) drew up a particular class of mental structure, named pre-inventive structure. The pre-inventive structure can be seen as an internal precursor to the final, externalized products of a creative act, generated with a particular goal in mind or just as a vehicle for open-ended discovery (Ward et al., 1999). Examples of pre-inventive structures are symbolic visual patterns and diagrams, representations of three-dimensional objects and forms, mental blends of basic concepts, mental models representing conceptual systems and verbal combinations that indicate new associations and insights. The different types of pre-inventive structure depend on the nature of the task.

The Geneplore model also suggests that the constraints of the final product in creative processes can be influenced by both the generative and the exploratory phase at any time (Ward et al., 1999). For instance, when constraints are imposed on resources, they can restrict the type of structures that could be generated. Paradoxically, when constraints are imposed on practicality, they might restrict the types of interpretations. Subsequently, the model seems to see that the two distinct processing stages, the generation and exploration, are applied in most instances of creative cognition (Ward et al., 1999). In the stages of generative processing, mental synthesis, mental transformation and exemplar retrieval lead to pre-inventive structures, which are then interpreted in the exploratory stage by assessing the emergent properties and implications. The forms involved in the pre-inventive structures include mental models and designs, and exemplars of novel categories. Once the stage of exploration is completed, the pre-inventive structures can be regenerated through new discoveries and insights that appear, until they develop to a final, creative idea or product.

8.3.3 Cognitive behaviour in group jazz

Cognition within group jazz seems to suggest multiple activities happening at the same time. Poole (1983) outlined a multiple sequence model relating to all the different activities as a unit of strands that generate at the same time. Bastien and Hostager (2002) adopted Poole's theory (1983) in a case study of group jazz concerts and developed three tracks – musical structure, social structure and communicative behaviour – in addressing the cognitive and behavioural components of change events in jazz performance. The 'musical structure' involves conventions and cognitions generated by music theory and music scores. 'Social structure' represents behaviour and communicative codes, and 'communicative behaviour' includes non-verbal and verbal signs (Bastien & Hostager, 2002, p. 21). Poole (1983) also developed the concept of break points in his model, which suggested that there are points in time when changes will take place across all tracks, musical structure, social structure and communicative behaviour. This would impact on change in direction and the nature of group activities.

In the above sections I have examined improvisation processes and a number of factors affecting the quality of improvisation that are reported in the literature. In the following section some of these ideas are further discussed drawing on data from a recent empirical study.

8.4 Exploring musical improvisation in three contexts

The inquiry reported in the next sections is part of a larger study of improvisation across music genres and practice contexts (Hsieh, 2009). In this chapter I will focus on the development of improvisatory skills in three different contexts:

1. Improvisation as an individual in familiar and unfamiliar genres: an experienced classical musician learning to improvise
2. Improvisation as a duo between a novice and an expert: free style improvising as a duo
3. Improvisation by novices in an expert group: novices and experts learn as a group to improvise across genres

In recent years a range of methods have been adopted for researching musical improvisation. From an educational perspective, a case study methodology can facilitate our understanding of the relationships between musical practices and musical learning, and assist when planning future musical activities. In the present inquiry, a multi-methods approach was employed and each of the practice contexts was explored to consider specific constructs in the development of expertise in music and improvisatory related skills. A range of methods and data collection techniques was used, including a self-case study, interviews and observations. Semi-structured interviews were undertaken with novice and expert improvisers concerning their perceptions about improvisation in ensemble rehearsals and with multi-genre compositions.

8.4.1 Improvisation as an individual in familiar and unfamiliar genres

The main purpose of the self-case study was to understand how an individual musician learns to improvise in a new musical genre. It used self-regulated practice during the process of learning to improvise of an experienced classical musician, based on a planned sequential model: (a) sight-reading; (b) memorizing; and (c) improvising over eight weeks. I was the participant, a novice improviser with extensive formal Western classical music training. The self-case study used two commissioned musical compositions matched in length, harmony and structure, one in a classical genre, the other in jazz. In addition, I carried out a series of self-reflective observations over eight weeks on my practising with the two pieces.

I practised memorizing and improvising spending two hours daily on the two stimuli, and each day I varied the order of these two foci. I usually started with the more familiar genre (classical) and after each session wrote down all the activities in a practice dairy and verbalized my thoughts into an audio recorder.

8.4.2 Improvisation in a duo between a novice and an expert

The second context was chosen to explore how Western classical and jazz musicians worked as a duo, and whether there was evidence of transferred musical skills and applied practice and learning strategies in free improvisation. Two classical and two jazz musicians were selected to participate in this element of the research, and they were paired across styles. They used two notated pieces of music, one in blues style and one in a more Western classical genre.

The two expert improvisers were professional jazz musicians who had been active on the London jazz scene for a number of years. Both were trained classically in school up to A level music and specialized in jazz when they entered music conservatories. Additionally, both of the jazz specialists were composers and bandleaders as well as instrumentalists. The two novice improvisers were professional classical musicians who had worked respectively as a violinist and a flautist in professional orchestras and string quartets. During this duo playing each participant was given as much time as they felt was necessary to prepare for the duo improvisation. When all the participants felt comfortable enough to undertake the task, it was recorded using a video digital camera.

8.4.3 Improvisation by novices in an expert group

In the third context 14 classical and jazz musicians took part in learning to improvise for a specially commissioned large ensemble work rehearsal series that took place over a period of two months. Nine of the musicians were specialists in jazz performance and worked as professional players on the London jazz scene. Five of the musicians were classical trained, but had some experience in the Irish folk music tradition or other world music practices. These 14 musicians formed a large ensemble group for the research study and decided to call themselves Fringe Magnetic Ensemble. The ensemble was male dominated; 12 members were males and only two female. The instruments in the ensemble were trumpet, flugelhorn, piano, clarinet, flute, bass clarinet, violin, cello, double bass, drums and percussion. Each musician was required to learn and perform an individual improvisation as well as a group improvisation for the commissioned musical work. The music stimuli were especially commissioned for jazz and classical musicians performing composed and improvised music together as an ensemble. Eleven sessions of rehearsals were recorded on a digital camera. Each lasted between 50 and 70 minutes.

8.5 Discussion

8.5.1 Improvisation as an individual in familiar and unfamiliar genres

From the data derived from the self-case study, I as a novice improviser who had expertise in classical piano performance depended mostly on my short-term working memory when improvising individually from a jazz piece. The emphasis on short-term working memory appeared to be due to (1) my low level of domain knowledge acquisition and (2) a high level of performance anxiety in relation to learning to improvise in an unfamiliar genre. A similar outcome with improvisation was evidenced on the classical piece, even though the level of my knowledge acquisition and general domain familiarity was much higher within the classical genre. The main learning strategies that I adopted were (a) applying an analytic strategy during the improvisation process and (b) imitating elements from the given musical themes. When comparing my solo improvisation in both classical and jazz music, I was able then to apply a wider range of relevant learning strategies with the classical music stimuli.

There has been little research investigating the novice improviser's use of learning strategies while learning to improvise. The research by Sudnow (1978), who studied himself as an adult professional classical musician acquiring jazz improvisation skills, comes closest to my methodological approach. In his study he reported an applied strategy as 'frantic playing' where he had to give up cognitive control and let his hands find the most appropriate notes instead. As a result, Sudnow (1978) concluded that experts do better in their own domain and that it is difficult to transfer skill development and knowledge acquisition between musical genres. In terms of the elementary stages of an improvisation learning process, Johnson-Laird (1988) suggested that in the early stages of learning to improvise processes draw on short-term memory in order to produce an acceptable improvisation of a more mechanical nature. Sudnow's study (1978) and the present research differ in terms of research design. Sudnow focused on jazz improvisation, whereas the present research applied different systematic methods, such as the use of planned self-regulated practice and tasks related to two matched music pieces (specially designed to have similar structures and musical design). The self-case study demonstrated that the novice improviser experienced greater difficulties in learning to play and improvise on the jazz music piece. The lack of relevant domain knowledge in jazz and limited performance experience and skills in relation to this particular genre were clearly influential. The process of self-regulated learning to improvise in an unfamiliar genre meant that existing skills could only be used at a more basic level than was the case with the classical music piece. In addition, the process created enormous anxiety that further interfered with the development of related musical skills as I had limited strategies for coping with the anxiety in real time. For me, it seemed that musical skills and domain knowledge were not easily transferrable between different musical genres.

8.5.2 Improvisation in a duo between a novice and an expert

Several issues in the ways that musicians with classical and jazz backgrounds engaged in duo improvisation emerged from the data analysis from the second practice context. The data suggest that the classical improviser was able to utilize both conscious and automated influences from contemporary music compositions when developing strategies for duo improvisation. Timing was also an essential component, as it provided a clear framework to improvise upon.

Participants with a jazz background employed identical strategies when learning to improvise as a duo, drawing on conscious and automated processing and timing. In terms of musical structure in the duo improvisation, the jazz expert tended to take charge of the melody line. There were also differences among improvisers from classical and jazz musical backgrounds in terms of their strategy development in duo improvisation performance. These differences related to the nature of their acquired knowledge and the usage of a composing approach. The jazz experts worked with a much tighter set of constraints than those working within a classical genre. For the classical musicians, the structures related to harmony and timing were less constrained than those used in traditional jazz formats.

In the small group context of the duos, the individual characteristics of the two group members influenced the process of improvisation. The expert improvisers were more likely to take risks, and when the other duo member appeared to be less adventurous and more limited in producing musical ideas, this had the effect of hindering the development of strategies in the expert's improvisation. Csikszentmihalyi (1991) suggests that risk-taking and flow could hold the key to achieving an optimal level of musical communication in improvisation. In addition, Barrett observes that a key characteristic of professional jazz improvisers is their display of 'provocative competence' (2002, p. 139). Here, the musicians make a deliberate effort to break away from their habitual performance comfort zone in order to reach a higher level of musical creativity. Comparing earlier studies of experts' characteristic risk-taking and the data derived from this study, a common theme emerges. Expert improvisers are able to shift from habitual creative performance practice, such as repeatedly using a familiar musical routine, in order to produce new musical ideas. The findings of the present study revealed that the more experienced improvisers believed that risk-taking was fundamental to a higher level of small group creativity.

It was also found that in a small group such as a duo, the style of leadership could have a significant impact on the process and product of improvisation. In learning to improvise as a duo, the more experienced improviser was more likely to be the leader. Two contrasting styles of leadership were shown by the participants: *supportive* and *dominant*. The adoption of a supportive leadership style increased the quality of the duo improvisation, the expert providing a solid bass harmony, which led to a coherent musical structure. In contrast, a dominant leadership style had a negative impact on the quality of the improvisation as it appeared to increase conflict between the participants and limited the musical choice of the group members by imposing restricted rules. The findings suggest that the style of leadership is an important factor in creating an effective organizational improvisation.

Previous research has suggested that member characteristics in duo performance groups range from *conflictive* to *compromising* (Murnighan & Conlon, 1991). Moreover, researchers have referred to the benefit of a 'servant' leadership style (Greenleaf, 1977). A directive leader can have a negative impact on improvisation if he or she imposes visible and obtrusive control upon the group. The findings of the present research evidenced that conflictive group characteristics and a dominant leadership style reduced the level of small group creativity. The expert jazz improvisers participating in the duos had had some training in the classical genre so perhaps it is unsurprising that most of them were able to work in both jazz and classical genres. For example, one expert jazz improviser was able to accommodate the limitations of the novice improviser's jazz domain knowledge by creating a musical improvisation based on a classical music theme.

In the small group improvisation, the role of the expert was crucial in determining the way that the novice could develop their skills. In one duo, the novice provided a supporting bass line that included random long notes because the improvisation was in an unfamiliar genre (jazz) and the expert adopted a dominant role. The novice improviser's limited domain knowledge acquisition was clearly a factor here. In the duos, the expert improvisers seemed to utilize conscious and automated influences from learned musical compositions. They used a sense of time/temporal cues or musical structure to provide a clear framework. A number of communication strategies were adopted by the expert improvisers when relating to other musicians, including the evaluation strategy of 'talking about doing' used to review the process and the product, although the jazz experts were more concerned with acquiring a collective musical style.

8.5.3 Improvisation by novices in an expert group

From the observations and interviews carried out in the study of ensemble rehearsals and group improvisation in a multi-genre musical task, there was evidence of novices adopting similar strategies as in the duo contexts, for instance using long notes as a supporting accompaniment. There was also evidence of imitating the given musical themes. While the experts were able to be in the 'groove' and assert their individual creativity, the large group size and limited performance experience and related musical skills appeared to inhibit the novices' developing improvisatory skills. In the large group improvisation a range of strategies were reported to be used by the leader and individual group members. There was interaction generated between musicians' engagement with the musical structures and allied verbal and non-verbal communicative behaviour throughout the entire ensemble improvisation learning process. There was also at least one turning point where higher levels of creativity and coherence seemed to emerge, akin to a 'break point' (Poole, 1983; Bastien & Hostager, 2002), when changes seemed to occur simultaneously across musical, social and communicative tracks. The leadership of the group appeared to be crucial in facilitating the development of the group's improvisatory capacity. The cross-genre nature of the music and its structure, in theory, should have enabled all participants to make a similar contribution to the emerging improvisation. Interestingly, across the sessions, experts and novices tended to produce almost identical improvisations in each session, and there was little further development once the initial ideas had been established. Furthermore, the initial ideas developed tended to be in the genre where the individual had the most existing expertise.

Overall, the present research has reported that existing musical skills were reduced in their effectiveness in the unfamiliar musical genre, such as jazz, when learning to improvise individually. More specifically, in the case of a novice improviser such as myself, many different skills were affected, and learning to improvise in both new and existing genres appeared to follow a staged process. In terms of developing individual creativity, novice improvisers experienced more difficulties in unfamiliar musical genres when creating solo improvisation performances; less original musical ideas could be produced when improvising on the given jazz musical piece.

8.6 Implications for music education

The current study has some implications for students and music educators. The data suggest that the development of improvisation skills in adult musicians has a strong connection to the growth of musical experiences and expertise. Therefore postgraduate music students would benefit from opportunities to develop improvisation skills as part of their courses, as essential skills education. This would help music students to understand the strength and weakness of their existing musical skills and domain knowledge, as well as provide an opportunity to assert their individual creativity.

It has also been suggested that duo improvisation can be valuable in developing improvisation skills if the leadership strategy from the expert improviser is appropriately supportive, allowing the duo to listen to each other, utilizing their relevant domain knowledge and developing a sense of group creativity. Musical opportunities might be based on duo performances, helping students to develop improvisation strategies and a deeper level of musicianship. At undergraduate and graduate levels, the research offered insights into the difficulties that non-jazz musicians can experience when asked to improvise, and implies that course designers responsible for leading music studies such as 'jazz for non-jazz specialists' would need to recognize and facilitate effective ways to overcome students' problems and likely anxiety. The study outlined the importance of information flow in jazz performance and of applying effective communication strategies. Students of jazz studies are offered coaching in performance skills as an essential part of their courses. These may incorporate understanding of the importance of communication and information flow.

This inquiry has offered an example of how improvisation can be developed through combining different genres in cross-genre compositions. Additionally, it has found that involving experts from different musical genres can influence the development of existing musical skills, domain knowledge acquisition and individual creativity. For students who are interested in learning music from different genres and engaging in practical experiences of improvisation, the development of the experimental performance Fringe Magnetic Ensemble illustrated some of the difficulties they may encounter (Hsieh, 2009). It is hoped that this work can assist classical specialist music students to be aware of diverse possibilities and strategies for developing improvisation skills in individual and group contexts.

References

Amabile, T. M. (Ed.) (1983). *The social psychology of creativity*. New York: Springer-Verlag.

Barrett, F. (2002). Creativity and improvisation in jazz and organizations: Implications for organizational learning. In M. P. Cunha, K. N. Kamoche & J. V. Cunha (Eds.), *Organizational improvisation* (pp. 135-162). New York: Routledge.

Bastien, D. & Hostager, T. (1988). Jazz as a process of organizational innovation. *Communication Research*, 15(5), 582–602.

Bastien, D. & Hostager, T. (1992). Cooperation as communicative accomplishment: A symbolic interaction analysis of an improvised jazz concert. *Communication Studies*, 43(2), 92-104.

Bastien, D. & Hostager, T. (2002). Jazz as a process of organizational innovation. In M. P. Cunha, K. N. Kamoche & J. V. Cunha (Eds.), *Organizational improvisation* (pp. 14-28). New York: Routledge.

Berliner, P. (Ed.) (1994). *Thinking in jazz: The infinite art of improvisation*. Chicago: University of Chicago Press.

Crossan, M., Lane, H., White, R. E. & Klus, L. (1996). The improvising organization: Where planning meets opportunity. *Organizational Dynamics*, 24(4), 20-35.

Csikszentmihalyi, M. (Ed.). (1991). *Flow: The psychology of optimal experience*. New York: Harper & Row.

Cunha, M. P., Kamoche, K. N. & Cunha, J. V. (Eds.) (2002) *Organizational improvisation*. New York: Routledge.

Finke, R. A., Ward, T. B. & Smith, S. M. (1992). *Creative cognition: Theory, research and applications*. Cambridge, MA: MIT Press.

Gordon, E. E. (1993). *Learning sequences in music: Skill, content, pattern. A music learning theory* (4th edition). Chicago: GIA Publications.

Greenleaf, R. K. (1977). *Servant leadership: A journey into the nature of legitimate power and greatness*. Mahwah, NJ: Paulist Press.

Hallam, S. (Ed.) (2005). *Music psychology in education*. London: Institute of Education, University of London.

Hatch, M. J. (1997). Jazzing up the theory of organizational improvisation. *Advances in Strategic Management*, 14(2), 181-191.

Hatch, M. J. (1999). Exploring the empty spaces of organizing: How improvisational jazz helps redescribe organizational structure. *Organization Studies*, 20(1), 75-100.

Hsieh, Su-Ching (2009). Cognition and musical improvisation in individual and group contexts. Unpublished PhD dissertation, Institute of Education, University of London.

Johnson-Laird, P. N. (1988). *The computer and the mind: An introduction to cognitive science*. Cambridge, MA: Harvard University Press.

Johnson-Laird, P. N. (Ed.) (1994). *Human and machine thinking*. Hillsdale, NJ: Lawrence Erlbaum.

Johnson-Laird, P. N. (2002). How jazz musicians improvise. *Music Perception*, 19(3), 415-442.

Kenny, B. J. & Gellrich, M. (2002). Improvisation. In R. Parncutt & G. E. McPherson (Eds.), *The science and psychology of music performance: Creative strategies for teaching and learning* (pp. 117-134). Oxford: Oxford University Press.

Kratus, J. (1996). A developmental approach to teaching music improvisation. *International Journal of Music Education*, 26(1), 3-13.

Leck, H., with Jordan, F. (2009). *Creating artistry through choral excellence*. Milwaukee, WI: Hal Leonard.

Moorman, Ch. & Miner, A. (1995). *Walking the tightrope: Improvisation and information in new product development. Report No. 95-101*. Cambridge, MA: Marketing Science Institute.

Moorman, Ch. & Miner, A. (1998). The convergence between planning and execution: Improvisation in new product development. *Journal of Marketing*, 62(3), 1-20.

Murnighan, J. K. & Conlon, D. E. (1991). The dynamics of intense work groups: A study of British string quartets. *Administrative Science Quarterly*, 36(2), 165-186.

Poole, M. S. (1983). Decision development in small groups: III. A multiple sequence model of group decision development. *Communication Monographs*, 50(4), 321-341.

Pressing, J. (1988). Improvisation, methods and models. In J. A. Sloboda (Ed.), *Generative processes in music: The psychology of performance, improvisation and composition* (pp. 129-178). Oxford: Clarendon Press.

Pressing, J. (1998). Psychological constraints on improvisational expertise and communication. In B. Nettl & M. Russell (Eds.), *In the course of performance:*

Studies in the world of musical improvisation (pp. 47-67). Chicago: University of Chicago Press.

Solomon, L. (1986). Improvisation II. *Perspectives of New Music*, 24(2), 224-235.

Sudnow, D. (Ed.) (1978). *Ways of the hand: The organization of improvised conduct*. Cambridge, MA: Harvard University Press.

Ward, T. B., Smith, S. M. & Finke, R. A. (1999). Creative cognition. In R. J. Sternberg (Ed.), *Handbook of creativity* (pp. 189-212). Cambridge: Cambridge University Press.

Weick, K. E. (1998). Introduction essay: Improvisation as a mindset for organizational analysis. *Organization Science*, 9(5), 543-555.

Weick, K. E. (1999). The aesthetic of imperfection in orchestras and organizations. In M. P. Cunha & C. A. Marques (Eds.), *Readings in organization science: Organizational change in a changing context* (pp. 166-184). Lisbon: ISPA.

Chapter 9

Music therapy: a resource for creativity, health and well-being across the lifespan

Leslie Bunt

9.1 Introduction

Music contains potential capacities to engage an individual or a group in therapeutically creative and socially communicative processes. To begin, explanation of some of the terminology in this chapter's title may be helpful. 'Resource' is used in its fullest holistic sense, demonstrating how music therapy can provide a child or adult with a full range of actions and potentialities across various domains defined thus: 'Music therapy is the use of sounds and music within an evolving relationship between client/patient and therapist to support and develop physical, mental, social, emotional and spiritual well-being' (Bunt & Hoskyns, 2002, pp. 10-11). The 'creativity' within such a resource is fundamental to engagement with processes within music therapy, contributing to a child's or adult's ongoing development of self and identity (MacDonald et al., 2002). 'Health' is construed not solely in relation to sickness but to an ongoing process and an individual's search for meaning in the world. Involvement in music, particularly improvisation, can contribute to the development of this flexible identity as well as being a resource closely linked to an individual's quality of life (Ruud, 1998). 'Well-being' is likewise construed as part of an ongoing process and balanced continuum with qualities including: 'interpersonal contact...a sense of community...fostering of a sense of self...transcendence or the loss of a sense of time...a balance of activity and relaxation' (Boyce-Tillman, 2000, p. 14). We can add pleasure, power, release, enjoyment and fun, qualities often reported regarding music therapy sessions.

While emphasizing this broad notion of creativity and ongoing balanced processes within health and well-being we must be mindful that many children and adults coming to music therapy are living with profound health problems, disabilities and difficulties, facing daily issues of struggle, loss and pain. Music therapy can contribute to how an individual adapts and copes with each unique situation.

9.2 Examples from practice and some theoretical underpinnings

In any music therapy session there will be the potential for a creative meeting to occur within the music, both client and therapist alike testing out new ways of acting and being (Bruscia, 1998). Music therapists Mércèdes Pavlicevic and Sandra Brown discovered that, in contrast to improvising together as two musicians, when exploring the roles of music therapist and client there were different ways of relating: 'it was not the music that dictated the improvisation, but how we experienced the other person, the client, in the music' (Pavlicevic, 1997, pp. 66-67). This kind of evolving relationship with a therapist contains and supports the client (or patient in some contexts) across the various domains as mentioned above.

While the relationship through the music is central to music therapy, theoretical links have also been made with other disciplines including psychology, psychotherapy, neurology and sociology. Some common theoretical concepts will be used to underpin briefly the following examples to illustrate three different social contexts for the work. These examples are illustrations of only some of the creative play and interactions that might take place in a music therapy encounter. Parallels between a child's curiosity in sounds, exploratory play and creative improvised music-making will be illustrated in the first two examples. In both of these and the following adult group example the emphasis will not be on final musical products but on socially communicative, psychological and contextually related processes. These three examples will also be referred to in later sections describing the evolution of the profession and as examples of stages in the development of music therapy research.

9.2.1 Early musical patterning

The context for the first example is hospital-based. The music therapist was part of an interdisciplinary child development team that included paediatric specialists in physiotherapy, occupational therapy, speech and language therapy and social work, working alongside a consultant paediatrician.

Baby A was referred to the team at six weeks for an assessment, given concerns that *in utero* a history of maternal alcohol abuse might have caused some brain damage (foetal alcohol abuse syndrome). Given the complexities surrounding her early history A had spent her first days in a specialist baby unit, being put up for fostering and potential adoption soon after birth. The following descriptions are drawn from video films of sessions and discussions with the staff team and A's foster mother who gave consent for the material to be presented in case studies.

A became very distressed and tense when handled by members of the team and her foster parents, and this was creating difficulties in establishing any early patterns of communication and secure attachments. She appeared to settle and become calmer when surrounded by sound, for example searching for the source when a pair of bright Indian bells was sounded. Given A's curiosity in the world of sound it was proposed that the music therapist work with the physiotherapist for an intensive series of joint sessions (two per week) initially to provide a musical frame for encouraging a range of physical movements, for example rising and falling vocal phrases to mirror A being helped to sit up and return to lying down and the use of a sustained pulse to reflect the pace of any of her movements. As A became more relaxed, secure and trusting she began to initiate more vocal and movement gestures. By six months she would track the sounds of instruments as they moved across her line of vision; reach out to explore the instruments with both hands, for example a small drum placed in front of her; indicate with a vocal sound when she wanted a particular sound to occur; and vocalize in small bursts of sound in the gaps between short melodic phrases. Elementary turn-taking dialogues began to be established: short flute melody – A's vocal response – new melody reflecting A's sounds – further reply from A. She also began to sustain her attention in short bursts while attending to longer simple melodies played to her.

The creative process expanded when the various activities were picked up and developed regularly by members of her foster family. This use of sounds and music to support social and emotional development in a very collaborative and holistic approach contributed to a very positive outcome to this early intervention (for more details of this case example see Bunt, 1994, pp. 77-79).

The underpinning here is fundamental, rooted in our human biology and neurological processing. The sounds themselves and the inherent alternating patterns within the short pre-verbal vocal and gestural exchanges (as described above) can become the building blocks for communicative development, linking to all future physical, language, social and emotional development. Much movement and rhythmic interaction anticipates these early vocal exchanges akin to what anthropologist Mary Bateson labelled 'protoconversation' (1979, p. 65). Synchronizing movements with A helped to reduce her physical tension and motivate her in creating her own vocal sounds and communicative gestures. Much research over the last few decades has indicated that babies from their earliest days not only demonstrate inherent self-synchrony in their movements but also make instant connections with the pulse and patterned-based nature of their caregivers' movements, vocalizations and facial expressions (an early review is Schaffer, 1977). It is as if a baby arrives in the world 'hard-wired' for creative communication, with music as a source for engagement, as proposed in developmental psychologist Colwyn Trevarthen's hypothesis of a 'fundamental intrinsic motive pulse...generated in the human brain' (2002, p. 25). After extensive analysis of audio recordings of mothers interacting with their young babies, Trevarthen's research colleague, the musician Stephen Malloch, proposed a theory of 'communicative musicality' which 'consists of the elements pulse, quality and narrative – those attributes of human communication, which are particularly exploited in music, that allow co-ordinated companionship to arise' (1999-2000, p. 32). Trevarthen's and Malloch's ongoing collaboration has provided a fundamental theoretical underpinning for music therapy practice (Malloch & Trevarthen, 2009; Trevarthen & Malloch, 2000). They also built on research that demonstrates that this interactive 'dance' between child and adult is very much two-way with both partners establishing and enjoying these closely interconnected and shared 'narratives' of emotionally expressive activity, as was demonstrated between A and the music therapist. These narrative episodes can be described using all the musical parameters of 'pulse, tempo, rhythm, accent, stress, loudness, silence, pitch and melody' (Bunt & Hoskyns, 2002, p. 71). A repertoire of shared meanings over time can thus be established.

9.2.2 Tuning in to the child

Seeing A at such an early age meant that possible difficulties in timing reactions, gross movement and potential communication problems could be addressed before any of these patterns became firmly established. The members of the team were able to work with the foster parents in creating activities to maximize A's potential across all aspects of her development.

Timing is also central to the next example. This setting is a community-based music therapy centre (see section 9.5 for more details of the registration of music therapists in the UK).

Paul (not his real name) attended with his nursery nurse for blocks of weekly half-hour music therapy sessions after referral by his paediatrician when 3 years old until he began full-time schooling just before his fifth birthday. He was diagnosed as being on the autistic spectrum, having difficulties in communication and forming relationships, speech and language delay, repetitive play and a need for keeping sameness (Wing, 1993). Short descriptions of some of his musical play are taken from sessions towards the beginning, middle and end of the music therapy process with changes in details being made to maintain anonymity.

At the start of one of the early sessions Paul explores the boundaries of the room, which contains a drum and cymbal, a large xylophone, some wind chimes on a stand, a box of smaller percussion instruments and an upright piano. He plays a few sounds by tapping the drum, makes a sweeping gesture across the wind chimes, moves past the cymbal and spins it briefly. The music therapist accompanies Paul's explorations with quiet and sustained piano chords, aiming to link together his musical fragments. The piano music is kept as unobtrusive as possible so as not to contribute to any increase in Paul's level of arousal and excitement. He is not interested in the box of smaller instruments, returns to spinning the cymbal and is joined by the therapist. Together more side-by-side interactive play on this preferred object is developed, spinning and then tapping the cymbal in turn. In this way Paul's repetitive spinning of a hard object was used as a creative kind of bridge to more shared and softer indirect communication.

Six months later Paul has become more accustomed to the setting and a repertoire of shared musical activities has been established. Early in a session from this period he vocalizes on a range of vowel sounds using his characteristic descending minor third (F-D). This is picked up on the piano and vocally by the therapist and extended into a greeting song that matches the tempo, quality and loudness of Paul's sounds. He appears to recognize that the piano sounds are connected to his sounds and responds to the singing of his name by looking more towards both the therapist and his nursery nurse, with some smiling, especially in the gaps between the phrases. The trainee music therapist, on placement at this time, begins to play sustained D's and A's as a drone on her violin. She also matches some of Paul's vocalizations with descending glissandi. Paul appears attracted by the sounds, moves across to the violin, sitting in front of the trainee while she plays. He takes the bow and moves it across the strings in a clear focused movement. He holds the trainee's wrist as they bow together. He seems very aware of the way that the speed and weight of gestures create sounds of different qualities and energies. He spontaneously vocalizes in synchrony with the gestures. He stands up, touches and then plucks the strings. He then sits again and is very still and attentive while the trainee plays the violin to him.

A further six months have elapsed and Paul is preparing to start school when he will continue with weekly music therapy with the school's visiting music therapist. After a preliminary exploration of the room at the start of a later session Paul takes the two drum sticks offered by his nursery nurse and, responding to her encouragement, plays the large drum for a succession of his most extended episodes of engaged play to date. His whole body seems to be moving in synchrony with his drumming as he looks towards the music therapist who supports his playing with strong and rhythmic piano playing. This then moves into another favourite musical activity, taking turns to roll a rainstick across the floor from one person to the other. There is a feeling here of more confident co-created play and the beginnings of more sustained direct communication with another person.

The ongoing interactions between child and caregiver/therapist allow the child to explore an emerging sense of self. These take place within the evolving context of a relationship and, in the context of music, a shared creative encounter with another, all without emphasis on words. Daniel Stern (1985) has explored how a child develops a sense of self through these kinds of interpersonal interactions, beginning with these non-verbal levels. Some of Paul's difficulties in timing his responses, in being able to take control of his actions and in differentiating between his world and the world of the other might relate to what Stern calls the development of a 'core self' (1985, pp. 69-123; Wigram et al., 2002, p. 86). Paul also presented difficulties in recognizing which emotions were part of his own internal experience and which were part of others around him, relating to Stern's development of the 'subjective self' (1985, pp. 124-161; Wigram et al., 2002, p. 86).

In Paul's case it was clear that by tuning in to his tempo and specific way of exploring the instruments the music therapist was able to meet him at his level of play and to build the creative evolution of the interactions from this point of contact. This relates to Stern's notion of 'affect attunement' (1985, pp. 138-161), which is not simply the adult imitating the child's gesture but attempting to 'read' empathically the feelings that lie behind any gestures (in the early sessions Paul's short bursts of fragmented playing and single gestures). The therapist vocalized or played an instrument incorporating similar levels of loudness and duration to Paul's sounds yet also adding a different musical response, often including a slight extension to the length of sounds. Stern points out that these 'attunements' can take place across different modalities, for example, as in this case, a child's drum sound matched by an adult's piano sounds. At the start of the middle session Paul appeared able to recognize his own sound world both as part of the therapist's response and also as something new. He began to incorporate some of the therapist's responses and aspects of the joint activity into his own play and interactions.

For children such as Paul, where problems in communication and some lack of both self and interactional synchrony are potentially isolating, 'the engagement of their musicality by another can be a lifeline to human sociality' (Malloch & Trevarthen, 2009, p. 6). Pavlicevic (1997) has drawn on both Trevarthen's and Stern's work in her notion of 'Dynamic Form', bringing together both the personal/emotional and musical. The fundamental nature of 'communicative musicality' and processes in synchronizing with both self and other can be observed within the musical flow of a session. When problems in communication occur music therapists can observe their musical correspondences. They not only observe and 'read' any problems in communication but, through interacting using a range of musical responses and resources, can contribute to processes of 'musical repair' (Ansdell & Pavlicevic, 2005, p. 195).

Psychoanalyst Donald Winnicott (1974) examined the way that a child begins to use toys and other objects to explore creatively the intermediate states between 'me' and 'not me', 'self' and 'other'. This transition and separation stage is a delicate one, and for children on the autistic spectrum who need to learn that what is outside of their skin boundary is not part of them it is even more fragile and difficult Tustin (1992). In Paul's case we can observe how he used the violin as a means for exploring the immediate playful environment outside of himself. The violin (and later the rainstick) was also used as a vehicle for indirect communication with another person without the overwhelming and potentially too arousing experience of direct communication. It seemed that the violin could appear both part of Paul and part of the outside world, a transitional object in a Winnicottian sense (Winnicott, 1974). As in Winnicott's explorations of a child's use of a special blanket or teddy bear, the violin existed in this transitional space between subjective and objective worlds. It also involved the subjective play of another. As observed in a child's play the transitional object is invested in all manner of feelings as in the way Paul explored a range of different creative ways of exploring the use of the bow, the strings and the violin itself.

As a means of drawing together the links being developed between creativity, development of self and attunement the psychoanalyst Kenneth Wright writes:

> Attunement is a key concept in understanding creativity for several reasons: first, it enlarges our conception of what it means to get something back in a transformed and enlivening way; second, it clearly reveals the structure of such an interaction; third, it offers a glimpse of how such an interaction might strengthen the foundations of the self and enhance the sense of personal vitality; and fourth, it offers a model for later kinds of interaction with a similar function, not least the process of artistic creation. (2009, p. 68)

9.2.3 The development of social processes and a group's sense of cohesion

The context for the final example is a centre for cancer care where people living with cancer attend a one-off music therapy group as part of a residential programme of therapies and consultations. The session occurs at the midpoint of the week's programme. To protect anonymity the following description is an amalgamation of material from different weeks.

A group of eight adults assemble for their 90-minute music therapy session. The music therapist begins by inviting each member to choose an instrument as a form of introduction. Group members play their chosen instrument and describe verbally any associations with the sounds. These might be connections with aspects of the natural world or to specific memories of people and places. Some share how they are feeling; others feel comfortable just playing; one would prefer it if the group could all play together. The therapist begins to play a gentle heartbeat pulse on a drum as a means of introducing some sense of structured support and gradually the members of the group create overlapping improvised musical patterns. One member wishes to play faster and changes the tempo and there are further variations in tempo and loudness as other members of the group initiate changes. There is a palpable increase in energy in the room and a move from individual exploration of chosen instruments to more listening and responding to each other. After this first improvisation one or two members comment that they felt their individual sounds were drowned out. The therapist invites them to play to each other and for other members to join the mood created by these interactive exchanges. A gradual sense of playing as a group emerges. More words are shared to describe the feelings evoked by this second group improvisation. Connections are made to the rapidly changing feelings of living with cancer and the metaphor of the journey of a river in all its different moods is suggested as a way of articulating and releasing some of these feelings. Each group member selects a range of instruments to represent the various stages of the river's journey. The music starts tentatively and quietly, gathers momentum, moves to a loud and chaotic climax before evening out with long flowing melodies and a resultant feeling of expansion and calm. Spontaneous verbal comments occur, making connections between the music and the diverse feelings: sadness, fear, confusion, frustration, anger and an ongoing search for acceptance and peace. The therapist suggests some listening as a way to close the session. After checking out individual musical preferences the slow movement of Bach's *Concerto for two violins* is proposed, music that has both a sense of predictability and echoes of the quiet undulations at the end of the river improvisation. The group members are invited to recline in their comfortable chairs, close their eyes, take some deep relaxing breaths, focus on the quiet and expansive feelings that accompanied the end of the previous improvisation and begin to listen to the music. After a final round of comments relating to the feelings and associations evoked by the music and whole session it is time to end.

Supporting theory now shifts from one-to-one to a group-based perspective. Irvin Yalom, a leading group psychotherapist, has identified several core 'therapeutic factors' in group work (Yalom & Leszcz, 2005). These can be viewed in microcosm in this amalgamated example, even though it was a one-off group. The factors include:

- 'instillation of hope': demonstrated once the group members felt sufficiently comfortable to touch the instruments and confident in the knowledge that there was no right or wrong way of playing, facilitating creative and playful exploration that could be potentially beneficial to all;
- 'universality': demonstrated by the way that sharing of problems and making music together, including joint negotiation of discovery of the creative potential of the various instruments, contributed to bringing a sense of unity to the group;
- 'altruism': demonstrated by the sense of care and concern shown by the members of the group for each other, playing for each other and agreeing on a common metaphor for the final improvisation;
- 'development of socializing techniques', 'imitative behaviour', 'interpersonal learning': all demonstrated through the non-verbal nature of transaction via the musical structures through group members exploring novel ways of playing, of interacting and of learning from each other and from the very experience of creating music together;
- 'group cohesiveness': demonstrated by instantaneous music-making, by the group listening experience and the sustained silences that brought people together after both improvising and listening;
- 'catharsis': demonstrated by the venting of a wide range of feelings, both difficult and positive ones, particularly during the final theme-based improvisation, the group members feeling able to risk such explorations within the safety provided by the therapist, other members of the group and the whole setting (developed from Bunt, 1994, pp. 26-29; Yalom & Leszcz, 2005, pp. 1-2).

Bruscia's elaborations on the changes and growth from 'intrapersonal' and 'intramusical' perspectives (the individual explorations of the instruments at the start of this example) to more 'interpersonal' and 'intermusical' ones (playing to and for each other and the group improvisations) (1998, pp. 127-128) are further contributions in understanding how creative and social processes are framed in group music therapy. The responses during this example indicate the different 'connections' people make between emotions and music (Juslin & Sloboda, 2001, pp. 91-96; Juslin & Sloboda, 2010). There were the individual 'associative connections' between the sounds of particular instruments either while improvising or listening, 'iconic connections' when musical elements were linked to an external event as in the 'river' improvisation and 'intrinsic connections' when links were made (both while improvising and listening) between the group members' emotions 'and both surface and deep structural aspects of the music' (Bunt & Pavlicevic, 2001, p. 185).

Within the contained boundaries of time and space in this session the members of this group therefore created something new, ideas emerging within a socially interactive process, 'both as a means to connect with others and to share expressively significant ideas' (Young, 2005, p. 291).

The creative nature of music, in particular improvisation, is central to all three case examples. Aspects of Malloch and Trevarthen's 'communicative musicality' and emerging individual and group musical and creative identity are fundamental to all three. Each example can be underpinned by different theoretical perspectives linking with developmental, psychological, psychotherapeutic or social processes. At the heart of all three examples are emotional connections to music made by the children and adults, facilitated by the attendant yet musically active music therapist.

9.3 Socio-cultural context

These three case examples were embedded in different socio-cultural contexts. Examining the development of music therapy as a profession can be viewed as a case study in itself; the evolution of the profession has adapted to shifting social and cultural contexts. At root, music's connection to healing and medical practices has been observed since time immemorial. Historically the use of music as a healing force has been described within the magical, mythological, religious, philosophical and scientific frameworks of different periods (Bunt, 1994; Gouk, 2000; Horden, 2000; Wigram et al., 2002). But it was not until the middle of the twentieth century, while addressing the rehabilitation needs of returning US veterans from the Second World War, that the profession of music therapy began to take shape. In order to move beyond the general assumptions that listening to live music could be beneficial for patients, challenges were made to musicians to undertake further training and to justify perceived outcomes across a range of physical, emotional, cognitive and social parameters. Training and professional associations become established, firstly in the United States. In the UK the first training course was established in 1968, the professional association in 1976 and the first governmental career and grading structure in 1982 (Bunt, 1994; Darnley-Smith & Patey, 2003).

Traditionally music therapy has been practised in contexts where major disorders in communication can be found. Music therapy began to develop an early presence within large institutions for adults with learning difficulties and mental health issues and in special schools for children with wide-ranging learning difficulties and behavioural problems. In 2006 a survey of music therapists carried out by the UK-based charity MusicSpace Trust (with funding from the government's Department of Health) indicated that these were still the major areas of practice (MusicSpace Trust, 2007). The areas that ranked highest in percentage of total hours of work with adults and children per week were learning difficulties, autistic spectrum disorders, mental health issues and emotional and behavioural difficulties. There were indications of more work developing in the areas of neurology, cancer and palliative care and preventative work in mainstream schools. Preventative and crisis intervention work in mainstream schools was also noted in another survey of therapists employed by MusicSpace, alongside work with children with attention deficit hyperactivity disorder (Bunt, 2006).

Such developments in practice have occurred alongside underpinning by theories drawn from medical, behavioural, psychotherapeutic and humanistic approaches (Ruud, 1980). Recent challenges have emerged to situate music therapy outside of the boundaried private space of hospital ward or specialist unit in more community-based social contexts (Stige & Aarø, 2011). There were aspects of this pattern observed in the three examples above.

Some of the original pioneers of music therapy were deeply committed to this more community-based aspect of music therapy, which is currently being re-assessed with the creative approaches that form Community Music Therapy, reframing music therapy within 'musical community' (Pavlicevic & Ansdell, 2004). Connections have been made with so-called 'new musicology', particularly Christopher Small's formulation of 'musicking', a creative act where all manner of relationships are set up between sounds and people (Ansdell, 2004; Small, 1998). Further links have been made with sociologist Tia de Nora's explorations of how the creative resources within music can be used by individuals in everyday life (De Nora, 2000). Her work mirrors increasing shifts within music therapy practice to explore how a whole range of music from different cultures can be used not only 'in the service of human communication' but also 'in the service of human collaboration' as a means to build communities (Pavlicevic & Ansdell, 2009, p. 362).

9.4 Some key research findings

By returning to the three case examples central to this chapter some patterns in the development of music therapy research can be highlighted, mirroring some of the shifts in the social and cultural context explored in the previous section. A strong physiological and developmental research base has already been noted in the combined music therapy and physiotherapy approach with Baby A. Exploring how listening to different kinds of stimulating and relaxing music influenced changes in such areas as respiration, heart rate, electrical resistance of the skin and muscle tone contributed greatly to the early acceptance of music therapy, particularly in the United States (Bunt, 1994; Ruud, 1980; Wigram et al., 2002). Meta-analyses and reviews of the use of music in medical and dental contexts have been carried out and the emergence of a whole body of research on the cognitive neuroscience of music has begun to inform music therapy practice (Peretz & Zatorre, 2003; Standley, 1995). For example, Michael Thaut has made major contributions in the understanding of the relationship between neural processing and the timing of a range of motor functions. His research has demonstrated how music therapy can be used effectively not only with children but also to assist the rehabilitation of adult patients who have gait disorders resulting from Parkinson's disease, stroke, traumatic brain injury or the effects of ageing. 'Rhythmic Auditory Stimulation' has helped in the recovery of more stable walking patterns for these groups of patients (Thaut, 2005). The popular writings of the neurologist Oliver Sacks (2007) have done much to bring these positive contributions into public consciousness.

The requirement to indicate the impact of the work and for the focus to be on measurable outcomes has increasingly become a feature of music therapy research, especially so given the current external pressures of evidence-based practice (Edwards, 2002, 2005; Pavlicevic et al., 2009). Some of the author's early research began to address issues of outcome in a series of interrelated studies with young children with learning difficulties. Time-based measures and video analysis were used to compare periods of individual music therapy with no music therapy and the further control of play sessions with a well-known adult. Significant results were found in the development of vocal sounds and turn-taking. There were also positive increases in the amount of looking towards the adult, the 'child's imitative skills and ability to initiate an activity' (Bunt, 2003, p. 187).

Music therapy for children on the autistic spectrum has continued to be an important focus both in practice (as in the example of Paul) and in research. One systematic review of studies in this area has been accepted by the Cochrane Collaboration, a database established to collate evidence from randomized controlled trials (RCTs). The review is based on three studies on music therapy for autistic spectrum disorder where daily music therapy for one week indicated that music therapy might improve these children's communication skills (Gold et al., 2006). The review called for more research and recently Jinah Kim carried out a small scale RCT, finding 'significant evidence supporting the value of music therapy in promoting social, emotional and motivational development in children with autism' (Kim et al., 2009, p. 389).

Within music therapy there is also a developing tradition of qualitative research, mixed-methods and more arts-based approaches (Wheeler, 2005). In relation to our third case example a series of interrelated studies began to address the question of how engagement with the group music therapy session may be beneficial for people living with cancer. The first stage involved a counsellor who explored the constructs emerging from individual responses to the question 'Music and Us?' posed before and after the music therapy session. This was carried out across six groups, similar to the case example. A main finding was the shift from pre-session words describing the individual effects of music, for example 'relaxing', 'energising', to post-session words describing the effect of taking part in the group, for example 'group togetherness' and 'communication' (Bunt & Marston-Wyld, 1995, p. 48). There were also comments relating to temporarily transcending pain while engaged in the music.

The second stage used a mixed-methods approach to explore questions relating to experiences in both improvisation and listening sessions. Results arose from both physiological and psychological data, alongside quotes relating to the actual experience of the participants. Physiological data from a limited sample of nine participants included increases in salivary immunoglobulin A (a possible indicator of immunity) after one listening session. Standardized psychological tests indicated a decrease in tension and energy after the listening and a corresponding increase in energy and sense of well-being after improvisation sessions for 29 participants (Burns et al., 2001).

The third stage was grounded in a qualitative approach and involved 23 lengthy telephone interviews carried out by research colleagues after the group sessions. This stage included positive results, but 'framed by personal biographies...situated within socially constructed notions of aesthetics' and cultural and musical identity (Daykin et al., 2007, p. 349). For example, a sense of creativity was found to be important but 'choice and enrichment' were contrasted with how interviewees related the 'limitation and disempowerment' connected with their cancer diagnosis (Daykin et al., 2007, p. 364). There was much discussion as to whether music was both 'good' and 'meaningful', often with comparisons being made to different styles of music. Links were made with personal biographies and the notion of 'being musical' or not. Concepts of 'talent' and personal biography came together at times with the session being a place where such notions could be explored. For example, the theme of 'latent creativity' was quite common, with some participants keen to re-introduce music into their lives. For these participants music was able to foster a sense of 'hope', transcendence and looking-forward, with effects noted after the session. However, contrastingly, for some the experience evoked feelings of 'regret and loss', particularly relating to earlier musical experiences or unhappy musical memories. Such results emphasized the sensitivity and care needed to be shown by the music therapist facilitating such a group experience (for further elaboration of the themes, see Daykin et al., 2007).

9.5 Implications for policy and practice

The profession of music therapy can be proud of its achievements in just over half a century. In the UK a major development occurred in 1997 when the profession worked with art and drama therapy to become registered as creative therapies within the Health Professions Council, moving towards further standardization and regulation of practice and protecting legally both the public and standards of proficiency and practice (Bunt & Hoskyns, 2002).

Coupled with this regulatory move have been continuing calls for justification, cost-effectiveness and demonstration of clinical impact and outcome. In spite of being a relatively small profession music therapists have embraced these challenges with quite a substantial number of published RCTs, systematic reviews and meta-analyses. A recent breakthrough for people living in England and Wales is that music therapy is now included with the other registered arts therapies in the National Institute for Health and Clinical Excellence (NICE) guidelines to be considered for 'all people with schizophrenia, particularly for the alleviation of negative symptoms' (NICE, 2009, 1.3.4.3, p. 21).

Jane Edwards (2005) has pointed out that both music therapy trainees and professional practitioners need to have working knowledge of studies that underpin different areas of practice and to be aware of the pros and cons of different kinds of evaluation and research procedures. But there are problems if future policy decisions require dogged allegiance to the RCT and clinical trial. The nature of a small profession presents difficulties in recruiting large enough samples and adequate resources. Individual responses to music, the personal styles of different therapists, the wide-ranging variations within the populations with which music therapists work and the constraints of intervention protocols are all issues to surmount. Edwards also cautions about keeping the research 'relevant to the real-world context in which music therapy is practised' (2005, p. 296 and see also Edwards, 2002).

There are other ways of indicating evidence. This was echoed by Professor Sir Michael Rawlins (2008), the Chairman of NICE, who has argued for a wider range of approaches to analyse evidence and that alongside RCTs decisions could be made, for example, from well-run observational studies in relation to the benefits and potential risks involved with any therapeutic intervention. And music therapists may not be the most appropriately trained people to carry out this kind of research. There are other colleagues who have a whole range of appropriate research skills with whom it is both challenging and rewarding to collaborate to aid development of policy.

The case examples in this chapter have charted some of the current range of music therapy practice. Exploring the continuum of the private boundaried therapy space to more community-based and less boundaried contexts has implications for further dialogue and collaborative research with, among others, sociologists, musicologists, social psychologists and anthropologists (Pavlicevic & Ansdell, 2009). It has been argued that there is a potential danger of the profession's isolation if music therapy continues to concentrate on medical, biological and psychological models of care and practice without addressing the wider social, political, organizational, musical and cultural processes within which the work is embedded (Procter, 2004).

We need to continue to tell the creative stories of the people with whom we work and our own stories as musicians working in these different contexts, drawing from alternative notions of cultural, musical and social capital. We need to keep the stories and the vibrant relationships alive in our practices and to celebrate the synthesis of form and structure and freedom and expression in the work. We can leave the final word to one of the UK's pioneers of music therapy, Juliette Alvin, who in her last television interview (BBC, 1983) considered that the development of music therapy would very much depend on the development of music, which, after all, she noted, connects us to whom we are as human beings.

Acknowledgement

Some of the material for this chapter has been developed from a presentation to a conference on Music Health and Happiness, Royal Northern College of Music, Manchester, November 2008.

References

Ansdell, G. (2004). Rethinking music and community: Theoretical perspectives in support of community music therapy. In M. Pavlicevic & G. Ansdell (Eds.), *Community music therapy* (pp. 65-90). London: Jessica Kingsley.

Ansdell, G. & Pavlicevic, M. (2005). Musical companionship, musical community: Music therapy and the process and value of musical communication. In D. Miell, R. MacDonald & D. J. Hargreaves (Eds.), *Musical communication* (pp. 193-213). Oxford: Oxford University Press.

Bateson, M. C. (1979). 'The epigenesis of conversational interaction': A personal account of research development. In M. Bullowa (Ed.), *Before speech: The beginnings of interpersonal communication* (pp. 63-77). Cambridge: Cambridge University Press.

Boyce-Tillman, J. (2000). *Constructing musical healing: The wounds that sing*. London: Jessica Kingsley.

British Broadcasting Corporation (1983). *Music as therapy: Part 2 of The music child*, a television documentary produced by Keith Alexander for BBC Scotland.

Bruscia, K. E. (1998). *Defining music therapy* (2nd edition). Gilsum, NH: Barcelona.

Bunt, L. (1994). *Music therapy: An art beyond words*. London: Routledge.

Bunt, L. (2003). Music therapy with children: A complementary service to music education?, *British Journal of Music Education*, 20(2), 179-195.

Bunt, L. (2006). Music therapy for children. In G. E. McPherson (Ed.), *The child as musician: A handbook of musical development* (pp. 273-288). Oxford: Oxford University Press.

Bunt, L. & Hoskyns, S. (Eds.) (2002). *The handbook of music therapy*. Hove: Brunner-Routledge.

Bunt, L. & Marston-Wyld, J. (1995). Where words fail music takes over: A collaborative study by a music therapist and a counselor in the context of cancer care. *Music Therapy Perspectives*, 13(1), 46-50.

Bunt, L. & Pavlicevic, M. (2001). Music and emotion: Perspectives from music therapy. In P. N. Juslin & J. A. Sloboda (Eds.), *Music and emotion: Theory and research* (pp. 181-201). Oxford: Oxford University Press.

Burns, S. J., Harbuz, M. S., Hucklebridge, F. & Bunt, L. (2001). A pilot study into the therapeutic effects of music therapy at a cancer care center. *Alternative Therapies*, 7(1), 48-56.

Darnley-Smith, R. & Patey, H. M. (2003). *Music therapy*. London: Sage.

Daykin, N., McClean, S. & Bunt, L. (2007). Creativity, identity and healing: Participants' accounts of music therapy in cancer care. *Health: An Interdisciplinary Journal for the Social Study of Health, Illness and Medicine*, 11(3), 349-370.

De Nora, T. (2000). *Music in everyday life*. Cambridge: Cambridge University Press.

Edwards, J. (2002). Using the evidence based medicine framework to support music therapy posts in healthcare settings. *British Journal of Music Therapy*, 16(1), 29-34.

Edwards, J. (2005). Possibilities and problems for evidence-based practice in music therapy. *The Arts in Psychotherapy*, 32(4), 293-301.

Gold, C., Wigram, T. & Elefant, C. (2006). Music therapy for autistic spectrum disorder. *Cochrane Database of Systematic Reviews 2006*, Issue 2. Art. No. CD004381. DOI: 10.1002/14651858.CD004381.pub2.

Gouk, P. (2000). *Musical healing in cultural contexts*. Aldershot: Ashgate.

Horden, P. (2000). *Music as medicine: The history of music therapy since antiquity*. Aldershot: Ashgate.

Juslin, P. N. & Sloboda. J. A. (Eds.) (2001). *Music and emotion: Theory and research*. Oxford: Oxford University Press.

Juslin, P. N. & Sloboda, J. A. (Eds.) (2010). *Handbook of music and emotion: Theory, research, applications*. Oxford: Oxford University Press.

Kim, J., Wigram, T. & Gold, Ch. (2009). Emotional, motivational and interpersonal responsiveness of children with autism in improvisational music therapy. *Autism*, 13(4), 389-409.

MacDonald, R. A. R., Hargreaves, D. J. & Miell, D. (2002). *Musical identities*. Oxford: Oxford University Press.

Malloch, S. N. (1999-2000). Mothers and infants and communicative musicality. *Musicae Scientiae*, Special Issue: Rhythms, Musical Narrative, and the Origins of Human Communication, 29-57.

Malloch, S. & Trevarthen, C. (2009). Musicality: Communicating the vitality and interests of life. In S. Malloch & C. Trevarthen (Eds.), *Communicative musicality: Exploring the basis of human companionship* (pp. 1-11). Oxford: Oxford University Press.

The MusicSpace Trust (2007). *A systematic review of the current provision of music therapy services carried out by registered music therapists in the UK*, currently available for download from www.musicspace.org.uk (accessed 11 February 2011).

National Institute for Health and Clinical Excellence (2009). *Schizophrenia: Core interventions in the treatment and management of schizophrenia in adults in primary and secondary care. NICE clinical guideline 82*. Developed by the National Collaborating Centre for Mental Health – see www.nice.org.uk/nicemedia/live/11786/43608/43608.pdf (accessed 2 January 2011).

Pavlicevic, M. (1997). *Music therapy in context: Music, meaning and relationship.* London: Jessica Kingsley.

Pavlicevic, M. & Ansdell, G. (Eds.) (2004). *Community music therapy.* London: Jessica Kingsley.

Pavlicevic, M. & Ansdell, G. (2009). Between communicative musicality and collaborative musicing: A perspective from community music therapy. In S. Malloch & C. Trevarthen (Eds.), *Communicative musicality: Exploring the basis of human companionship* (pp. 357-376). Oxford: Oxford University Press.

Pavlicevic, M., Ansdell, G., Procter, S. & Hickey, S. (2009). *Presenting the evidence* (2nd edition). The Nordoff Robbins Research Department, available for download from www.nordoff-robbins.org.uk (accessed 11 February 2011).

Peretz, I. & Zatorre, R. (Eds.) (2003). *The cognitive neuroscience of music.* Oxford: Oxford University Press.

Procter, S. (2004). Playing politics: Community music therapy and the therapeutic redistribution of music capital for mental health. In M. Pavlicevic & G. Ansdell (Eds.), *Community music therapy* (pp. 214-230). London: Jessica Kingsley.

Rawlins, M. D. (2008). *De testimonio: On the evidence for decisions about the use of therapeutic interventions. The Harveian Oration of 2008.* London: Royal College of Physicians.

Ruud, E. (1980). *Music therapy and its relationship to current treatment theories.* St. Louis, MO: Magnamusic Baton.

Ruud, E. (1998). *Music therapy: Improvisation, communication and culture.* Gilsum, NH: Barcelona.

Sacks, O. (2007). *Musicophilia, tales of music and the brain.* New York: Picador.

Schaffer, H. R. (Ed.) (1977). *Studies in mother–infant interaction.* London: Academic Press.

Small, Ch. (1998). *Musicking: The meanings of performing and listening.* Hanover, NH: Wesleyan University Press.

Standley, J. (1995). Music as therapeutic intervention in medical and dental treatment: Research and clinical applications. In T. Wigram, B. Saperston & R. West (Eds.), *The art and science of music therapy: A handbook* (pp. 3-22). Chur, Switzerland: Harwood Academic.

Stern, D. (1985). *The interpersonal world of the infant: A view from psychoanalysis and developmental psychology.* London: Academic Press.

Stige, B. & Aarø, L. E. (2011). *Invitation to community music therapy.* New York: Routledge.

Thaut, M. H. (2005). *Rhythm, music and the brain: Scientific foundations and clinical applications.* New York: Routledge.

Trevarthen, C. (2002). Origins of musical identity: Evidence from infancy for musical social awareness. In R. A. R. MacDonald, D. J. Hargreaves & D. Miell (Eds.), *Musical identities* (pp. 21-38). Oxford: Oxford University Press.

Trevarthen, C. & Malloch, S. (2000). The dance of wellbeing: Defining the musical therapeutic effect. *Nordic Journal of Music Therapy*, 9(2), 3-17.

Tustin, F. (1992). *Autistic states in children* (revised edition). New York: Routledge.

Wheeler, B. (2005). *Music therapy research* (2nd edition). Gilsum, NH: Barcelona.

Wigram, T., Pedersen, I. N. & Bonde L. O. (Eds.) (2002). *A comprehensive guide to music therapy*. London: Jessica Kingsley.

Wing, L. (1993). *Autistic continuum disorders: An aid to diagnosis*. London: National Autistic Society.

Winnicott, D. W. (1974). *Playing and reality*. London: Penguin.

Wright, K. (2009). *Mirroring and attunement: Self-realization in psychoanalysis and art*. London: Routledge.

Yalom, I. D. & Leszcz, M. (2005). *The theory and practice of group psychotherapy* (5th edition). New York: Basic Books.

Young, S. (2005). Musical communication between adults and young children. In D. Miell, R. MacDonald & D. J. Hargreaves (Eds.), *Musical communication* (pp. 281-299). Oxford: Oxford University Press.

PART III
Paths for further enquiry

Chapter 10

Action-research on collaborative composition: an analysis of research questions and designs

Gabriel Rusinek

10.1 Introduction

Composing individually or collaboratively in small groups has become an established activity in the national curricula or educational standards of many countries, and a central part in some of them. The term 'composition' here does not refer to the creation of music by professionals in classical or popular genres. Instead, it refers to a pupil-centred learning procedure that seems to facilitate motivation and meaningful music learning, consisting in the non real-time generation of music which is new for the pupils who are generating it. Composition flourished in school music after proposals such as Schafer's in Canada (1965), and Paynter and Aston's in the United Kingdom (1970), which in the 1960s and 1970s aimed at nurturing music education with some of the creative ideas of avant-garde music (for a historical perspective, see Cox, 2004). It was eventually incorporated into mainstream music education, and the increasing awareness of its educational potential has generated an abundant research literature (for accounts from various countries, see Barrett, 1998b; Espeland, 2007; Leung, 2007; Odam, 2000; Odena & Welch, 2007; Rusinek, 2007a; Strand, 2006).

Composing is not always a lonely activity, in spite of the romantic, mythical views of the individual composer that abound among classical music audiences, music curricula and textbooks. Music is frequently composed in collaboration with others in folk and pop music. Moreover, daily exposure to the media has made the image of pop musicians composing collaboratively become part of children and adolescents' out-of-school worlds. In this chapter, views of creativity, of group creativity and of musical creativity will be considered in relation to collaborative composition and its implications as a pupil-centred learning procedure. There are fewer reports documenting research on collaborative composition than on individual composition. Many of the studies were carried out by music educators in educational contexts where they acted as teachers to the pupils or as facilitators. A sample of these reports will be reviewed, describing the creative projects and their research questions and designs. Finally, methodological issues in relation to the value of the knowledge accumulated with this research approach will be discussed, with the aim of assisting future investigations on how pupils interact and develop skills through collaborative composition.

10.2 Learning through collaborative composition

10.2.1 Composing as a creative activity

Inducing pupils to compose implies believing that they can be creative and that one of the aims of schooling must be fostering creativity (for analyses of teachers' or policy-makers' views in different locations, see Leung & McPherson, 2002; Odena, 2001). This is not necessarily the 'historical' or 'big' creativity – or 'Creativity' with a capital letter – displayed by professional artists, scientists or inventors, but 'everyday' or 'small' creativity. Among the many views of what can be considered creative, the *consensual* and the *systemic* are interesting for this discussion. After analysing the interjudge reliability of independent ratings of creative products in many domains, Amabile (1982) concluded that a product or idea is creative if expert observers agree it is creative. According to Csikszentmihalyi's systemic view (1988), those expert observers make up a social field that eventually decides whether the cultural domain will or will not be modified by the variations produced by certain individuals.

Creativity seems to be related to motivation. Research by Hennessey and Amabile (1988) has shown that creative people are intrinsically motivated, and that creativity can be constrained by external pressures. However, some pupils manage to be creative in spite of deadlines, evaluations or rewards, which are external pressures inherent to school contexts. Further research by Hennessey has revealed that enabling extrinsic motivation can even support creativity, because it is the individual's interpretations of the external contingencies that determine 'whether performance will be undermined, enhanced, or remain unchanged' (2003, p. 197).

Learning in groups is commonly thought to foster pupils' motivation and creativity. However, Nemeth and Nemeth-Brown (2003) have found that in certain conditions group interaction can inhibit the individuals' ability to generate creative ideas, for example when they think that those ideas might be met with negative reactions and self-censor them. Hennessey (2003) also observed that creativity can diminish if the group members reduce efforts because there is no expectation of individual accountability for the group's outcome, if their intrinsic task motivation is supplanted by the extrinsic need to appear competent or if they compete among themselves.

Musical creativity (for reviews, see Barrett, 2005; Burnard, 2007; Hickey, 2002; McPherson, 1998; Webster, 1992) in a school context is understood here as a *generative* creativity (Sági & Vitányi, 1988). Different to professional composers' *constructive* creation, pupils generate musical variations through operating intuitively with a small repertoire of musical elements, in the same way people can generate unlimited sentences with a limited repertoire of words

(Chomsky, 1965). Using Csikszentmihalyi's systemic view (1988) to discuss children's musical creativity in spontaneous music-making, Barrett (2005) argued that children themselves were the field when they were the controllers of the setting, for example when making music informally. However, this might not be the case when children compose in a school context. Within Amabile's consensual view, appropriate observers are 'those familiar with the domain in which the product was created or the response articulated' (1996, p. 33). In order to know who appropriate observers in relation to pupil's compositions were, Hickey (2001) applied the consensual assessment technique (Amabile, 1982) and found that music teachers' independent ratings of their creativity were highly correlated, while ratings made by professional composers were not. This suggests that the music teachers were the appropriate observers, and therefore they might constitute the field in a systemic view of school composition.

10.2.2 Composing in groups as a learning procedure

Composition is a learning procedure in tune with main-trend teaching approaches in countries with well-established pupil-centred, constructivist pedagogies. On the contrary, it opposes main-trend approaches in countries with traditional teacher-centred pedagogies – or is considered an innovation at best. In both situations, teachers who include composition proactively in their teaching are in fact acknowledging the importance of creating as a specific mode of musical knowledge (Stubley, 1992), and therefore they expand more traditional approaches to music education limited to just appraising and performing. Composing can be conceptualized as a problem-solving activity (Berkley, 2004; Burnard & Younker, 2004; DeLorenzo, 1989; Wiggins, 1994) and as an aesthetic problem (Barrett, 1998a). Pupils must use their musical skills and understanding, as well as their divergent thinking, to find an appropriate musical solution for an open-end problem – the compositional assignment.

When teaching composition, tensions might appear between process and product. In his study of children composing a 'school opera', Ocaña (2008) observed that although the process was important for himself as a teacher and relatively important for the parents, the children were more concerned with the final product – the public performance of their creation. When researching, however, both focuses are complementary. Barrett (1998a) analysed children's compositional products to comprehend their aesthetic decision-making when it was not evidenced in their verbal responses. On the other hand, Wiggins (1999) observed the verbal and musical interactions that constitute the compositional process as a window to comprehend children's musical thought. Fautley's model of the group composition process (2005) includes an initial confirmatory stage and the generation and exploration of musical ideas, followed by the organization, work-in-progress performance, revision, transformation and modification of those ideas, and sometimes a final performance. In her extensive review, Wiggins (2007) groups the compositional processes in two broad stages: a first stage when musical ideas are generated, including pupils' spontaneous music-making and the exploration of musical elements, and a second one when those ideas are set into context, including their refinement through repetition, development and revision.

When composing in groups, pupils operate in their 'zone of proximal development' assisted by their peers (Vygotsky, 1978). This peer interaction leads to a shared understanding (Rogoff, 1990) of music and to a development of their autonomy. Miell and MacDonald (2000) observed more successful musical collaborations when there was friendship in the groups in their study, because of the high level of mutual engagement facilitated by that friendship. Based on previous research on distributed cognitions (Salomon, 1993), Fautley (2005, p. 44) distinguished two types of interaction within group composition: a *shared* composition, characterized by verbal negotiation, joint planning and 'fitting together' individual thematic materials and instrumental resources, and a *distributed* composition, characterized by a synergy of the individual ideas that through non-verbal explorations cohere into a single unity.

As with music education advocacy in general, there are claims that composition develops skills transferable to other contexts (e.g. Byrne et al., 2001). However, advocacy claims must be considered cautiously, according to Bresler's demythologizing meta-analysis of numerous arts advocacy research papers (2002). Precaution is also suggested by Bowman when he argues that we should stop trying to justify the presence of music education in the school curriculum because of non-musical benefits, in favour of documenting how it 'shows us about the profoundly embodied and socioculturally-situated character of all human knowing and being' (2004, p. 31). Collaborative composing can be viewed under this philosophical perspective, and also under Elliott's praxial contention that, being music not just sound but human interaction *through* sound, the role of music education must be 'inducting students into musical ways of life' (1996, p. 2). The value of collaborative composing, I therefore maintain, is that it lets pupils not only think *in* music (Wiggins, 1999) but think *as* musicians. Pupils' intuitive knowledge becomes apparent, and it does so within an *authentic* learning situation (Brown et al., 1989) because they must face challenges that, at an elementary technical level, are parallel to those faced by professional composers and performers.

10.3 Action-research on collaborative composition

10.3.1 Action-research in music education

Part of the research on collaborative composition has been carried out by teachers in their own classrooms and by lecturers within teacher training programmes, and also by university-based researchers in school projects where they acted as facilitators. These strategies of inquiry (Denzin & Lincoln, 1994) have the particularity that the researchers always act as participant observers, and receive denominations such as 'teacher-research', 'practitioner-research' or 'action-research'. Such terms have subtly different meanings because of the research traditions they derive from. Teacher-research is a genre of practitioner-research, where the teacher – as an educational practitioner – investigates in his or her own classroom. The research carried out by teachers has been criticized (for an early positivist critique, see Hodgkinson, 1957) for possible methodological hindrances such as the danger of teachers' subjectivity not being contrasted or their lack of theoretical and methodological bases. However, it has proved an enormous potential of practical transferability for learning improvement and teachers' professional development.

The term 'action-research' is perhaps a broader concept, which besides teacher-research also includes university–school collaborations, where university-based researchers come into a school setting and co-research with the teachers or themselves become involved in teaching. It was developed in other social sciences with the idea that research had to be carried out not only to understand but also to transform social conditions through recursive 'plan-act-observe-reflect' cycles. Although there are different versions of these cycles, they include identifying the problems, planning an *action*, collecting data systematically to evaluate the action and modifying the plan consequently after reflecting on the data collected (for extensive methodological discussions, see Noffke & Somekh, 2009).

At the first Qualitative Methodologies in Music Education Research Conference held at the University of Illinois in 1994, Roberts encouraged music teachers to engage in research in their own classrooms and with their own agenda in order to improve music education, because external researchers 'seldom really challenge their conclusions in the context in which they are exposed, but rather consider their enterprise finished once the findings are published' (1994, p. 27). Two articles have reviewed the characteristics of the action-research studies in music education carried out since then. Cain (2008) found that the studies in the sample he selected had integrated research and action, were collaborative and had led to powerful learning for the participants, although none accomplished all the methodological principles detailed by Somekh (2006), for example few were cyclical. Strand (2009) reviewed another sample of action-research studies, which focused on the teaching of composition, and analysed the teachers' reports from a narrative viewpoint. She found that the narrations were stories where teaching composition was considered a means, where the processes and products were evaluated taking into account children's viewpoints, and where teachers expressed personal growth and professional transformation.

For this chapter, a sample of nine studies completed since 1994 about collaborative composition was selected in order to include different school locations and contexts, educational levels, compositional tasks and musical media. The reports show research carried out by music educators in their own classrooms, or acting as facilitators in other educational contexts, independently of the denomination they used for the chosen strategy of inquiry (Denzin & Lincoln, 1994). The sample excludes, then, investigations carried out by music educators in their classrooms or elsewhere about *individual* composition, and investigations about any type of composition carried out by external, non-participant observers.

While academics' motivation to undertake research may vary from building educational theory to promoting social change, teachers' main motivation is usually improving their own teaching practices. Thus, being a teacher researcher demands a delicate balance not just between the time spent in teaching and in researching, but between teacher and researcher identities. While in some reports the description of the educative action takes precedence over the analysis of the research data, in others the methodological issues cast a shadow on the teaching itself. Therefore, the description of the projects and of the composition assignments will be considered first, followed by an analysis of the research questions and designs.

10.3.2 The compositional projects

Within the nine reports, two document instrumental composing activities in primary schools (see Table 10.1 for a summary of the nine contexts). Wiggins' project (1994) took place over a period of five months in an American school where she was working as a music teacher. One class of fifth-grade pupils was involved in three composition assignments with classroom instruments during ten sessions of that period, which alternated with sessions dedicated to analytical listening and performing of music that served as stimulus. The first assignment consisted of a piece that 'builds excitement' (Wiggins, 1994, p. 238) through changes of tempo, range and number of voices; the second was a piece with an ABA form with optional introduction, bridge or coda; the third was a variation on a proposed theme to be assembled in a whole-class theme-and-variation composition. Also in an American school where she was teaching, in Hamilton's project (1999) three sixth-grade music classes were involved in composing during a semester using pitched and unpitched percussion instruments, and electronic keyboards. They first improvised and composed based on a chord progression; then they created an 'original opera'; finally they composed a piece using invented notations.

As in Hamilton's dissertation (1999), two other papers document the creation of 'operas' by primary pupils. Hove-Pabst (2002) travelled to a one-room rural school in Wyoming (USA) for two weekly sessions during eight weeks to organize an 'original opera' project. Her role in the project included inducting the creation processes, developing musical skills and conducting the rehearsals and the performance, with the classroom teacher's assistance. The children were involved in writing the story and converting it into a libretto, composing the songs, making the costumes and the scenery, writing publicity and, finally, performing for an audience. In a Spanish state primary school near Madrid where he worked as a music teacher, Ocaña (2008) undertook the challenge of teaching all the subject areas of a fifth-grade class as a generalist, through a one-year 'school opera' project. During the first, preparatory cycle, children composed instrumental pieces with Orff instruments to develop their creative and musical abilities. During the second cycle, the children invented a story and wrote the libretto of the 'opera', composed arias, recitatives, dances and an overture, and prepared the costumes and the scenery. The third cycle was dedicated to the production, including rehearsing, making the publicity and performing in the school for their peers and at a local theatre for the parents and the community.

Table 10.1   The compositional projects and their contexts

Researcher	Country	Context	Compositional project
Wiggins (1994)	USA	Primary school	Instrumental composition (10 sessions for composing out of 31 sessions)
Hamilton (1999)	USA	Primary school	Instrumental improvisation and composition, and an 'original opera' project (a semester)
Hove-Pabst (2002)	USA	Rural school	'Original opera' (16 sessions and a performance); the university-based researcher conducted the creation and rehearsal with the teacher's assistance
Ocaña (2008)	Spain	Primary school	'Original opera' (one school year), the music teacher taught as a generalist
Allsup (2003)	USA	Secondary school	Composition with band and pop-rock instruments (11 weekly sessions); the university-based researcher acted as 'facilitator' within a school instrumental programme
Rusinek (2007b)	Spain	Secondary school	Instrumental composition, to be performed at a local theatre (12 sessions)
Hewitt (2002)	UK	University (teacher education)	20 generalists and 19 specialists created a short piece of music (four hours)
Major (2007)	UK	Secondary school	No project reported (composing activities according to English National Curriculum)
Faulkner (2003)	Iceland	Rural school	No project reported (composing was a regular activity)

Two articles document projects carried out in secondary schools. Allsup's project (2003) involved nine pupils aged 14-17 within a band programme in an American high school. They met for 11 weekly two and half hour sessions to create 'original music', with the researcher as facilitator. The pupils elected to split into two random groups, of which one chose not to use their primary band instruments but to work in a garage band style using electric guitar and bass, synthesized piano and drums. The other group chose to create music for band instruments, in a working style that ranged from classical to jazz. In my own project (Rusinek, 2007b), at a Spanish secondary school, 100 pupils aged 15-17 composed pieces 'of at least two minutes' using pitched and unpitched percussion instruments, and recorders. Each of the four participating ninth-grade classes was divided into three groups, which worked in separate rooms for two weekly 50-minute sessions during six weeks, and finally performed their compositions at a local theatre.

Hewitt's study (2002) was carried out within the context of a teacher training programme at a Scottish university, with 20 'generalist' students – preparing to be primary teachers – and 19 'specialists' – having studied music at university level for at least three years. The task, which they accomplished organized into nine smaller subgroups over four hours, was to bring a non-musical stimulus to the subgroup and then create a short piece of music based on it.

Finally, two among the reviewed papers do not describe any specific project. Major (2007) writes about composing activities framed within the National Curriculum in an English secondary school where she was teaching, but without detailing the characteristics of the assignments. Faulkner (2003) does not detail the assignments either, writing instead about a small rural school for 6-16 year olds in Iceland where he was teaching, and where composing had been a regular activity for many years.

10.3.3 The research questions and designs

In this section, the research questions – sometimes stated as 'aims' of the study and other times as 'themes' or 'issues' – and the research designs are analysed. A first group consists of teachers who investigated in their own classrooms, within the context of a specific project – the 'action' – which is described in the article, and where the research design follows intimately that 'action'. Wiggins (1994) called her strategy 'action-research' and 'classroom inquiry'. She collected data through qualitative methods to observe how 'phenomena related to music cognition, representation of musical ideas, and the role of interaction in musical learning' (Wiggins, 1994, p. 234), previously identified in laboratory settings, manifested in children's learning in a real classroom setting. Two selected 'target children' carried tape recorders with lapel microphones throughout the 31 sessions, while the whole class was also being videotaped because the researcher was working as the teacher of the class. Additional data to the 57 audio recordings and 20 videotapes collected were field notes, interviews with the target children's parents, written papers reflecting work done by the children and papers written by the target children to check their 'typicality' within the class. Triangulation was sought through formal and informal interviews with the target children about the emerging issues and through 'peer debriefing' with four colleagues, who were asked to read the data and criticize her interpretations. The researcher also sought to gain credibility through a prolonged engagement of five months in a ten-month relationship with the children, through persistent observation and through looking intentionally for the refutation of her interpretations with negative cases.

With a similar design but expanded to three classes instead of one, Hamilton (1999) called her investigation an 'ethnographic study' with the author serving 'as teacher-researcher'. She was interested in pupils' learning and in their cognitive processes while composing individually, with partners and in small groups. Her research questions also focused on the role of play and of peer interaction in pupils' learning experiences. Data were collected over 16 weeks. Six target pupils – two in each class – carried micro tape recorders and a video camera recorded the whole class situation. Additional data included artefacts such as the pupils' work and pupil and teacher journals. The data were examined through time allocation analysis, coded event data analysis and musical analysis, and the interpretations were corroborated through triangulation of data sources.

Also as a teacher-researcher, in my own study (Rusinek, 2007b) I tried to comprehend the significance attributed to composing by four classes of secondary pupils, many of whom presented learning difficulties and behaviour problems. I collected data through qualitative methods, including participant observations of the small groups' rehearsals, non-structured individual interviews with 30 pupils, sound recordings of the compositions, video recordings of the rehearsals and concerts, and the examination of pupils' informal preliminary and final scores. The corroboration of the interpretations was sought through triangulation of data sources.

The aim of Ocaña's one-year three-cycle action-research study (2008) was to integrate music as a subject within a fifth-grade curriculum through the creation of a 'school opera'. His research questions focused on what strategies the pupils developed to compose collaboratively, on what expressive resources they developed within the creative process, on how their perspectives towards music as a subject changed when they composed their own pieces and on what educational value and impact on the community an opera project could achieve. He collected data through participant observations, semi-structured individual interviews with 19 pupils, eight parents and four other teachers, and video-stimulated group interviews with the fifth-grade class and with all the school teachers. He also examined the pupils' written materials and compositions, which he fully transcribed for a musical analysis. The corroboration of the interpretations was sought through triangulation of informants, data sources and observers.

At a college level, Hewitt (2002) was interested in examining the differences in processes and products between music graduates and pre-service generalists without music training beyond secondary school level when engaged in a compositional task for small groups. No strategy of inquiry was stated, although from the reading of the article it seems that the author was researching within pre-service programmes at his university. The data were collected through video recordings, group discussions and semi-structured interviews with a small number of students.

A second group in the sample consists of studies that refer retrospectively to group composition activities that took place in a school context, and where the research design did not follow a specific 'action'. Faulkner named his study 'idiographic' and multi-method, and used an assortment of terms to describe the methods, such as qualitative, phenomenological, ethno-musicological and related to grounded theory (2003, p. 104) and to case study (2003, p. 110). In relation to composing experiences his own pupils had had during previous years, he wanted to comprehend their 'personal and psychological perception of composing in the classroom – processes, products, effects, effectiveness, meaning and value – and to examine the significance of social context and social agency' (Faulkner, 2003, p. 104). Data collection, carried out in five stages, consisted of a questionnaire for sixth- to ninth-grade pupils and a written assessment of video portfolios of their own compositions created over six to eight years, and semi-structured interviews with 12 pupils and with two ex-pupils who were aspiring professional musicians. In relation to regular compositional activities taking place in her classroom at the time of the study, Major's three-cycle action-research main issues (2007) were the nature of children's responses when talking about composing work in music lessons, the role of musical vocabulary and conceptual learning as manifest through their talk, and the role of the teacher in nurturing a better quality of talk. She also wanted to know whether children's thinking about and understanding of the music could be more complex than their talk about it, as shown by their musical products. The first cycle involved video-recording one music lesson with her seventh-grade students and another with a colleague's sixth-grade class. The second involved video-recording sixth- and eighth-grade small groups composing, video-stimulated interviews with members of those groups and individual interviews with tenth-grade pupils. The third involved asking four sixth-grade subgroups to demonstrate their compositions to each other and to talk about them without teacher intervention.

A third group of studies in the sample consists of university-based researchers who carried out an educational project in a school – an 'action' – acting as facilitators of the creative processes. In spite of being a participant observer who even provided musical instruction, Hove-Pabst curiously named her strategy of inquiry a 'case study' (2002, p. 98). Her aim was to assess the effectiveness of 'original student opera' as part of an arts education curriculum, in terms of integration of subject matter and relevance to the lives of the pupils. Data collection methods included field notes, informal conversations with the pupils and interviews with two pupils and the classroom teacher. She also gave questionnaires to parents and community members who attended the performance, and compiled children's journal entries.

Allsup (2003) was concerned with the notion of democracy as community-in-the-making, and although this notion is central in the action-research literature, he called his study 'ethnographic' with 'philosophical inquiry, collaborative inquiry, and participant observation' approaches. His aim was to reconceptualize instrumental music programmes at American schools to include 'more opportunities for creativity, self-expression, and cultural relevance' (Allsup, 2003, p. 24). Allsup's questions are both philosophical and pedagogical, focusing on how the participating groups evolve and define themselves through the practice of composing and analysing music, on what the choices reflect or signify, on how the experience might affect individual growth as well as community-making and on how such a project would be congruent with philosophies of democratic education. Data were collected through field notes, interviews, emails and instant messages, and recordings of musical and verbal interactions, and of spontaneous conversations.

10.4 Discussion

The reviewed reports document compositional activities in a variety of geographical locations, including Iceland, the United Kingdom, the United States and Spain. They were carried out in various educational contexts, such as primary urban and rural schools, secondary schools and universities. The educational settings include general music lessons in music classrooms, projects involving other subject areas, instrumental programmes and teacher training programmes. Diverse compositional assignments were carried out within those settings, ranging from instrumental composition with classroom, orchestral and rock band instruments to the creation of 'school operas'.

Although some of the studies reviewed here were named 'teacher-research', 'practitioner-research' or 'classroom-inquiry', they may all be considered action-research studies and present characteristics similar to those reviewed by Cain (2008) and Strand (2009). However, it is not clear why some were classed as 'ethnography' or 'case study' when the researchers – both classroom teachers and university-based researchers involved in a creative project where they acted as facilitators – were not external observers but *native*, participant observers.

The sample presents a variety of research designs that can constitute a starting point for other teachers willing to investigate their own teaching of composition. Within the designs, there is a coincidence in giving preponderance to the pupils' perspectives in the data collection. However, there is no such coincidence in how the interpretations are corroborated. While some of the reviewed reports present sophisticated triangulation methods including triangulation of data sources, of informants and of observers, others do not detail any procedure. This might hinder support of the credibility of an investigation carried out by an educator on his or her own practice. With no corroboration presented, the readers of a report might doubt whether the findings reconstruct a learning situation taking into account all its participants' viewpoints, and might think, instead, that perhaps they are relating exclusively the teacher's perspective. A weak corroboration – independently of the value of the documented educational practices – can also give the impression that the research is being utilized as a tool for an indulgent self-evaluation, given that engaged teachers often firmly believe in the way they teach. Faulkner, worried by claims about group composition being ineffective, concludes that 'pupils are reported as perceiving composing in this particular classroom as effective and enjoyable' (2003, p. 120). In a similar manner, Hove-Pabst, whose 'original opera' project aims were worded as an evaluation, confirms in the results the expected integration of subject areas as well as 'evidence of relevance to the children's lives' (2002, p. 101). There are also expressions of 'educational value', pupils' higher musical engagement and 'benefits for the community' in Ocaña's report (2008). Another outcome that might potentially hinder credibility is presenting findings that might be too obvious, as for example when Hewitt (2002) concludes that the pre-service generalist teachers were more concerned than the music specialists about their lack of ability to conduct performances, to evaluate compositions and to use conventional notation. In the same way, while some reports acknowledge having looked for negative cases, others do not. And equally important, while some looked for credibility through prolonged engagement and observations – up to a full school year – one was content to present data from a four-hour project.

It seems that we are not necessarily building on previous studies' design successes and limitations. The methodological issues discussed speak for the necessity of reviewing more carefully those successes and shortcomings, to avoid reinforcing a view of action-research as being poorly theoretically and methodologically grounded. Nevertheless, and despite these methodological hindrances, the knowledge accumulated by this small sample of reports exemplifies the potential of researching as a participant. Investigating peer interaction as an essential characteristic of collaborative composition, Hamilton (1999) identified two opposite functions: on the one hand sharing and furthering knowledge, and on the other distracting from learning. To understand the interaction among pupils through talk, Major (2007) developed and applied a useful typology that distinguishes between exploration, description, opinion, affective response, evaluation and problem-solving. As interaction also occurs through playing, Hamilton (1999) observed that pupils played not only to further knowledge, but to refresh their minds by alternating play and work, to distract each other from work or to fill time. Wiggins (1994) did not observe in her study many instances of random exploratory play but, instead, she found that successful strategies moved from a holistic initial planning to a detailed development of motivic ideas, and went back to reassembling and rehearsing the piece as a whole.

Interaction leads to collaboration of different types. In my own study (Rusinek, 2007b) in a mixed-abilities secondary school, I observed that pupils with good academic achievement tended to be more intrinsically motivated and collaborated with an awareness of the features of their learning process, accepting or rejecting their peers' ideas without taking personal offence and sharing responsibility for the final product. Conversely, in the work of pupils with low academic achievement there were many events of learning boycott, and motivation seemed to be more extrinsic, confirming Hennessey's redefinition of the intrinsic motivation principle of creativity (2003), commented on above. For example, the motivation in a highly conflictive group made up of at-risk, disaffected pupils was activated by the project's external rewards and in another group by the pupils' identification with television musical models. Allsup (2003) found that the traditions of the genre chosen by each group to compose shaped its interactions. Pupils showed a preference for the type of collaboration characteristic of jazz and pop music – which they viewed as 'fun, nonobligatory, self-directed, and personally meaningful' (Allsup, 2003, p. 24) – because it facilitated interpersonal relationships, peer learning and peer critique, and an atmosphere of mutual care.

The findings in the reviewed reports contribute to what we know about the characteristics and educative potential of collaborative composition, and they can make up an expandable knowledge base for many music educators. And for those music educators willing to contribute to the advance of such knowledge base through investigating in their own classrooms, the research questions in the reports provide an idea of what has been asked about pupils' interaction and musical learning when composing in groups, and what has not yet been asked. Ultimately, researching as participant observers can not only contribute to further knowledge on collaborative composition, but also potentially facilitate a double empowerment. It can empower music educators, as Regelski (1994) contends, because researching in their classrooms gives them back the control of the curriculum. And it can empower pupils, because composing in groups gives them control over their own learning.

References

Allsup, R. E. (2003). Mutual learning and democratic action in instrumental music education. *Journal of Research in Music Education*, 51(1), 24-37.

Amabile, T. M. (1982). Social psychology of creativity: A consensual assessment technique. *Journal of Personality and Social Psychology*, 43(5), 997-1013.

Amabile, T. M. (1996). *Creativity in context: Update to* The social psychology of creativity. Boulder, CO: Westview Press.

Barrett, M. S. (1998a). Children composing: A view of aesthetic decision-making. In B. Sundin, G. E. McPherson & G. Folkestad (Eds.), *Children composing* (pp. 57-81). Malmö: Malmö Academy of Music.

Barrett, M. S. (1998b). Researching children's compositional processes and products: Connections to music education practice? In B. Sundin, G. E. McPherson & G. Folkestad (Eds.), *Children composing* (pp. 10-34). Malmö: Malmö Academy of Music.

Barrett, M. S. (2005). A systems view of musical creativity. In D. J. Elliott (Ed.), *Praxial music education: Reflections and dialogues* (pp. 177-195). New York: Oxford University Press.

Berkley, R. (2004). Teaching composing as creative problem solving: Conceptualising composing pedagogy. *British Journal of Music Education*, 21(3), 239-263.

Bowman, W. (2004). Cognition and the body: Perspectives from music education. In L. Bresler (Ed.), *Knowing bodies, moving minds: Towards embodied teaching and learning* (pp. 29-50). Dordrecht: Kluwer.

Bresler, L. (2002). Research: A foundation for arts education advocacy. In R. Colwell & C. Richardson (Eds.), *The new handbook of research on music teaching and learning* (pp. 1066-1083). New York: Oxford University Press.

Brown, J. S., Collins, A. & Duguid, P. (1989). Situated cognition and the culture of learning. *Educational Researcher*, 18(1), 32-42.

Burnard, P. (2007). Routes to understanding musical creativity. In L. Bresler (Ed.), *International handbook of research in arts education* (pp. 1199-1214). Dordrecht: Springer.

Burnard, P. & Younker, B. A. (2004). Problem-solving and creativity: Insights from students' individual composing pathways. *International Journal of Music Education*, 22(1), 59-76.

Byrne, C., Halliday, J., Sheridan, M., Soden, R. & Hunter, S. (2001). Thinking music matters: Key skills and composition. *Music Education Research*, 3(1), 63-75.

Cain, T. (2008). The characteristics of action research in music education. *British Journal of Music Education*, 25(3), 283-313.

Chomsky, N. (1965). *Aspects of the theory of syntax*. Cambridge, MA: MIT Press.

Cox, G. (2004). New sounds in class: Music teaching in UK schools in the 1960s, and its relationship to the present. Presentation to the 26th International Society for Music Education World Conference, Tenerife 11-16/7/2004. Proceedings in CD.

Csikszentmihalyi, M. (1988). Society, culture, and person: A systems view of creativity. In R. J. Sternberg (Ed.), *The nature of creativity: Contemporary psychological perspectives* (pp. 325-339). New York: Cambridge University Press.

DeLorenzo, L. C. (1989). A field study of sixth-grade students' creative music problem-solving processes. *Journal of Research in Music Education*, 37(3), 188-200.

Denzin, N. K. & Lincoln, Y. S. (1994). Introduction: Entering the field of qualitative research. In N. K. Denzin & Y. S. Lincoln (Eds.), *Handbook of qualitative research* (pp. 1-17). Thousand Oaks, CA: Sage.

Elliott, D. J. (1996). Consciousness, culture and curriculum. *International Journal of Music Education*, 28(1), 1-15.

Espeland, M. (2007). A Nordic perspective on creativity in music. In L. Bresler (Ed.), *International handbook of research in arts education* (pp. 1215-1217). Dordrecht: Springer.

Faulkner, R. (2003). Group composing: Pupil perceptions from a social psychological study. *Music Education Research*, 5(2), 101-124.

Fautley, M. (2005). A new model of the group composing process of lower secondary students. *Music Education Research*, 7(1), 39-57.

Hamilton, H. J. (1999). Music learning through composition, improvisation and peer interaction in the context of three sixth grade music classes. Unpublished doctoral dissertation, University of Minnesota.

Hennessey, B. A. (2003). Is the social psychology of creativity really social? Moving beyond a focus on the individual. In P. B. Paulus (Ed.), *Group creativity. Innovation through collaboration* (pp. 181-201). Oxford: Oxford University Press.

Hennessey, B. A. & Amabile, T. M. (1988). The conditions of creativity. In R. J. Sternberg (Ed.), *The nature of creativity* (pp. 11-38). New York: Cambridge University Press.

Hewitt, A. (2002). A comparative analysis of process and product with specialist and generalist pre-service teachers involved in a group composition activity. *Music Education Research*, 4(1), 25-36.

Hickey, M. (2001). An application of Amabile's consensual assessment technique for rating the creativity of children's musical compositions. *Journal of Research in Music Education*, 49(3), 234-244.

Hickey, M. (2002). Creativity research in music, visual art, theater, and dance. In R. Colwell & C. Richardson (Eds.), *The new handbook of research on music teaching and learning* (pp. 399-415). New York: Oxford University Press.

Hodgkinson, H. L. (1957). Action research – a critique. *Journal of Educational Sociology*, 31(4), 137-153.

Hove-Pabst, S. (2002). Children's original opera in a rural American schoolhouse: Integration and relevance in discovery learning music education. In M. Espeland (Ed.), *Samspel–ISME World Conference 2002. Focus areas report*. Proceedings in CD. Bergen: International Society for Music Education.

Leung, B. W. (2007). Teaching music composition in Hong Kong: An overview. In L. Bresler (Ed.), *International handbook of research in arts education* (pp. 1223-1224). Dordrecht: Springer.

Leung, B. W. & McPherson, G. (2002). Professional composers' and curriculum planners' perceptions about creativity in Hong Kong school music programs. *Music Educational International*, 1, 67-77.

McPherson, G. (1998). Creativity and music education: Broader issues – wider perspectives. In B. Sundin, G. McPherson & G. Folkestad (Eds.), *Children composing* (pp. 135-156). Malmö: Malmö Academy of Music.

Major, A. E. (2007). Talking about composing in secondary school music lessons. *British Journal of Music Education*, 24(2), 165-178.

Miell, D. & R. MacDonald (2000). Children's creative collaborations: The importance of friendship when working together on a musical composition. *Social Development*, 9(3), 348-369.

Nemeth, Ch. J. & Nemeth-Brown, B. (2003). Better than individuals? The potential benefits of dissent and diversity for group creativity. In P. B. Paulus (Ed.), *Group creativity: Innovation through collaboration* (pp. 63-84). Oxford: Oxford University Press.

Noffke, S. E. & Somekh, B. (Eds.) (2009). *The Sage handbook of educational action research*. Los Angeles: Sage.

Ocaña, Á. (2008). La composición de una 'ópera escolar' como elemento integrador del currículum. Unpublished doctoral report, Complutense University of Madrid.

Odam, G. (2000). Teaching composing in secondary schools: The creative dream. *British Journal of Music Education*, 17(2), 109-127.

Odena, O. (2001). How do secondary school music teachers view creativity? A report on educators' views of teaching composing skills. *Education-line* – see www.leeds.ac.uk/educol/documents/00003133.htm (accessed 3 January 2011).

Odena, O. & Welch, G. (2007). The influence of teachers' backgrounds on their perceptions of musical creativity: A qualitative study with secondary school music teachers. *Research Studies in Music Education*, 28(1), 71-81.

Paynter, J. & Aston, P. (1970). *Sound and silence: Classroom projects in creative music*. Cambridge: Cambridge University Press.

Regelski, T. A. (1994). Action research and critical theory: Empowering music teachers to professionalize praxis. *Bulletin of the Council for Research in Music Education*, 123(Winter), 63-89.

Roberts, B. A. (1994). Music teachers as researchers. *International Journal of Music Education*, 23(1), 24-33.

Rogoff, B. (1990). *Apprenticeship in thinking: Cognitive development in social context*. New York: Oxford University Press.

Rusinek, G. (2007a). Argentinian and Spanish perspectives on musical creativity. In L. Bresler (Ed.) (2007), *International handbook of research in arts education* (pp. 1219-1221). Dordrecht: Springer.

Rusinek, G. (2007b). Students' perspectives in a collaborative composition project at a Spanish secondary school. *Music Education Research*, 9(3), 323-335.

Sági, M. & Vitányi, I. (1988). Experimental research into musical generative ability. In J. A. Sloboda (Ed.), *Generative processes in music: The psychology of performance, improvisation and composition* (pp. 179-194). Oxford: Oxford University Press.

Salomon, G. (Ed.) (1993). *Distributed cognitions: Psychological and educational considerations*. Cambridge: Cambridge University Press.

Schafer, R. M. (1965). *The composer in the classroom*. Toronto: Berandol Music.

Somekh, B. (2006). *Action research: A methodology for change and development*. Maidenhead: Open University Press.

Strand, K. (2006). Survey of Indiana music teachers on using composition in the classroom. *Journal of Research in Music Education*, 54(2), 154-167.

Strand, K. D. (2009). A narrative analysis of action research on teaching composition. *Music Education Research*, 11(3), 349-363.

Stubley, E. (1992). Philosophical foundations. In R. Colwell (Ed.), *Handbook of research on music teaching and learning* (pp. 3-20). New York: Schirmer Books.

Vygotsky, L. S. (1978). *Mind in society: The development of higher psychological processes*. Cambridge, MA: Harvard University Press.

Webster, P. R. (1992). Research on creative thinking in music: The assessment literature. In R. Colwell (Ed.), *Handbook of research on music teaching and learning* (pp. 266-280). New York: Schirmer Books.

Wiggins, J. (1994). Children's strategies for solving compositional problems with peers. *Journal of Research in Music Education*, 42(3), 232-252.

Wiggins, J. (1999). The nature of shared musical understanding and its role in empowering independent musical thinking. *Bulletin of the Council for Research in Music Education*, 143(Winter), 65-90.

Wiggins, J. (2007). Compositional process in music. In L. Bresler (Ed.), *International handbook of research in arts education* (pp. 453-469). Dordrecht: Springer.

Chapter 11

Perspectives on musical creativity: where next?

Oscar Odena

11.1 Introduction

In this final chapter some overarching themes emerging from the volume's contributions are discussed. The themes identified, which are interconnected, are not exhaustive but capture broad issues that resonate across creativity studies in music education research and related areas. The first two themes concern the definition of musical creativity and the provision of musical creativity practices across different countries. Subsequent themes relate to the importance of emotional engagement for the effective implementation of these types of activities and with implications for practice. As most of the previous chapters focused on formal education settings, the contexts of musical creativity discussed here often refer to formal education. In light of the emerging themes the chapter concludes with a consideration of issues that would need further research.

11.2 Understanding musical creativity

The increased dissemination of all styles of music and musical practices through the globalized media and the internet has not facilitated a clearer definition of the concept of creativity in music. There seems to be at least two opposing views among people's general understanding of musical creativity: the *systematic* and the *romantic*. These views seem to correspond with the discourses of 'mastery' versus 'mystery' or 'absolute expertise', identified in research with advanced performers (Creech et al., 2010; Wilson & MacDonald, 2005). The *systematic* view involves a good deal of effort and persistence, where creative work is seen as a rational everyday affair. For instance, adult musicians follow an intense daily working schedule when preparing a new recording (especially if the recording studio is paid for by the day!). This is in opposition to the *romantic* view of creativity characterized by irrationality, mystery and unconsciousness. But a relevant idea for developing musical creativity emerging from this volume is that a period of focused effort is required in order to consider a musical problem. The final contestants in student music competitions, for example, are likely to have rehearsed for months prior to impressing the panel of adjudicators and the audience. This is not acknowledged in *romantic* explanations of the creative process, perhaps due to successful musicians not seeing this type of sustained effort as hard work – see, for instance, the mystical explanations of Harvey's composing in Deliège and Harvey (2006) and of Mozart's in Vernon (1970). Musicians' accounts of sustained creative work appear underpinned by motivation (e.g. McCutchan, 1999). While engaged in focused activities, highly motivated individuals' perception of time is minimized, a situation described as being in a state of *flow* (Csikszentmihalyi, 1996).

Even though social psychologists have defined the creative product as something that is assessed as novel and valuable (Amabile, 1996) there will always be a degree of paradox in defining musical creativity. The paradox is illustrated by the fact that a similar musical product could be assessed as novel for one learner and not very novel for another, depending on the learner's previous experiences. This may turn into confusion if we try to apply adult assessment criteria to children's work. It is the facilitator or teacher who would need to develop particular criteria for each learner or group of learners. Novelty and usefulness, nevertheless, would need to be seen as internally related rather than independent requirements. A creative musical product would need to be 'useful in a particularly novel way' for the learner and 'novel in a useful or appropriate way' for the activity (Klausen, 2010, p. 356). Therefore, not any combination of sounds and music structures will do: even if they are novel for the learner, they have to be useful in an appropriate way, determined by the parameters of the activity.

In the opening chapter Burnard argues against the limitations of a historical understanding of creativity linked with high-art orthodoxies that praise individual geniuses (reinforcing the romantic view). She advocates instead for an understanding of musical creativity *as it is practised* and considers the differing values and features that apply to different modes of creativity, including individual, collaborative and performance creativity. She suggests that teachers and students need to learn about musical creativity as a situated social activity, recognizing the existence of various modes in which musical creativity can be practised. Educators and learners would not need to define what creativity *is* but rather explain what constitutes the practices on which multiple creativities of music are based, asking *which* music, from *what* social and activity system it arises, and *who* are the artists or groups that inform and support it.

In contemporary music curriculum guidelines, creativity is seen as a skill to be developed by all students and is generally linked with composition and improvisation activities. Although the teachers' perceptions of creativity appear to be evidenced during these types of activities, performing and appraising are also activities in which students can develop their musical creativity skills (Odena et al., 2005). A situated understanding of musical creativity, shared with all those involved in the learning interaction, would be more useful than a romantic definition of creativity characterized by mystery and linked with the exceptionality of geniuses. Although there are still many unknowns about how musical ideas come into being, neuroscientists in recent years have uncovered how the musical brain works (Altenmüller & Gruhn, 2002; Hodges, 2006; Patel, 2009).

What seems clear is that the learner needs a strategy to preserve new ideas and a sustained period of effort to refine them, and that some ideas only come about while working (individually, collaboratively or alternating periods of individual and collaborative work). Despite all the complexities outlined above, a working definition of musical creativity may be explained as the development of a musical product that is novel for the individual and useful for the situated musical practice. For example, a professional musician repeating without emotion a pre-learned jazz solo during a concert would not be developing his or her musical creativity a great deal, whereas a student in a school jam session arriving for the first time at some of the same musical ideas as the professional performer would be doing something novel at an individual level and useful for the situated musical practice.

11.3 Musical creativity practices across countries

A number of different musical creativity practices are reported in the countries that form the context of the previous chapters. The variety of practices appears to be linked to the history of provision of these activities in and out of schools and with the pedagogical and teacher education traditions in each country – socio-economic factors are also relevant but would fall beyond the scope of this volume; interested readers can find an excellent introduction to the sociology of music education by Wright (2010), which features in the same series as this book.

Chapter 6 illustrates the comprehensive music school system of Minas Gerais, as well as some of the styles of the rich musical environment in which young people grow up in this Brazilian state. At the same time the author observes that generalist schools choose whether to offer music or not, resulting in some students not receiving any formal music education. Likewise, in Chapter 4 some recent developments in the provision of musical opportunities for children in Portugal are outlined, such as the Curriculum Enrichment Activities. However, the contributors explain that these after-school activities are non-compulsory and suggest that the children who are not attending could be lacking music education experiences at school as some classroom teachers rely on the after-school activities for this provision. Interestingly, at community level, musical activities in Portugal appear to be alive with a diversity of folk groups and philharmonic bands reported in the literature, which provide opportunities for musical engagement outside formal education settings (Boal-Palheiros & Resende, 2010; Ferreira et al., 2006). The students' personal music preferences in these two countries are not very different to other contexts and seem to be influenced by global trends (Boal-Palheiros & Hargreaves, 2001, 2004; LeBlanc et al., 2002). But in the cases above the children's communities could be providing additional opportunities for engaging in musical creativity practices outside school. Without trying to suggest a cause–effect relationship, it appears that in some places where young people have greater exposure to informal music-making activities in their communities music has less relevance as a formal school subject.

Musical creativity practices in schools seem also related to the pedagogical tradition in each country. In England, where there has been a strong tradition of creative music-making activity since the 1960s, secondary schools often have a number of rooms for the music department and a collection of instruments, allowing for whole classroom, small group and individual work – Mills and Paynter (2008) and Pitts (2000) offer detailed accounts of the development of creative music-making activities during the second half of the twentieth century. As exemplified in Chapter 2, secondary music school teachers in England generally have a music-related degree and a one-year postgraduate music education qualification, and they tend to bring their preferred practices and styles into generalist schools. Music is compulsory until age 14 and students can choose to continue afterwards, following a number of progression routes. For instance, they can take the A level course at ages 16-18, whose requirements include developing a portfolio of composition exercises and an original piece. In other English-speaking Western countries such as the United States and Australia opportunities for the development of musical creativity in schools seem to be facilitated by a long tradition of music provision coupled with a degree of freedom for educators to develop their own activities. In the United States music school provision is linked to the state and local financial conditions, which results in dissimilarities among schools. Some schools have well-equipped music technology rooms and composing as a regular activity, as in the school described in Chapter 5. In others, the emphasis leans more towards ensemble performance, an activity that drives many programmes focused on preparing orchestras, choirs and marching and jazz bands for competition in adjudicated festivals (Campbell, 2008; Radocy, 2001).

In countries where music is a recent introduction to compulsory education, the opportunities for developing musical creativity in formal settings appear to be more limited. For example, in Spain, following the 1990s education reform, music was made available as a curriculum subject until age 16. The government sent some percussion instruments to schools to promote student-centred practical activities, but teachers are still reported to continue with their teacher-centred pedagogy, characterized by a 'declarative knowledge' tradition and the widespread use of textbooks (Rusinek, 2008, p. 13). Teachers obtain a life contract once they have passed the state theory-based exams (*oposiciones*), after which they have few incentives for long-term personal development. Nevertheless, educators have a considerable degree of freedom when developing curriculum guidelines and some of the work reported is encouraging (see, for instance, the book on creativity in music education by Díaz and Riaño, 2007). Practices such as collaborative composition projects are being employed to engage disaffected adolescents, including some of the studies reviewed in Chapter 10, suggesting that the possibilities for creativity in the classroom are ultimately driven by the individual teachers. As observed in the previous chapter, composing in groups in the classroom opposes the accepted pedagogy in countries that have a teacher-centred education tradition. This type of activity allows for increased student autonomy, which may go against conventional school practices or, in the best-case scenario, be perceived as an innovation.

11.4 Emotion and purpose in musical creativity practices

Regardless of the education system tradition, a common theme that emerges across the chapters is the significant role of emotion in musical creativity practices. Chapter 4 explains how any musical activity is embedded in an emotional context and suggests that teachers would benefit from being aware and making use of the children's emotions when planning classroom activities. Chapter 9 reviews previous studies in music therapy and outlines the importance of establishing and enjoying shared narratives of emotionally expressive activity between child and adult for successful and meaningful music sessions. The author also explains Stern's notion of *affect attunement*, which in music therapy settings is not simply the adult imitating the child's gesture but attempting to read empathically the feelings that lie behind any gestures. This concurs with the notion of *empathetic creativity* described in Chapter 7. One of the outcomes of empathetic creativity would be the emotional link that emerges among musicians when they play and/or improvise together, sometimes generating a 'musical spark'. This spark can appear when groups of players, no matter what style and technical level, perform listening to and interacting with each other instead of just playing alongside each other.

In individual rehearsal and solo performances, the use of emotions may be linked with the player developing and communicating a personal meaning. It has been reported that a degree of rhythmic variation (or rubato) is linked to increased positive assessment of musicality in classical music performance (Johnson, 1997; Madsen et al., 2010). Similarly, in jazz improvisation a degree of variation when developing musical phrases or motifs is preferred to performing those motifs exactly as recorded by other players. The classical rubato and the jazz motifs may be developed by students working out their own emotional link with and understanding of the music and trying hard to communicate it. This requires internal (or intrinsic) motivation, to maintain the will while working towards the improvement of a musical product, in this case the different nuances in the student's own rubato or motifs. A driver of the individuals' motivation may be the sense of fulfilment in the pursuit of something novel and useful, even if the final outcome cannot be clearly defined from the outset.

Gardner (1983, 1993) in his theory of Multiple Intelligences described a number of capacities that he called intelligences. To the more familiar mathematical, linguistic, bodily, musical and spatial intelligences – which are traditionally developed in schools as Maths, Language, Physical Education, Music and Arts and Design – he added *personal* and *interpersonal* intelligences. The latter would be the capacity to perceive the emotions and intentions of those around us. *Personal* intelligence (which he called intrapersonal) would be the capacity to perceive our own feelings. These two capacities converge in Goleman's concept of *emotional intelligence* (1995) and have been used when planning and implementing activities in education and professional development. It is argued that (a) the intelligences can be developed when two or more are used in combination with the personal and the interpersonal intelligences, and (b) such combined activities are more memorable. For instance, using drama strategies while studying music scores has been employed to enhance learning and decrease performance anxiety. A study by Odena and Cabrera (2006) reports how a group of five conservatoire students assigned five operatic characters to the melodic patterns of a difficult clarinet concerto and invented a short play for the characters. In subsequent sessions they rehearsed and performed the short play and the concerto, each student dressed up and performing only the melodic part assigned to the character (Cabrera et al., 2006; Odena, 2007). These activities, combining musical, personal and interpersonal intelligences, resulted in the participants' development of emotional links with the score and a reported decrease in performance anxiety.

Emotional links developed in group composition activities have been used as a tool to promote inclusion among students from different communities in post-conflict environments (Odena, 2009, 2010) and to facilitate the inclusion of socially vulnerable adolescents in conflictive neighbourhoods (Hesser & Heinemann, 2010). These examples illustrate the strong relationship between music and the emotions, which are particularly relevant during musical creativity practices and can impact on behaviour. Additional other-than-musical benefits include the importance of musical creativity practices such as sound play and experimentation for the development of emotionally rounded and healthy children (Welch, 2010). Educators may be more likely to make full use of this potential by including the musical features of the students' musical cultures and their practices as elements for classroom discussion from which to build on and develop music skills (Barrett, 2005). For instance, the electronic gadgets used by some musicians to build their song arrangements in real time while singing can be analysed in terms of musical features such as pitch, timbre and rhythmic patterns. The combination of these features with the accompanying voices may be the starting point to discuss harmony and arrangements, and this understanding may be later transferred to other practices, with the assistance of the students' emotional links with the music. Potential challenges may revolve around increased student voice, which may interfere again with accepted school practices, and with the need for educators to be curious and open to any new musical developments.

11.5 Implications for practice

Chapter 2 put forward four themes to take into account when thinking about musical creativity: (1) the personal characteristics of those involved in creative activities; (2) the environment most conducive for the development of creativity; (3) the creative process; and (4) its products. In this section some implications for practice are presented, broadening suggestions for secondary schools outlined elsewhere (Odena, forthcoming). Figure 11.1 includes points for consideration when facilitating the development of musical creativity presented under the above four themes, in view of this volume's contributions and recent literature (Burnard, 2007; Hallam, 2010; Hickey, 2009; Philpott, 2007; Sawyer & DeZutter, 2009; Shirley, 2009; Webster, 2009).

PERSON: DIFFERENTIATING FOR PERSONAL NEEDS

Level and type of challenge: individuals require suitable stimulating challenges in relation to their own previous learning. We do better when the activity fits how we think. It is important for facilitators to know the learners, to design activities with scope for developing all their potential. For instance, offering a variety of additional open-ended and challenging tasks (more instruments, different musical materials, extended structures), which will also facilitate the learners' ownership of their creative development.

ENVIRONMENT: THE CONTEXT FOR CREATIVITY

Resources: the potential for creativity may be enhanced by building rich and stimulating resources, which can be used to both initiate and support the creative process. These resources can be musical and extra-musical: a variety of recordings, instruments, films, computers and music software.

Time: individuals require time to satisfactorily complete their work, yet creativity in music cannot be given limitless time. Facilitators need to be sensitive to the learners' needs and flexibly adapt the expectations as an activity or project progresses.

Emotional environment: individuals need to feel capable of taking risks and sense that their contributions are respected and valued. This positive environment can be built and sustained through dialogue with constructive positive feedback.

THE CREATIVE PROCESS

Levels of structure: it is advisable to include various levels of structure when promoting creativity, depending on the task and the desired musical learning. For example, facilitators might set learners a free choice about which problems to solve and how to do it, open-ended tasks that channel the work through particular stimuli (a poem, an object) or structured problem-solving with a limited set of expressive and structural ingredients. All of the above may be done individually or in groups, where participants may learn from each other and generate a product in which no single individual determines the result. To increase efficiency, collective activities need to be carefully planned, combining them with individual thinking time and preserving the work produced along the way.

Students' support: facilitators need to assist the learners' technical development by questioning, prompting, modelling and setting up opportunities for other models to be heard, such as external musicians. Facilitators need to be creative, for instance 'jamming' with learners, and have to encourage further development of musical ideas, as novice musicians are likely to be satisfied with their work after a basic exploratory phase.

THE CREATIVE PRODUCT

Assessment: sharing the assessment of work and developing assessment criteria with the learners facilitates the emergence of further ideas and the development of self-assessment skills. For instance, in a composition project, asking participants to come up with musical examples that match each of the assessment criteria and letting them give constructive feedback to each other at different stages of the project.

Figure 11.1   Facilitating the development of musical creativity. Developed from Odena (forthcoming)

Although the recommendations in Figure 11.1 may appear to focus on composition they could be used for all types of musical activities, for instance when exploring the use of musical elements (tempo, dynamics and so on) to give different emotional qualities to the performance of a song or when appraising these qualities in other people's performances. Intrinsic motivation appears to be a driver for successful students (Odena, 2001) and this could be facilitated rather than inhibited by offering learners a degree of choice in terms of activities and materials. The role of the facilitator should be to fire up the individuals' curiosity to learn, developing rather than inhibiting their interests.

The learners' development of music-making skills can be assisted by appraising how music and sound is made and used by others. The components of sound and music permeate most daily human activities. Music and sounds are used in audiovisual marketing as well as many other contexts to add an emotional dimension to objects and social phenomena, from consumer products to sports, political and religious gatherings. Music can be a tool for manipulation when used 'in conjunction with an intellectual message, adding new and powerful emotional dimensions to it' (Strandberg & Wallin, 2006, p. x). For example, rhythm and volume can induce a wide range of emotional reactions, including calmness and stress. Harmony combined with instrumentation is often used in the media to support emotions such as joy or sadness, while melodic themes or leitmotifs are linked with characters (Gustems, 2005). Developing an increased awareness to critically listen to these uses of music in daily live seems very relevant for education in the internet age and has the potential to assist learners' development of their own musical creativity.

11.6 Issues for further study: where next?

It is hoped this volume has contributed to the understanding of musical creativity, drawing on current debates in music education research and closely related areas. As in other social sciences, systematic inquiry often produces more questions than answers. Nevertheless, it is this process that suggests what questions need addressing and how to frame them better. For example, some music therapy inquiry lines focused on emotions have not yet been fully explored in mainstream education settings. In Chapter 9 there are references to sessions in which participants found that some activities evoked feelings of regret and loss, relating to earlier musical experiences or unhappy musical memories. Such results highlight that educators need sensitivity and care in order to avoid early negative musical experiences that may hamper future musical creativity development. For instance, imposing songs that evoke happy feelings to the facilitator but not necessarily to the students or imposing activities that assist the learning preferences of a majority but not all of the participants may inhibit the development of musical creativity.

An overview of general creativity studies by Sternberg suggests that people with creative abilities who are 'never taught or assessed in a way that matches their pattern of abilities, may be at a disadvantage in course after course' (2006, pp. 5-6). The subsequent labelling of the minority as 'non-creative' could result in lower self-esteem and unhappy memories linked with formal music education. Cases of 'lifelong perceptions of musical disability' due to teachers' negative comments and public humiliation in front of peers have been documented in studies of signing development (Welch, 2001, p. 15). How to best assist the growth of musical creativity skills in learners of all ages who may have lacked previous opportunities for musical engagement or may have had early negative experiences is an issue that requires further study.

Musical creativity development in informal settings and what may be learned from it for formal education (Green, 2008) is also a topic with scope for further inquiry, particularly in countries where opportunities for informal musical engagement abound outside schools. The impact of teacher education developments on the pedagogical traditions of different countries is another area for continuing exploration. Comparative music education is a field that is relatively underdeveloped but has the potential to increase awareness of good practice internationally (Tate, 2001). Other questions to explore further include what may be learned from studying musical creativity practices across genres (Chapter 8) and from projects that succeed in apparently unsupportive environments. Exploring success factors in unsupportive settings with a lack of resources could be useful for advancing practice in places without a strong tradition of creative music-making activity.

Public forums such as the publications and conferences organized by the International Society for Music Education (www.isme.org) and other national and international professional associations around the world offer good opportunities for exchange and collaborative studies across different countries. How current and future educators may develop their own pedagogy for creativity, taking into account their local needs and personal aspirations in an increasingly globalized world, is a challenge for all those involved in music education. This is one challenge that we should rise to and cherish.

References

Altenmüller, E. & Gruhn, W. (2002). Brain mechanisms. In R. Parncutt & G. E. McPherson (Eds.), *The science and psychology of music performance: Creative strategies for teaching and learning* (pp. 63-81). Oxford: Oxford University Press.

Amabile, T. M. (1996). *Creativity in context: Update to The social psychology of creativity*. Oxford: Oxford University Press.

Barrett, M. (2005). A systems view of musical creativity. In D. J. Elliott (Ed.), *Praxial music education: Reflections and dialogues* (pp. 177-195). Oxford: Oxford University Press.

Boal-Palheiros, G. & Hargreaves, D. J. (2001). Listening to music at home and at school. *British Journal of Music Education*, 18(2), 103-118.

Boal-Palheiros, G. & Hargreaves, D. J. (2004). Children's modes of listening to music at home and at school. *Bulletin of the Council for Research in Music Education*, 161-162 (Summer–Fall), 39-46.

Boal-Palheiros, G. & Resende, R. (2010). The practice of Portuguese traditional music in primary schools. In G. Mota & A. Yin (Eds.), *ISME Proceedings of the 23rd international seminar on research in music education* (pp. 66-71). Changchun, China: North East Normal University and International Society for Music Education.

Burnard, P. (Ed.) (2007). Section 11 Creativity. In L. Bresler (Ed.), *International handbook of research in arts education* (pp. 1173-1290). Dordrecht: Springer.

Cabrera, L., Lluna, J. E. & Odena, O. (2006). Teatralizar la partitura para aprender major: Un estudio sobre 'La Flauta Mágica' como imagen interpretativa del concierto de clarinete de Mozart [Dramatizing the score to improve learning: A study of 'The Magic Flute' as performance image of Mozart's clarinet concerto], *Eufonía. Didáctica de la Música*, 36(1), 113-123.

Campbell, P. S. (2008). *Musician and teacher: An orientation to music education.* New York: W. W. Norton.

Creech, A., Papageorgi, I. & Welch, G. (2010). Concepts of ideal musicians. *Journal of Research in Music Performance* (Spring), 1-18.

Csikszentmihalyi, M. (1996). *Creativity: Flow and the psychology of discovery and invention.* New York: Harper Collins.

Deliège, I. & Harvey, J. (2006). Postlude: How can we understand creativity in a composer's work? A conversation between Irène Deliège and Jonathan Harvey. In I. Deliège & G. A. Wiggins (Eds.), *Musical creativity: Multidisciplinary research in theory and practice* (pp. 397-404). Hove: Psychology Press.

Díaz, M. & Riaño, M. E. (Eds.) (2007). *Creatividad en educación musical* [*Creativity in music education*]. Santander: Universidad de Cantabria.

Ferreira, R., Mota, G. & Seabra, F. (2006). Growing up in a philharmonic band: A cultural perspective. In H. E. Price (Ed.), *Proceedings of the 21st international seminar on research in music education* (pp. 45-51). Bali: Research Commission of the International Society for Music Education and Hong Kong Baptist University.

Gardner, H. (1983). *Frames of mind: The theory of multiple intelligences.* London: Heinemann.

Gardner, H. (1993). *Multiple intelligences: The theory in practice.* New York: Basic Books.

Goleman, D. (1995). *Emotional intelligence: Why it can matter more than IQ.* New York: Bantam Books.

Green, L. (2008). *Music, informal learning and the school: A new classroom pedagogy.* Farnham: Ashgate.

Gustems, J. (2005). Escuchar los anuncios: Una aproximación al uso de la música y del sonido en la publicidad televisiva [Listening to adverts: An approximation to the use of music and sound in TV adverts]. *Eufonía. Didáctica de la Música*, 34(1), 91-100.

Hallam, S. (2010). Music education: The role of affect. In P. N. Juslin & J. A. Sloboda (Eds.), *Handbook of music and emotion: Theory, research, applications* (pp. 791-817). Oxford: Oxford University Press.

Hesser, B. & Heinemann, H. (Eds.) (2010). *Music as a natural resource: Solutions for social and economic issues*. New York: United Nations.

Hickey, M. (2009). Can improvisation be 'taught'? A call for free improvisation in our schools. *International Journal of Music Education*, 27(4), 285-299.

Hodges, D. A. (2006). The musical brain. In G. E. McPherson (Ed.), *The child as musician: A handbook of musical development* (pp. 51-68). Oxford: Oxford University Press.

Johnson, C. M. (1997). A comparison of the perceived musicianship of skilled musicians and their respective rhythmic timings in performances of Mozart. *Bulletin of the Council for Research in Music Education*, 133, 45-51.

Klausen, S. H. (2010). The notion of creativity revisited: A philosophical perspective on creativity research. *Creativity Research Journal*, 22(4), 347-360.

LeBlanc, A., Fung, C. V., Boal-Palheiros, G., Burt-Rider, A. J., Ogawa, Y., Oliveira, A. & Stamou, L. (2002). Effect of strength of rhythmic beat on preferences of young music listeners in Brazil, Greece, Japan, Portugal, and the United States. *Bulletin of the Council for Research in Music Education*, 153/154 (Summer/Fall), 36-41.

McCutchan, A. (Ed.) (1999). *The muse that sings: Composers speak about the creative process*. New York: Oxford University Press.

Madsen, C. K., Geringer, J. M. & Johnson, Ch. M. (2010). Effect of instruction in appropriate rubato usage on onset timings and perceived musicianship of Mozart & Bach performances: A CRDI replication. In G. Mota & A. Yin (Eds.), *ISME Proceedings of the 23rd international seminar on research in music education* (pp. 38-43). Changchun, China: North East Normal University and International Society for Music Education.

Mills, J. & Paynter, J. (Eds.) (2008). *Thinking and making: Selections from the writings of John Paynter on music education*. Oxford: Oxford University Press.

Odena, O. (2001). Developing a framework for the study of teachers' views of creativity in music education. *Goldsmiths Journal of Education*, 4(1), 59-67.

Odena, O. (2007). Recitar suonando [Enacting a story when performing], *Musica Domani*, 142(March), 17-21.

Odena, O. (2009). *Early music education as a tool for inclusion and respect for diversity: Study paper for the Bernard van Leer Foundation*. University of Brighton and Bernard van Leer Foundation – see https://uhra.herts.ac.uk/dspace/handle/2299/4982 (accessed 1 February 2011).

Odena, O. (2010). Practitioners' views on cross-community music education projects in Northern Ireland: Alienation, socio-economic factors and educational potential. *British Educational Research Journal*, 36(1), 83-105.

Odena, O. (forthcoming). Creativity in the secondary music classroom. In G. E. McPherson & G. Welch (Eds.), *The Oxford handbook of music education*. New York and Oxford: Oxford University Press.

Odena, O. & Cabrera, L. (2006). Dramatising the score: An action-research investigation of the use of Mozart's Magic Flute as performance guide for his clarinet Concerto. In The Society for Music Perception & Cognition (SMPC) and European Society for the Cognitive Sciences of Music (ESCOM), *Proceedings of the 9th international conference on music perception & cognition* (pp. 310-315). Bologna, Italy: SMPC & ESCOM.

Odena, O., Plummeridge, Ch. & Welch, G. (2005). Towards an understanding of creativity in music education: A qualitative exploration of data from English secondary schools. *Bulletin of the Council for Research in Music Education*, 163(Winter), 9-18.

Patel, A. D. (Ed.) (2009). Part 4: Music and the brain. In S. Hallam, I. Cross & M. Thaut (Eds.), *The Oxford handbook of music psychology* (pp. 169-216). Oxford: Oxford University Press.

Philpott, Ch. (2007). Creativity and music education. In Ch. Philpott & G. Spruce (Eds.), *Learning to teach music in the secondary school: A companion to school experience* (2nd edition) (pp. 119-134). London: Routledge.

Pitts, S. (2000). *A century of change in music education*. Aldershot: Ashgate.

Radocy, R. E. (2001). North America. In D. J. Hargreaves & A. C. North (Eds.), *Musical development and learning: The international perspective* (pp. 120-133). London: Continuum.

Rusinek, G. (2008). Disaffected learners and school musical culture: An opportunity for inclusion. *Research Studies in Music Education*, 30(1), 9-23.

Sawyer, R. K. & DeZutter, S. (2009). Distributed creativity: How collective creations emerge from collaboration. *Psychology of Aesthetics, Creativity, and the Arts*, 3(2), 81-92.

Shirley, I. (2009). Teaching creatively. In J. Evans & Ch. Philpott (Eds.), *A practical guide to teaching music in the secondary school* (pp. 45-53). London: Routledge.

Sternberg, R. J. (2006). Creating a vision of creativity: The first 25 years. *Psychology of Aesthetics, Creativity, and the Arts*, S(1), 2-12.

Strandberg, Ö. & Wallin, B.-A. (2006). Foreword: Manipulating music – a perspective of practicing composers. In S. Brown & U. Volgsten (Eds.), *Music and manipulation: On the social uses and social control of music* (pp. x-xi). Oxford: Berghahn Books.

Tate, P. (2001). Comparative perspectives. In Ch. Philpott & Ch. Plummeridge (Eds.), *Issues in music teaching* (pp. 224-237). London: RoutledgeFalmer.

Vernon, P. E. (Ed.) (1970). *Creativity: Selected readings*. Harmondsworth: Penguin.

Webster, P. (Ed.) (2009). Part 8: Composition and improvisation. In S. Hallam, I. Cross & M. Thaut (Eds.), *The Oxford handbook of music psychology* (pp. 401-428). Oxford: Oxford University Press.

Welch, G. (2001). *The misunderstanding of music: An inaugural lecture*. London: Institute of Education University of London.

Welch, G. (2010). *Professor Graham Welch interviewed by Gloria Patricia Zapata Restrepo (part 1 of 4)*. Held at the Institute of Education University of London – see www.youtube.com/watch?v=Knjrm8UMC2k&feature=play er_embedded (accessed 1 February 2011).

Wilson, G. B. & MacDonald, R. A. R. (2005). The meaning of the blues: Musical identities in talk about jazz. *Qualitative Research in Psychology*, 2(4), 341-363.

Wright, R. (Ed.) (2010). *Sociology and music education*. Farnham: Ashgate.

Index

References to tables and illustrations are in **bold**